FREUD'S CONVERTS

FREUD'S CONVERTS

Vicki Clifford

*To Janice & Derek
with love
Vicki*

KARNAC

First published in 2007 by
Karnac Books Ltd
118 Finchley Road, London NW3 5HT

Copyright © 2008 Vicki Clifford

The rights of Vicki Clifford to be identified as author of this work have been asserted in accordance with §§ 77 and 78 of the Copyright Design and Patents Act 1988.

All rights reserved. No part of this publication may be reproduced, stored in a retrieval system, or transmitted, in any form or by means, electronic, mechanical, photocopying, recording, or otherwise, without the prior written permission of the publisher.

British Library Cataloguing in Publication Data
A C.I.P for this book is available from the British Library

ISBN-13: 978-1-85575-536-9

Edited, designed, and produced by
Florence Production Ltd, Stoodleigh, Devon
www.florenceproduction.co.uk

Printed in Great Britain
www.karnacbooks.com

CONTENTS

ACKNOWLEDGEMENTS		vii
PREFACE		ix
PROLOGUE		xi
Introduction		1
1	Science and Status	10
2	The Construction of Freud	21
3	(i) Freud's Legacy	42
	(ii) Contemporary Psychodynamic Psychotherapy	80
4	(i) The Construction of Carl Rogers	115
	(ii) Person-Centred Theories and Practice	121
5	Roger's Legacy	138
6	(i) Post-Secular Psychotherapy	169
	(ii) Post-Feminist Responses	191
Conclusion		195
BIBLIOGRAPHY		200
INDEX		213

This book is dedicated to all those people who have ensured my many good hair days!

ACKNOWLEDGEMENTS

I would like to say that the following is by no means representative of the many people who have supported me both academically and otherwise. I thank all those who have shared in the evolution of this project. It is impossible to say thank you enough to Professor Alistair Kee, whose shoulders must be the strongest and most exploited in academe. His commitment to this work has never abated. Such generous giants are very rare and I am honoured to have had the pleasure to work with him. Dr Steve Tilley deserves particular thanks also for being such a committed supervisor. Many thanks to my friend and colleague Dr Jeremy Carrette, whose insights and challenges were essential to keep me from remaining in my comfort zone. Professor Richard Roberts I thank for his gentle criticism. Professor Dan Gunn I thank for his many practical tips. My friend Dr William McCrea has been utterly unconditional in his support I am indebted to him for this. I thank my colleagues at the University of Stirling, in particular Dr Alison Jasper for her enthusiasm. I am grateful to my colleagues at No.21 Counselling Agency with whom I had so many thought provoking conversations, and to those independent practitioners who listened to my ideas and gave their criticisms and generous support. In particular Jonathan Wood. Thanks to Murray McGrath, Dr Hugh Montgomery and Dr Karen Kerner who, in the early days, were particularly generous with their time. It would not have been possible without access to the Tavistock Clinic Library, New College Library in the University of Edinburgh, Royal Edinburgh Hospital Library and the librarians who patiently and courteously attended to my needs. Thanks to Ruaraidh Macintosh for his endless questions.

Special thanks to my family in particular to Diane, Edward, Alexander & Eugenia.

Finally, thank you to Robin Chapman Campbell who has cheerfully lived with this project and has kept me sane: although this may be disputed.

PREFACE

This project was conceived while I was training to become a psychotherapist. I was intrigued by the frequency with which my colleagues and the literature in the field, drew on language which is more traditionally used within religious discourse. Later as a practitioner, I observed that when my clients struggled to find words to describe their experiences they were also drawn to religious language. In addition to my training in psychotherapy I have a degree in Religious Studies. The synthesis of these two fields has afforded me a position which may best be described as a hybrid and which consequently has given me a peculiar awareness of the analytical dimensions of spirituality and psychopathology. In its rudimentary stages this project explored the structures and functions of psychotherapy and counselling, uncovering clear parallels with religion. However, as the project unfolded more subtle and nuanced resemblances were uncovered, both in the tradition and in contemporary developments. A recurring question has been why it is that psychotherapists and counsellors, who locate themselves within the natural and medical sciences, rely so much on language which would associate them with the realm of religion. Both "science" and "religion" are slippery terms which, once defined, lose much of their potential—in the way that an eel may lose its "eelness" once it has been pinned down. The Gaelic poet Sorley Maclean once said of his work "what is lost in the translation is the poetry". My continuing interest in this project is because some of the most original developments in contemporary theory and practice have broken through inherited stereotypes and are redefining the relationship between psychotherapy and religion.

PROLOGUE

Freud in a letter to Jung (1908):

> We are certainly getting ahead; if I am Moses, then you are Joshua and will take possession of the promised land of psychiatry, which I shall only be able to glimpse from afar. . . .[1]

In a later letter Freud states:

> It is strange that on the very same evening when I formally adopted you as eldest son and anointed you—in *partibus infidelium*—as my successor and crown prince . . .[2]

Wilhelm Stekel a follower of Freud stated:

> I was the apostle of Freud who was my Christ![3]

Webster argues:

> in scientific terms the reasons for adopting his theories were, as I have tried to show, no better than the reasons which might be given for imitating his way of talking or over his neurotic habits. In both cases we are confronted not by a reasoned decision but by an act of irrational submission to the power of Freud's personality and to the capacity he had for projecting himself both in his life and his writing as a prophet, sage, healer and even redeemer.[4]

Max Graf the father of young Hans, one of Freud's patients, described Freud as:

head of the psychoanalytic church[5]

George Weisz:

The group's elitism and sense of exclusiveness, combined with an eschatological vision of reality which made adherence to the group an experience approaching religious conversion; and, more important, an exaggerated reverence for the founder which transcended the normal bounds of scientific authoritarianism.[6]

Peter Gay claimed:

Jones took some pains to disabuse the public of the reputation for intolerance that Freud had acquired, and in particular he attacked the analogy that compared psychoanalysis to a religious movement, with Freud a new . . . [7].

Ernest Jones:

Freud was of course the Pope of the new sect, if not a still higher Personage, to whom all owed obeisance; his writings were the sacred text, credence in which was obligatory on the supposed infallibilists who had undergone the necessary conversion, and there were not lacking the heretics who were expelled from the church. It was a pretty obvious caricature to make, but the minute element of truth in it was made to serve in the place of reality which was far different.[8]

Rogers states

When I am at my best, as a group facilitator or a therapist, I discover another characteristic. I find that when I am closest to my inner, most intuitive self, when I am somehow in touch with the unknown in me, when perhaps I am in a slightly altered state of consciousness in the relationship, then whatever I do seems to be full of healing.[9]

Rogers argues:

> Our relationship transcends itself and becomes part of something larger[10] ...
> This kind of transcendent phenomenon is certainly experienced at times in groups in which I have worked, changing the lives of some of those involved.[11]

Further:

> I realise that this account partakes of the mystical. Our experiences, it is clear, involve the transcendent, the indescribable, the spiritual. I am compelled to believe that I, like many others, have underestimated the importance of this mystical, spiritual dimension.[12]

Notes

1. McGuire, W. (ed.) (1991) *The Freud Jung Letters*. Penguin Books. Letter no-125F, p. 133.
2. Ibid. Letter no. 139F, p. 144.
3. Webster, R. (1995) *Why Freud was Wrong: Sin, Science and Psychoanalysis*. Harper Collins, p. 305.
4. Ibid., p. 3.
5. Ibid., p. 310.
6. Ibid., p. 308. Webster here uses a quotation from George Weisz in Sulloway, F.J. (1979) *Freud Biologist of the Mind: Beyond the Myth of Psychoanalysis*. London: Fontana.
7. Gay, P. (1988) *Freud: A Life for Our Time*. New York/London: W.W Norton & Co., p. 175.
8. Ibid.
9. Kirschenbaum, H. & Land Henderson, V. (1990) *The Carl Rogers Reader*. London: Constable, p. 137.
10. Ibid., p. 137.
11. loc. cit.
12. loc. cit.

Introduction

I have set out the quotations above as a way of illustrating that psychotherapy has an issue to be addressed: psychotherapy today functions as a religious movement. This because despite Freud's overt rejection of religion he none the less relied on it and exploited religious figures and language for his own ends. Those quotations from Freud himself are evidence of this. Psychotherapists have difficulty in coming to terms with this and deny or exclude religion from their remit. This is ironic given that they are trained to uncover the denials and repressions of their clients. In other words they are capable of exploring the defences of others but are blind to their own: the area of religion has proved to be particularly problematic.

Freud's overt criticism of and theoretical rejection of religion has resulted in a turbulent relationship between psychotherapy and religion whether or not the practitioner claims allegiance to Freud. To exemplify this point the case of Carl Rogers and his adherents have been used in this study for the purposes of comparison. Although Rogers, like Freud, is an inspirational character he has not commanded the same amount of interest as Freud and consequently the weight of material on each is unequal. However, the choice of approaches which appear here is only illustrative of phenomena which exist across the wider psychotherapy community and other approaches would have illustrated similar journeys.

The aim in this work is to uncover the religious aspects of psychotherapy by first using a historical critical reading of two approaches and by deconstructing psychotherapy as an ideology. This is necessary for the discussion which follows in which an exploration of contemporary psychotherapy shows how difficult it has been for practitioners to embrace religion and the spiritual. This is critical and it points to the new openness to religion among some forward thinking psychotherapists who recognise the importance of the spiritual and its dimension of the transcendent. This project is unusual as religious studies scholars usually remain faithful to the study of identifiable religion and religiousness and rarely trespass into areas where they would traditionally be unwelcome. For example, it is common to have a psychology of religion but to reverse this and look at the religious study of psychology is much less common. Those scholars who have ventured into studying the religion of psychology have, it seems, delivered results which demonstrate more than a little of their Judaeo Christian bias. Scholars of religion are familiar with defending religion against the attacks of psychology now is the time for scholars of religion to offer their assistance to psychotherapists with their religious problem. I have been drawn into this field because of my training in both religious studies and psychotherapy.

People have relationships to Freud, or to their chosen founder, which are different to what they say they are. What you see is not what you get. In order to explore this area I have drawn on two traditions of psychotherapy, the psychodynamic and person-centred. The balance of information is unequal by virtue of shear volume of work about Freud and psychodynamic theory, although quantity does not equate with quality and there is a good deal of repetition in the Freudian literature. Freud's central position is also due to his influence on the person-centred tradition and his responsibility for the conception of the psychodynamic approach. The frequency in the literature, whether theoretical, biographical or autobiographical, of both Freud and Rogers and their followers, of language which one would expect to find in religious discourse was such as to be worthy of exploration.

Although the comments in the prologue are of differing orders, some are by Freud and Rogers, and others about Freud, the use of religious language is undeniable even if uttered with a sense of irony or condescension. To say that language is religious is to imbue words with meaning which have a cultural context. For example, when

Freud describes Jung as Joshua and himself as Moses he draws on the biblical tradition, the Judaeo Christian tradition with which he was most familiar. In making such comparisons Freud does not really mean that they are Joshua and Moses but that their relationship stands up to such comparison. There is an element of tongue in cheek about what Freud says but there is also the arrogance of using such heroic figures as comparisons. Freud also compared himself to Hannibal and to St Paul. However, can we deduce from this that he believed that his stature was in their league? We shall see.

Freud was aware that the psyche or, as he would call it the unconscious, had historically been a matter for religion. The psyche had been the concern of religion because it was other worldly, unseen, unidentifiable. But what does it mean to say that something is religious? (It appears that, if some exponents of religious studies had their way, the word religion would be eliminated.[1]) The use of the word religion is peculiar to the user and their particular anthropological lens determines what it means. Wittgenstein noted that the use of a word determines its meaning.

To support any claim about the religiousness of the movements of Freud and Rogers it would be useful to be clear about the use of religion for this work. There is little to gain in trying to define religion, as noted, how the word is used is what matters. In this work the word is used in what may be regarded as a common sense way. For example, if I speak to other English speakers about religion they do have some idea of what I mean. Of course it is their idea and will differ from my own but there will at least be an understanding a family resemblance. The family resemblance between organised religions and psychotherapy is uncanny. However, the religiousness of psychotherapy is more subtle than such a reductionist reading would lead us to believe.

Whilst this is not a project about language the notion of linguistic hygiene is worth noting. This is the idea that each discipline should use the language which is their own and not trespass into the language of other disciplines. So that the frequency of religious language in a subject which claims to be science[2] as does psychotherapy would not occur. My interest is that psychotherapists use the language of religion because they do not have appropriate terms of their own. This is because what is going on in therapy has more in common with religion than therapists admit. The continued active exclusion of the common features of religion and psychotherapy by contemporary psychotherapists is explored below.

The use of irony has allowed an unquestioning acceptance of language which is supposed to be so far removed from their field that it is overlooked. The language that Rogers uses in his quotations is more to describe his experience and the process of therapy than in the case of Freud, which is to borrow from the Judaeo Christian traditions. Rogers describes what he experiences and feels and does not make comparisons of himself or his followers with historical heroes. His concern seems to be to reflect what he is doing. Freud, on the other hand, in comparing himself and others with historical figures, set a trend which his critics and his followers have continued. Why? He did not compare himself with heroic scientists such as Newton or Darwin although others since his death have made such comparisons.

As mentioned above, there is an inequality of weight given to each tradition. The biographical literature on Sigmund Freud appears infinite and on Carl Rogers there is very little[3]. They each contributed to the biographical literature by writing their own confessional work, again following in the tradition of religious thinkers. It is the content of these works which, arguably, sets them apart and encourages their readers to view them differently to other great minds. The choice of literature has been determined by availability therefore those chapters on contemporary psychotherapy are dependent on those practitioners who have published. With the exception of Adam Phillips, who has published extensively, there is limited availability in each tradition.

The biographical literature on Freud can be loosely divided into two groups, critics and devotees, with only the occasional maverick who on first reading appears to occupy some middle ground but ultimately ends up in the devotee's camp. Frederick Crews, Richard Webster, Adolf Grunbaum, and Jeffrey Masson are regarded as the most vehement of Freud's recent critics, and although they appear intent on demonising him, ultimately they cannot. Ernest Jones, Frank Sulloway, Ronald Clark, Paul Roazen are the most often cited of those who deify him. Fritz Wittels wrote the only known biography of Freud which Freud read, and although Freud did not want Wittels to publish he still wrote a foreword for it. We shall see that "paradoxical" is the best way to describe Freud. Peter Gay's works on Freud are scholarly in their attempt to be objective but the reader is left in no doubt about the author's allegiance to Freud.

Whilst this may not be a project to reclaim the humanity of Freud it is fair to point out that those who write about him rarely do so without taking sides. The reasons for them doing this are part of the work, as both Freud and Rogers, although Rogers to a different degree, suffer from either deification or demonisation. Their humanity has become obscured by layers of construction both by themselves and by others. The way in which Freud and Rogers have been bipolarised is not peculiar to them: it is part of a process to which many significant thinkers have been subjected. Freud, in particular, played a significant part in his own construction and therefore he must take some responsibility for what has become of him. It is interesting to note that even in the public domain, that is, the non-analytic community, Freud is rarely described with indifference.

The bipolarisation of Freud and Rogers appears to happen across the board. Whilst practitioners trained in a variety of traditions, psychodynamic, person-centred, cognitive behavioural, gestalt and others who acknowledge their training in one approach would not confirm any specific orientation in practice. Interviews with many of them were invaluable in corroborating this thesis albeit in anecdotal form. The mention of Freud raises passions unparalleled by other thinkers. We seem to love or hate him as if we knew him and yet the man we think we know is a construct. Freud is often regarded with suspicion, described as a charlatan or the man who is always on about sex. I have even had him described to me as "the man who has caused more destruction to the human race than any other single human being" and, by a clinical psychologist, as "having no sense of humour". I encountered a similar response to Rogers by those who, although familiar with him, are not of a person-centred persuasion. Although Rogers is not the household name that Freud is, none the less, within the field, he engenders responses which go beyond the so called objective.

We are fortunate that both Freud and Rogers wrote about themselves. Although these primary sources give us insights into the minds of each they were both clever men and had their own motivation for such writing. As we shall discover below, each was capable of economy with the truth and Freud in particular was aware of what he could do to shape how he and psychoanalysis would be received. Freud and Rogers were selective, as were their followers and critics, about what became known about them. The result is a fascinating tapestry of stories which even if they are outright lies, have become part of the mythology and are consumed by a process of decontextualisation which has produced a kind of faction. The process of uncovering the other Freud and Rogers, for there are doubtless multiple layers of each, only serves to reconstruct them. The material for construction is in the first instance selected by the parents of the child who treat them in specific ways. Both Freud and Rogers were singled out by their parents, although each for different reasons. The child finds ways of responding to this and then eventually his followers and critics respond to this construct of a human being. Each person builds with what they have selected then adds to this their own embellishments. They may exclude aspects which they are either blind to, a version which could be regarded as benign, or they may actively delete aspects of the life which do not quite fit with their mission, as has been the case in psychotherapy. Scholars come along and begin to deconstruct this product and then reconstruct it in their own image. This process is continuous and the product is never complete, as the next wave of scholarship endeavours to find the real founder. The motivation behind such scholarship is, in part, a quest for truth and authenticity, the evidence of this process is no better exemplified than in the quest for the historical Jesus. People want the real thing and set about their scholarship in the belief that there is such a thing.

The delusion, to which I refer in my opening question, is that those involved in psychotherapy are blinded by virtue of their position inside[4] their tradition. The theory of psychotherapy aims to expose a reality which is, as yet, unknown, but they cannot see the wood for the trees and there is an aspect of their process which is unavailable to them by virtue of their occupying it. Each therapist chooses a school with which they have an affinity and in so doing becomes a disciple of the school and to the founder. This discipleship has been described as being like that of the Greco-roman schools of philosophy[5] but it may be argued that this is not the case. For sure the work of Plato and Aristotle, among others, has been celebrated, but their followers seem more concerned with their words than their characteristics. Whilst the philosopher or the artist may engender a following who want to copy his work or even the way that he dresses, there is less evidence that the same deification or demonisation occurs with them as with Freud. Perhaps a closer comparison may be made with that of the eastern guru where the disciple lives with the master in the hope of learning not only a mental training but a particular way of living. As for the scientist, it is unlikely that he will copy the way their predecessors spoke, or the way they dressed, or for that matter the way they smoked. Freud's followers have engaged in all of these. Freud is, as noted, often compared to Marx and Darwin for the magnitude of his work but these two do not engender the extremes of devotion and demonisation which Freud does. This is not to say that followers of Marx and Darwin do not respond passionately to them. We need only observe any march in Red Square to sense the passion of Marxists. A follower of Freud or indeed Rogers becomes an insider with a peculiar relationship to their founder which has religious fervour. The analogy of psychotherapy and religion goes beyond those overt criteria such as scripture, doctrine, ritual, myth, community, which may serve to define religion but tell us little of the subtleties of how it functions.

The prologue illustrates that psychotherapy has more to it than those practising it have been able to analyse effectively by virtue of their position as practitioners. This means that they are so caught up in the traditions of psychotherapy, that they are no longer able to view it dispassionately. There are of course people who are themselves hybrids, who are part psychotherapist and part other things, who may find it easier to have a view from outside. There is no view from nowhere.

Chapter One examines psychoanalysis and Freud's determination to have his work accepted as science. This I do by asking "what was at stake for Freud if psychoanalysis was not accepted as science?" Why did it matter so much that psychoanalysis was located in science? What of the context of Freud's work in Vienna? Rogers suffered from the same desire as have his followers. Was theirs the same motivation? As we shall see, it is of little use to define science any more than it is to define religion because, as noted, their meanings are determined by their use. Even if one argues that Freud and Rogers were not concerned with real or hard science, those metaphors which perpetuate the status of science, it is the behaviour of those involved which has determined this project.

Chapter Two explores the construction of Freud. The Freud that is for public consumption is a fabrication made up in part by his family, himself, his followers, critics and the media. There is no definitive Freud. Whilst it may be said that the whole is greater than the sum of his parts, with Freud there have been parts which are regarded as more significant than others. The selection of what is important depends upon the presuppositions of the viewer.

Chapter Three turns to Freud's legacy. The community which still declares an allegiance to Freud has a difficult inheritance to negotiate and the way in which each follower responds to this legacy is influenced by their commitment to Freud. A selection of contemporary psychotherapists whose views differ on what they do and where psychotherapy should be located illustrates their diversity. From their work it appears that psychoanalysis is defined more easily by what it is *not* rather than what it is.

Chapter Four explores the work of Carl Rogers as person-centred therapy is held in opposition to Freud's psychodynamic psychotherapy. The construction of Rogers follows a similar path to that of Freud, although we have as yet fewer layers of Rogers to disentangle. Although he has not commanded the same degree of interest as Freud it is too early to dismiss his impact as superficial. Rogers' work was also developed in a context and, as with Freud, religion was a specific taboo.

Chapter Five examines Rogers' legacy. The community which still declares an allegiance to him demonstrate parallel themes to that of Freud and the Freudians.

The front runners of the person-centred approach have until recently displayed similar resistance to developing certain aspects of Rogers', work but are beginning to take risks. This process is one where some followers develop the work of the founder and posit their own version of his work. This process accelerates after the death of the founder.

Chapter Six introduces the ideas of the "post-secular" and explores how these may impact on psychotherapy. The inextricable links between the history of philosophy, psychology, and psychotherapy appear to have gone through a cycle with the consequence that practitioners are returning, albeit rather tentatively, to the idea of spiritual practice without dogma. Their new found openness to the spiritual does not, however, translate into their rejecting the structure which they have built for themselves as a religious institution.

Notes

1. Lancaster University December 2003 had a conference asking questions about the state of religious studies. Is it a field? A Discipline? Should it be either at all? Should it become cultural studies? With each question there was the clear message to disconnect religious studies from theology as if the two are not inextricably linked. And the most controversial comment was that there is no such thing as religious studies.
2. Elliott, A. (ed.) (1999) *Freud 2000*. London: Polity. Elliott and Frosh (1995) *Psychoanalysis in Context*. London: Routledge. Bollas, C. (1999) *The Mystery of Things*. London: Routledge.
3. I have attempted to take into account the major trajectories and trends in both traditions
4. The insider outsider debate is on going in religious studies and we are aware that to make a distinction such as this is itself a binary tactic. None the less it serves to highlight those who are blinded by a position which is motivated by tacit knowledge. The author has both insider and outsider perspectives which allow her a position which is not hampered by fear of the accusation of being irrational or religious.
5. Ellenberger, H.F. (1970) *The Discovery of the Unconscious: The History and Evolution of Dynamic Psychiatry*. London: Fontana.

CHAPTER ONE

Science and Status

In 1993 *Time* magazine claimed "Freud is dead"[1]. However, over a decade on the evidence is to the contrary. Attention to Freud by both Freudians and psychodynamic practitioners, if we can use publications about him as a measure of interest, shows little sign of abating. Interest from elsewhere, the media, and his critics in particular, also indicate that interest in him is very much alive, although it is not unusual to find Freud in discussions about God, which is what the article in *Time* is about. If Freud had been successful in his mission, to have psychoanalysis accepted as science, his work would more often be found on the scientific pages of the popular press and of scientific journals than on those pages where it is most often found in discussions about religion.

As will be discussed below a good deal of criticism about Freud and his psychoanalysis is in relation to the "lack of scientific validity" of his theories and of the attitude of Freud and his followers to him and his work. The attitude is illogical, and ranges from reverential at one end to demonising at the other. Attitudes to Freud and psychoanalysis are rarely balanced and rarely from a perspective which is dispassionate. Perhaps this becomes more understandable when we notice that Freud had an unbalanced view of himself and his work which he modelled effectively. At times his self belief was countered by over whelming self doubt. Such swings in attitude appear normal for the prophet, which is often how Freud has been viewed. He is compared to religious leaders, gurus, comparisons which Freud himself also indulged in.

Freud was a scientist whose research was in the field of neuroanatomy for twenty years before he developed psychoanalysis. He was "a man in a white coat" kind of scientist. He was a modernist, a biological determinist who resisted cultural explanations for human behaviour. His work on psychoanalysis was motivated by the tradition of determinism. Biological determinism was very much in vogue in Freud's time: thus he saw humans and their behaviour as a result of their biology. Freud's thinking was revolutionised when he visited the Salpêtrière School in Paris where he was privileged to work with Jean-Martin Charcot who demonstrated, through his work on hysteria, that the mind functions or rather it "behaves as though anatomy did not exist or as though it had no knowledge of it"[2]. That Freud was in the company of such eminent scientists as Charcot goes part of the way to explaining his need to have psychoanalysis accepted as science. However, it would be unwise to define Freud only in these terms because although he was a scientist he was other things at the same time, including a self proclaimed "atheistic Jew" and one of religion's major critics. This makes it more paradoxical that his determination to have psychoanalysis accepted as a new science was such that it became a quest which itself was beyond reason:

> I started my professional activity as a neurologist trying to bring relief to my neurotic patients. Under the influence of an older friend and by my own efforts I discovered some important new facts about the unconscious (unsighted or inside?) life, the role of instinctual urges and so on, after these findings through a new *science*, psychoanalysis, a part of psychology and a new method of treatment for the neurosis. I had to pay heavily for this bit of good luck. People did not believe in my facts and thought my theories unsavoury. Resistance was strong and unrelenting. In the end I succeeded in acquiring pupils and (bringing about?) an international psychoanalytic association. But the struggle is not yet over.[3]

The above quotation is a transcription of the only known recording of Freud, in English, in which he leaves us in no doubt that even at the end of his life, when he recorded this, he was still determined to have psychoanalysis regarded as a new science. He knew that he would have to part-company with traditional sciences but was still determined to stay in the sciences. Although he claims that he had "succeeded", he also assures us that the "struggle" would continue. As we shall see below Freud was inconsistent about how he regarded what he did. As noted, he fluctuated between self assurance and self doubt about his place in the academy. He could not have foreseen just how problematic his comment on his "new science, psychoanalysis", would be for his biological and theoretical descendants and we can only speculate as to what was in his mind when he said "the struggle is not yet over".

However, no one can deny that he was right in his prediction that psychoanalysis would continue to struggle to be a science. Many practitioners today still regard psychoanalysis as a science but their arguments are unconvincing if we hold to a notion of science which is about empiricism and proof[4]. Psychoanalysts continue the justification of their scientific validity in debates, conferences, journals and books, which is testimony to Freud's work not yet being a *fait accompli*. Their continued "unrelenting struggle" to convince the world of their scientific validity is, a sign that psychoanalysts still protest too much.

The reasons which Freud had for claiming that psychoanalysis had scientific status are different to the reasons offered by contemporary Freudians. In Freud's time and culture science was a more dynamic term. Contemporary psychoanalysts, whilst clinging to the desire to be scientists, have the complication of their relationship with Freud and the huge body of traditions which they inherit. In other words, the ambitions of contemporary psychoanalysts, seeking to be scientists, are tainted by the desire to be true to the claims of their founder. Today's psychoanalysts live in an era where science enjoys a different kind of supremacy to that which it held in Freud's time and consequently contemporary psychoanalysts are battling to be accepted by what could be regarded as an out dated model.

Apart from the obvious lack of empirical evidence one of the stumbling blocks for psychoanalysis as science is that if it was/is science followers of psychoanalysis would have little difficulty in rejecting Freud and/or his findings and moving on. This is not the case. Psychoanalysts and psychotherapists of a psychodynamic nature revere Freud and his work in ways which contradict what we understand as a scientific paradigm[5] which traditionally demands the fall of the existing theory as it gives way to the new theory[6].

Neither Freud nor his work has engendered this kind of take over. Even those who have left the Freudian camp do not dismiss his ideas completely but build on them regardless of their flaws. And as will be demonstrated below, even those opposed to Freud rely on the psychoanalytic model to deconstruct him. Freud commands the kind of reverence which other great men of science, Charles Darwin, being an obvious example, do not enjoy. In fact, even to explain psychoanalysis as art, which Peter Gay and Susie Orbach have tried, does not explain their reverence for Freud. People who may want to paint like Picasso or Monet, who even copy their ways of dressing, smoking, speaking and even walking, as has been the case with Freud[7], would rarely have such difficulty in accepting their mistakes both theoretical and personal. A point worth noting is that even some who claim to be anti-Freudian, who voice their distaste for all things Freudian, are ultimately unwilling to depart from him.[8]

Whilst scientists endeavour to usurp their predecessors by disproving their theories the psychoanalyst holds fast to Freud and his work and is cautious not to disprove Freud or offend his memory. This is where the activity of delusion by contemporary psychodynamic practitioners is most present, by virtue of its glaring absence.[9] In Freud's time psychoanalysts who developed his ideas were accused, by Freud, of being heretics. Today's psychoanalysts still have this legacy to consider if taking a similar risk. As I hope to demonstrate below, to be seen to contradict Freud is not acceptable if you want to remain a psychoanalyst. From his grave Freud still directs his movement. Freud stated that to be a psychoanalyst one had to believe in what have come to be regarded as his four pillars[10]. In making this statement he was creating a dogma which his followers have found difficult to challenge, at least overtly[11]. This we shall explore in a later chapter. This said the parallels between Freud and religious founders whose words and actions become sacred and as such unquestioned by those who wish to be followers become understandable.

In Freud's time science had become the God of all things: to be scientific was beyond just being a man in a white coat. There were social, political and financial implications which were peculiar to being a scientist. To be a scientist held status which out weighed those who would once have been competitors. If one was a scientist this had implications for what one was not. For example, science was not art and certainly not religion. Science would eventually have answers, would explain the universe in ways which religions had not. To be religious, to believe in the unexplained, was regarded as superstitious and undesirable. But more than this, belief in things beyond science carried further connotations of being unintelligent. Freud found science and religion irreconcilable and his followers have maintained the same attitude. These beliefs, although out dated to a degree, have left a legacy for those who continue to debate about the divide between science and religion. Such debates are as compelling as ever but warrant a discussion which is beyond the scope of this project.

As we know from Freud's work and correspondence his views on religion were less than flattering. Few people who are religious would regard Freud's oft quoted view of "religion as a universal obsessional neurosis"[12] as complimentary. Freud did say this but, when viewed in the context of his other work, he also regarded religion as necessary if only as a way of preventing anarchy. For Freud and many others to be a scientist was to demonstrate evolution: science and atheism had become bed fellows. Science for Freud was a secular practice which excluded religion and did not rely on faith, and although this is now more of an area of contention, for Freud science, atheism, and the secular were allies, if not synonymous. This is ironic given that history shows that science was largely the domain of men of religion, for example, Galileo, Newton and even Darwin himself did not reject the possibility of God[13]. Lest we forget, Freud was a modernist given to grand theories, who used large brush strokes for his theories: to universalise religion as neurosis was but one of his brush strokes. As we shall see below, Freud was selective particularly in his choices about what was deemed an obsessional neurosis. For example, his own cigar smoking was omitted. His famous retort when challenged about his cigar smoking that "sometimes a cigar is just a cigar" is but one example of this.

By and large today when people talk of science they imply qualities such as truth and objectivity, implied in which is distance and reason, detachment from the object of study, but ultimately the ability to reason without the burden and this is how it was and still is viewed—of subjectivity. These are the illusions[14] under which science has demanded status. Science and the secular have become almost synonymous, in so far as to be secular carries values and status which overlap with science. So when Freud made his famous claim that he had discovered a new branch of the science of psychology he was also making an alliance with the secular. This is the legacy which his followers have to contend with. Freud as a self proclaimed atheistic Jew, or as the title of Peter Gay's book states, "A Godless Jew"[15], has made it extremely difficult for his descendants to view religion in a positive way. The irony of Gay's title has yet to be fully explored! If you are a God you do not need the idea of other Gods.

Although Freud's claim about his new science has been the cause of immense controversy both during his life and since his death, scholars have noted that the notion of science for Freud working in Europe did not hold the same ideals of empiricism[16] as in the United Kingdom. Whilst this work is not about a religion versus science debate it is useful to question what drove Freud's determination to reinvent science so that psychoanalysis could be accepted. Freud knew what was expected of a scientist, he had been one for twenty years before he discovered psychoanalysis, and his new work did not fit the criteria of empiricism or objectivity.

Freud's works have been divided in various ways. For example, his works on religion have been regarded as an independent canon. These works were a form of armchair anthropology, derived from books rather than field studies. Added to this were Freud's observations of patients and his inferences and comparisons of obsessional behaviours with that of religious ritual. Freud's findings relied on his interpretation and inference of individual cases which could not be repeated and as such were not empirical in the way science demanded. Freud's notion of science was stretching the common use of the word.

What is often marginalised is the context in which Freud felt it necessary to make such a claim and what was at stake if he did not. Freud was neurotic, had many illnesses and was at times bordering on hypochondria[17]. He was, as is often noted, an insecure academic seeking approval. There is plenty of evidence which points to his not fitting in[18]. However, he also countered this with demonstrations of unparalleled self-belief. Freud, unlike many of his contemporaries in science, did not enjoy the financial support of his family and therefore had a basic economic drive: he needed the money. When we discuss men such as Freud it seems impolitic to discuss such matters as income[19], although we may it seems discuss anything else related to them. Private medical practice was one way for Freud to earn a secure income and by specialising in psychiatry, an area which he identified as in need of development, he managed to do this. He could not indulge himself in a full time research post and support his wife and family. Practicing medical science was a position of social status. It was announced in a Viennese news paper that Privatdozent Freud, an eminent doctor, was to begin private practice in Vienna. Such was Freud's name in the University of Vienna for all he believed he was undervalued.

In Freud's time the scientist was by virtue of his title an objective observer too intelligent to believe in God. Freud's chosen area of practice, psychiatry, and in particular the unconscious, had a genealogy which was ambiguous. Medicine has not long been in the realm of science, in fact quite the contrary. In 1864, one of Freud's medical contemporaries, Moritz Benedikt, claimed that "hysteria could be cured by the confession of pathogenic secrets".[20] Freud in a joint paper with Breuer acknowledge this. (This is worth specific note as Freud is often accused of not giving credit to others, an accusation which may be partially true but not absolutely). Cure by confession without external prescriptions for punishment and which allowed the person confessing to abdicate responsibility for their behaviour was a departure from confession as it was experienced in the Christian tradition. Freud's development of Benedikt's idea lead to his own technique, but not before experimenting with Breuer's technique of hypnotism.

Freud worked with some of the most respected men in his field[21]. The University of Vienna had some of the most eminent thinkers of the time, many of international fame. Franz Brentano had a lasting influence on Freud and his work. Brentano encouraged Freud to revisit Feuerbach[22], some of whose ideas Freud adopted for his own theories. Brentano was both a believer and a Darwinist with whom Freud had enjoyed debating and who had led Freud to question his atheism. Freud had also worked with Charcot and Breuer, both regarded as pioneering medical researchers. Carl Claus taught comparative anatomy and gave Freud the opportunity to go to Trieste to do what turned out to be ground breaking research on eels, for which Freud gained a reputation for excellence. Ernest Von Brücke taught him physiology. Freud said that Brücke was the most influential man in his life. There are more, too numerous to list. But this gives us some idea of Freud's academic foundations. With this it is all the more remarkable that he was as academically insecure, as is often noted.

He was unsure of his own place in the academy and, as he himself notes, had to overcome "unrelenting resistance", and "struggle"[23], because people thought that his ideas were "unsavoury". At times he ascribed these difficulties to his being a Jew but he is inconsistent about this. He is, it appears, consistent about very little. Freud's desire to find a secure home for his work was a significant driving force for him. He did not want to be regarded as anything other than a scientist, although the paradox of Freud is his claiming, in that oft used quotation in a letter to Wilhelm Fleiss, that he was not a man of science at all but "a conquistador, an adventurer ..."[24] As suggested above, Freud had more to gain in private practice than as a research scientist, both in terms of status and income. He had experienced the humiliation of what he perceived as poverty, and consequently feared a return to this. The Freud family had relied on an uncle to support them financially and therefore Freud only had himself to support his research and his ever growing family. He had six children and so this was an important consideration. Economic as well as concerns about status were real for Freud and were certainly a part of what was at stake when he made his claim about his new science.

As noted, Freud's works on religion[25] are regarded as an independent canon and are testimony to his belief that religion was for people who were unable to think for themselves, people who abdicated responsibility for their behaviour. However, he was resigned to the fact that it was part of the social fabric necessary to maintain a civilized society. Freud turned to other thinkers who had rejected God, for example, Nietzsche, once a believer himself, in pronouncing the death of God, a metaphor for the death of religiousness, which gave people permission to believe that there had at least been such a thing to believe in. What Freud proclaimed seemed more extreme, God as man's invention without any possibility of existence was beyond blasphemy. For Freud God was the product of an over active imagination, a projection as Freud claimed, and as Feuerbach[26] had before him.

Freud has to be the most deluded of all and duped his followers into believing that what they were doing was scientific. Freud knew that to be successful he would have to make significant scientific discoveries and from early in his life he had reason to believe that he would. Added to this, is that science was where personal status could be found. Geologists had already made discoveries to "prove" that the earth was very much older than had been claimed by theologians. Darwin had "proved" that there was indeed a design in biology, evolution, which did not necessarily rely on a designer. Each of these theories caused major social fractures. The Christian God had been toppled from his established position and science became the replacement. To the question: What was at stake for Freud if science did not accept psychoanalysis? The answer is that he could have faded into oblivion, a place which many still argue he deserves. With some insight into Freud's early life we can see how he was motivated to prevent this. It was never in Freud's life plan to end in oblivion.

The Vienna in which Freud lived and worked for almost seventy eight of his eighty three years was, in the late nineteenth and early twentieth centuries, a hot house of creativity. Vienna was regarded as a "microcosm of enlightenment"[27], a place of heightened creativity, especially among Jews. This creativity has been ascribed to fear of the rise of National Socialism, and the overt anti-Semitism in places of power. Hitler and his work did not happen in a vacuum but was the culmination of a specific genealogy. Freud shared Vienna with many more creative intellectuals than those he encountered in his field within the university. For example, the philosopher Ludwig Wittgenstein, whose family converted to Christianity because of their fears of being Jewish in such a climate of instability, was Austrian[28] and in 1922 he published his famous *Tractatus Logico-Philosophicus* in Vienna. There was also Arnold Schonberg who became famous for the development of twelve tone music. Also a group of artists known as the Secession movement, one of whom was Gustav Klimt, flourished at the time. The Scottish architect and artist Charles Rennie Mackintosh planned to move to Vienna. It was almost incestuous. Doctors such as Freud were privy to what was going on beneath the surface and although there was a good deal of intellectual exchange this may be seen as a bi-product of political and social unrest. The date given to the beginning of this highly creative period coincides with an economic decline in 1873 and ultimately ended, so far as Jewish artists and intellectuals were concerned, with the annexation of Austria by Hitler's Third Reich. In the context of this multi-faceted enlightenment the work of Freud seems in some respects less daring. For example, in the field of sexuality he was less outrageous than Karl Kraus, Wilhelm Stekel or Otto Weininger who in 1903 published *Sex and Character* which had, according to Sulloway, "stunned the world"[29]. Weininger committed suicide the same year. With this in mind why did Freud become a household name when others in his city in his time were clearly more risqué than he was? This is one of the issues we shall proceed to explore.

Notes

1 Elizabeth Valklong President (1993) In: *Time Magazine*, November 29.
2 Sulloway, F.J. (1979) *Freud Biologist of the Mind: Beyond the Psychoanalytic Legend*. Great Britain: Fontana, p. 35.
3 This is a transcript of a recording which Sigmund Freud made in the year he died (1939). Those sections in brackets are difficult to make out as the recording is of poor quality and so I have taken a guess at what he may have said. The italics are my own for emphasis. The recording may be obtained from the Tavistock library. Tavistock Clinic, Belsize Park, London W3.
4 Elliott, A. & Frosh, S. (eds) (1995) *Psychoanalysis in Context* is a collection of papers many of which take for granted the scientific nature of psychoanalysis. London: Routledge. See also Elliott (ed.) (1999) *Freud 2000*.
5 Kuhn, T.S. (1970) *The Structure of Scientific Revolutions*. Chicago University Press.
6 Ibid. In addition, as I imagine Kuhn would testify, the task of the scientist is rarely (if ever) as "black and white" as the fantasy which is often held of it.
7 Many biographers note that some of Freud's followers did go to great lengths to copy his every gesture. Roazen (1975) p. 306. Webster (1995) pp. 307–8.
8 Webster, Masson and Crews some of the most vehement of his critics as we shall see below have difficulty giving him his last rites.
9 Derrida, J. (1972) *The Margins of Philosophy*. Chicago: University of Chicago Press (Translation 1982).
10 Jacobs, M. (1988) *Psychodynamic Counselling in Action*. London: Sage.

11 Islam has Five Pillars and Buddhism has Four Noble Truths and the Old Testament has the Ten Commandments. Acceptance of these foundations is a prerequisite for being a member of the community.
12 Freud, S., Volume 13. *The Origins of Religion*. Penguin Freud Library (here after PFL) includes his works on religion from 1907–1938, p. 40.
13 Charles Darwin was a religious man and claimed on his death bed that he had never denied that there had been a creator. He was read his last rites as a continued commitment to Emma, his wife, who was a devout Christian who feared that they would not meet again in the afterlife.
14 Religion is the "Illusion" which Freud writes of and by virtue of this position he cannot see his own illusions about science.
15 Gay, P. (1987) *A Godless Jew: Freud, Atheism, And The Making of Psychoanalysis*. New Haven/London: Yale University Press.
16 Bettelheim, B. (1982) *Freud and Man's Soul*. Whilst criticising the translation of Freud's work by the Stracheys also notes this distinction in the meaning of science.
17 Molnar, M. (1992) Translated, annotated with an Introduction. *The Diary of Sigmund Freud 1929–1939 A Record of the Final Decade*. Scribner New York. In these final years Freud limps from one ailment to another with differing degrees of severity.
18 Freud's disputes with Nothnagel, Brücke, Fechner and even Brentano, who made a lasting impression on him, are well documented. For a delicious explanation of this see Gay (1988) *Freud: A Life for Our Time*.
19 If Freud had been born into poverty we may regard him as even more heroic, in so far as his journey to fame and fortune would have had a more difficult start.
20 Ellenberger (1970) p. 46.
21 Different versions of who was responsible for Freud's trip to Trieste exist.
22 Gay (1988) pp. 28–9.
23 In a recording (available from the Library of the Tavistock clinic)which Freud made in 1939 he states that he had succeeded, eventually, with his struggle to gain psychoanalysis a place in the science of psychology.
24 Sulloway (1979) p. 477.
25 Vol. 13 PFL, *Totem and Taboo, Future of an Illusion, Civilisation and it's Discontents and Moses and Monotheism*.
26 Gay (1988)
27 Janik, A. & Toulmin, S. (1973) *Wittgenstein's Vienna*. Chicago: Elephant Paperbacks (Reprint 1996).
28 As a professor in Cambridge he was the most important figure in the English movement of Analytical Philosophy.
29 Sulloway, F.J. (1979) p. 224.

CHAPTER TWO

The Construction of Freud

So who is this man who has transcended the bounds of normal criticism? This chapter aims to deconstruct some of the stories about Freud which have become taken for granted, part of psychotherapeutic folklore. When studying a figure such as Freud one faces the challenge of the volume of information and consequently one has to be selective in a process which by definition is exclusive. The result of this is that it is unlikely that anyone will find a definitive Freud. The following, is one version of Freud. He was born on the 6th May 1856. Even this has been disputed with some believing it was March. Renée Gicklhorn is persuasive that May is more likely correct[1]. It was predicted from the moment of his birth that Sigismund Freud was destined for great things. Sigismund the name on his birth certificate he changed to Sigmund. However, he was known to the family as Schlomo[2], an old family name, sometimes translated as Schelomo, a Hebraic version of Solomon from shalom meaning peace[3]. His mother had pet names for him and called him "her little Sigi" and "her little Blackamoor"[4]. Although the validity of these has been questioned there is no reason that it has to be either/or: it was probably both and others.

Freud could trace his family back a long way. His family tradition was that of Hassidic Judaism, known for its mastery of allusion[5]. The inscription from Freud's father to him in the family bible is "To my son Schlomo". This is interesting in itself as traditionally the bible is handed down to the eldest son and although Freud was the first son of his mother Amalie Nathanson, his father Jakob Freud had been married twice before and had two sons by his first wife Sally. Ernest Jones, regarded as one of the most significant biographers, has made no reference to Jakob's second wife Rebecca, who died after three years of marriage, although she is believed to have brought the sons from his first marriage to live with their father and her in Pribor. Jakob's first wife did not want to move with Jakob when his grandfather offered him a position in the family wool business in Pribor, a town in Moravia now the Czech republic. Jakob's marriage to Rebecca was short. When Rebecca died he married Amalie, sometimes called Amalia[6], who was twenty years his junior.

When Freud was born he was already an uncle to his half brother Emanuel's son. Freud had seven siblings in addition to his two half brothers Emanuel and Phillip. He had a younger brother Julius who died in infancy in 1858, and who is, like Rebecca, have been omitted from some biographies[7]. Freud had a Catholic nanny for the first three years of his life, who took him to mass with her. She was accused of stealing from the family and was dismissed. Freud had five sisters Anna, Rosa, Marie, Adolfine and Pauline and then his younger brother Alexander whose name is believed to have been chosen by Freud. The Jones biography was subjected to major editing by Anna Freud, Freud's youngest daughter, regarded as her father's most devoted disciple. She is believed to have censored out information which would not show the family in a positive light. Anna was very protective of her father's memory and was intent on keeping it as untainted as possible.

Information about Freud and his family is plentiful, although selective. Working out the truths about Freud and of Freud is a difficult project. Biographers rely on previous biographies with each selecting, either consciously or unconsciously, information which fulfils their ideologically led questions. For example, those who want to show Freud as a heroic figure omit information regarded as less favourable whilst others dwell on the unfavourable in order to show him as a demon. Freud's biographers, what ever their motivation, have reused the numerous predictions believed to bear witness to the inevitability of his becoming great.

Of the many incidents in Freud's childhood there are three which he held to be significant and are therefore repeated by his biographers. The first was that he was born with a caul on his head, traditionally a sign of greatness. Fritz Wittels, the first of Freud's biographers, wrote of Freud that he had in fact been born covered in black hair, a feature which led his mother to call him "her little Blackamoor"[8]. Although one story need not exclude another, some stories are given more emphasis than others, indicative of a selection process which is of interest in itself. The second incident was when a gypsy/peasant woman told his mother that she had given birth to a child who was to become an important man in the world[9]. And the third, when Freud was an adolescent he was with his family in the Prater, a Viennese park, when an itinerant performer predicted that Freud would become a cabinet minister when he grew up.[10] This is the seen as the basis for his choice to study law. He changed his mind and studied medicine instead.

It may be difficult for the contemporary mind to realise the importance of such predictions. However, their significance becomes apparent below. These events indicate that even before Freud had taken his first breath he was believed to be special. It should therefore come as no surprise that he both behaved and was treated differently, almost with reverence, particularly by his mother and by many others who encountered him.

Freud, later in his life, claimed that the story of the peasant woman had been greatly significant in giving him his "thirst for grandeur"[11]. Although most people have memorable childhood stories Freud's have been emphasised, embroidered more than others. With such a destiny predicted it would have been difficult for Freud not to attempt to become important, (even had he chosen a different route of dissent). These predictions caused both Freud and his family to behave as if they were true,[12] thereby adding to Freud's self-belief. He was treated differently to his siblings, treatment which set him apart from them. If we believe at all in his own psychoanalytic principles—that childhood events continue to impact upon us throughout our adult lives—the way in which these stories were recounted to him would have had some bearing on his driven personality.

Freud was aware that he was the favoured child and talked of this in his adulthood.[13] Further examples of Freud being regarded as special and being singled out for favours are to be found in the dedication to him from his father in the family bible, mentioned above. Also, as an adolescent, he alone was given an oil lamp (a new invention) for studying, and another, at Freud's request another of his siblings was prevented from playing the piano because it disturbed him.

These stories are repeated again and again and are regarded in a positive light. There are others which paint a less rosy picture. For example, Freud as an adult recalled his father saying that he, Freud, would never make anything of himself. This became part of a recurring dream for Freud and indicates just how much the statement affected him. Another story which had a major influence on Freud was his father telling him that when he (his father) had been a child he was out walking, with a new cap on, when a gentile child hit his cap off his head and shouted "Jew get off the pavement!"[14] When Freud asked his father what he did his father replied that he had just picked up his cap from the dirt and walked on. This story made Freud angry and he acknowledged that it had had a lasting effect on him.

As a young man Freud had been very keen to have a career in research. However, as noted above the Freud family were not wealthy and depended on an uncle for financial support. This led Freud to resent his father as he was unable to support him in a career which did not pay enough to support a family life. Freud felt forced to go into private practice. For these reasons he regarded his father as something of a disappointment[15]. This story is somewhat anti-heroic and Freud's response to his father's death showed signs that none of these issues were resolved. The story of his father's cap being hit off by a gentile shows something of the relations between the Jews and the gentiles of the time as well as showing us something of the character of Freud's father, who unlike his son was not a revolutionary, but rather, a man willing to acquiesce.

Freud's autobiographical writings demonstrate that the combination of investment in, and expectations of, him was both difficult and enjoyable for him. Again, if we draw upon the principles of psychoanalysis, overt demonstration of self-belief is often interpreted as over compensation for deeply felt insecurity. Freud's family had high expectations of Freud. He always had something to live up to and was self critical if he did not succeed.

Whilst Freud seems to have done very well at school he was not regarded as a child prodigy or genius, although later in his career he, perhaps with a touch of irony, regarded himself in this light. Freud made no declaration of himself as a genius, however, he did, at times, deem himself to be in the same prophetic league as Moses and St Paul,[16] both powerful Jewish role models. Of course we can have no evidence of whether Freud was being ironic in his analogy, but even so it takes a certain kind of confidence to put ones self in the same category as such heroes. Freud was acutely aware of his Jewishness and although not a practicing Jew,[17] the influence of Judaism may be traced throughout his work[18]. But what do we mean by practicing Jew? He was a member of the B'nai B'rith a Jewish society to whom he lectured and used as a testing ground for many of his ideas. He remained a member during his whole life and acknowledged his debt to them for their support at times when he believed that he was being academically persecuted. Freud acknowledged the Jewish calendar and its festivals and his work follows in the tradition of Jewish mysticism with its convention of allusion[19]. He is also believed to have spoken Hebrew as an inscription from his father in the family bible is in Hebrew. In addition Bakan notes that a Professor Hammerschlag is believed to have taught him Hebrew.[20]

Freud, a self proclaimed atheist, became one of religion's most formidable critics. This was difficult for his wife Martha who was an observing Jew and a point of interest is that none of Freud's children married gentiles. Freud's criticism of religion is well known, as are his views on the ways in which it served a purpose, but his criticism did not prevent him from having numerous friendships with believers. He had many friends who were believers both Jewish and Christian. Of particular note is his relationship and correspondence with Oskar Pfister a Swiss pastor. From this we must infer that although he was anti-religion he was not a fundamentalist atheist and he maintained a significant connection to things Jewish throughout his whole life.

According to Thomas Szasz, Freud had differing views on his Jewishness, one for public and one for private life. This is not surprising as most people have public and private persona. What matters is to what extent Freud's public and private selves contradicted each other. Freud believed that his being Jewish was at times a hindrance and blamed this for holding him back, a notion which Sulloway claims is greatly exaggerated. For example, when he failed to receive promotion he blamed his rejection on being a Jew, believing that there was an anti-Jewish faction in the university.[21]

Contrary to Freud's belief in this anti-Jewish faction there is evidence which indicates that many other Jews were employed and in promoted positions at the time. His rejection was therefore more likely to have been because his work was regarded as having moved away from his more scientific neurological work and some of his ideas clashed with the social values and cultural climate of the time. His colleagues had particular difficulty hearing his theories on sexual abuse and infantile sexuality. His views were regarded by some as extremely controversial, in this late Victorian period. However, there were others whose writings were far more radical than Freud's[22] but who have faded into oblivion compared to him. Freud had an extra characteristic, best described as charisma, which allowed his followers to suspend their reason and become enraptured by the man.

As mentioned above, Freud did declare his Jewishness and this was at least to declare an awareness of an affinity with a cultural milieu. At times he believed that his being a Jew played a significant part in the success of his movement, but was equally aware that the psychoanalytic movement was in danger of becoming a ghettoized Jewish society. He believed that the dominance of Jews in the movement was not a good thing and one of his reasons for cultivating the kind of relationship which he did with Jung was in the hope of giving the society a gentile as a leader[23]. Freud engineered a plan that Jung was to become his successor in order that the psychoanalytic community would widen and become international. His desire was to found a world movement.

Freud's self-belief has been explored by many, for example, in Anthony Storr's *Feet of Clay*[24], an exploration of figures whom he regards as gurus, and in which there are chapters on both Freud and Jung.[25] Storr argues that Freud and Jung have many of the negative characteristics which would cause them to seek and find and enjoy guru status. However, Storr, by claiming that Freud also had altruistic characteristics, gives us some insight into the difficulty of categorizing a man such as Freud who is described as a despot[26] on one hand and somewhat altruistic on the other.

If Storr is correct it is unlikely that we would have stories about Freud's own feelings of awe towards some of his mentors, as gurus have difficulty in accrediting others' success. For example, as a student Freud was in awe, to the point of reverence, of Charcot.

Apparently on returning from Paris after studying with him Freud is described:

not so much a student reporting on a study trip as a zealot who had undergone religious conversion[27].

Both Ellenberger(1970) and Sulloway(1979) have comprehensive lists of those who were influential on Freud. From them we can see that he showed admiration for many, Charcot, Breuer, Brücke, Brentano, Jung among others. However, Charcot, Breuer and Liebault[28], (a practitioner of hypnosis) are most often cited as his mentors. Freud's teachers were numerous and must include those with whom he had no direct contact, other than through their work. He was exceptionally well read. For example, we know that he read Plato, Nietzsche, Benedikt, Bachofen, Feuerbach, and Darwin. He also read literature. Freud, like others, was in awe of many people but at times this faded when his own knowledge grew.

Throughout his life Freud worked hard, in his studies, in his research, in his practice, and also in his correspondence. According to Hans Sachs, one of his disciples, who spent a great deal of time with Freud over along period, Freud always had just a little more to give than any one else. Sachs gives examples of Freud's great physical as well as mental resilience.[29] Further evidence of this resilience is to be found in the final seventeen years of his life, when he continued to work with the same application as he always had. He did this despite having cancer of the mouth, on which he had numerous surgical procedures, some say as many as thirty three, which were a source of great pain to him. He wore a prosthesis, a source of deep discomfort which interfered with his speech, and he had to have daily treatment (administered by Anna his youngest daughter) to clean his wound. His cancer was, even then, attributed to his dependence on large cigars. He found them difficult to give up but claimed that he managed to cut down on the number.

The picture of Freud which we are beginning to build indicates that he was, as is often the case, much more complicated than his critics and admirers have been able to illustrate independently. The paradoxical character of Freud comes to light through the combined biographical works, and his autobiographical writing. As much as they try[30], it has not been possible for his biographers to separate the man from the myth[31]; they are now one and the same. Freud also had difficulty in separating himself from the growing myths, and it is no wonder that he became just as guilty of creating and perpetuating them as anyone. When people around you are intent on elevating your position it is easy to come to believe, delude yourself, that what they say is right rather than taking the opportunity to counter them and asking what their need for such elevation is. This would have happened if Freud had applied his own psychoanalysis.

Freud had difficulty in settling as a scientist and found some tension between himself as a scientist and as an adventurer. For him, these did not necessarily go hand in hand and it is worth quoting him in full:

> "for I am actually not at all a man of science" he once told his friend Fliess, "not an observer, not an experimenter, not a thinker. I am by temperament nothing but a conquistador, an adventurer, if you wish to translate this term—with all the inquisitiveness, daring, and tenacity characteristic of such a man."[32]

It seems that Freud's difficulty was in believing that he could be both a scientist and a "conquistador" at the same time. This problem appears to be, of integrating different paradigms, a problem which echoes the on-going struggle in psychoanalysis and other therapies. The tension created by the need for scientific[33] recognition on the one hand and the subjective human qualities required for successful practice on the other is still around for today's therapists.

The notion of psychoanalysis as science is perpetuated by many of the biographers. For example, Ernest Jones in defence of psychoanalysis as science states:

> Mediocre spirits demand of science a kind of certainty which it cannot give, a sort of religious satisfaction. Only the real, rare, true scientific minds can endure doubt, which is attached to all our knowledge.[34]

This statement, in claiming that only "true scientific minds can endure doubt" is but one example of a follower protesting too much. If psychoanalysis is not a science then what is it? The alternatives which have been suggested are dismissed. Psychoanalysts have more to gain, as Freud had, by being regarded as scientists. Perhaps the "grain of truth" which Jones, in the prologue, claims there is behind the notion of psychoanalysis as religion is beginning to mature.

However, it is evident that Freud himself was aware that the techniques and skills of the practitioner were of little consequence if the relationship between patient and practitioner had no rapport. The efficacy of psychoanalysis relies on the faith of the patient in the practitioner and the practitioner in the patient. For example, Paul Roazen states:

As rationalistic and intellectual as Freud sounds, he was also concerned to show that what turns the scale in a patient's therapeutic struggle is not his intellectual insight—which is neither strong enough or free enough for such an achievement—but simply and soley his relationship to the doctor[35].

Whilst being aware of the importance of theory for the wider recognition of psychoanalysis, Freud knew that no amount of theory could make therapy successful if the patient/doctor relationship was mismatched. This should leave us in no doubt that he believed that there is something more required for the process of therapy than good textbook practice, a "something" which remains out with the reach of scientific study. In fact Freud did not behave as a scientist in any traditional sense with regard to either his subject or his patients and was aware of his effect on his patients and his ever increasing band of followers, who responded to Freud as if he was an indispensable giant. Freud realised that he was part of this therapeutic process, his powerful "aura" was necessary for the cultivation of the transferential relationship, a relationship which he cultivated with patients as well as his followers. Such behaviour was/is not expected of men of science. It is this behaviour which raises the question of the nature of psychoanalysis. Scientists are not supposed to influence their work with their personalities. The psychoanalytic movement was built from Freud's personality. Freud was offering salvation and became the *One* for whom the psychoanalytic community existed. The community functions as a *sangha* does with a leader whom they follow and whom they cannot hope to usurp.

Freud's work sits more comfortably in the field of metapsychology. It is not repeatable in the way that empiricism requires as it relies on interpretation. Freud's life is also based on interpretation. Thus what we have of Freud is tantamount to a body of mythology. It is useful to understand that there is mythology in Freud's work, and of, Freud. That is, Freud drew upon ancient myths for inspiration for his theories, the most famous of which is Oedipus Rex. In addition to this there are numerous myths about Freud which have a different function to those which he adopted for his theories.

Myths about Freud have served to construct a history which, as noted, both deifies him, and or demonises him. The effect of these myths has been that any notion of a real Freud is lost in favour of a make believe heroic figure[36]. As we can see from above Freud, from the beginning of his life was used to special attention. This continued throughout his life and indeed after his death. Many commentators note the different myths of Freud; in fact Sulloway devotes a section of his book to "The Myth of the Hero". The hero has always had an important role in myths and has been the subject of much interest for a long time. For example, Thomas Carlyle wrote a series of lectures on the hero in history and the way in which our attitudes to heroes has changed[37]. Our heroes were once Gods with extraordinary qualities and powers, where as now they have evolved into humans with different extraordinary qualities. These new Gods have come to be so by a process of adulation and their adaptation to it. One of the consequences of enjoying such adulation is that they become seduced by economics and power. There are exceptions to this, for example, Mother Theresa and Nelson Mandela who defy such cynicism.

What is meant by myth is determined by its use. Contemporary use of myth differs from even a decade ago. It functions today as a substitute for lie. For example, there is a trend in popular culture to state that something is a myth when it is untrue. For example, the notion of the nuclear family is heralded a myth: any notion of normal is deemed a myth, perfection is also a myth. Almost without exception, when used in the media myth is used as a form of condescension, or irony, with connotations of fabrication. My own use of the word is unlike this contemporary popular use which sees myth as synonymous with lie. The myths of Freud have constructed a Freud with multiple personalities. Each version of Freud, including his own, has had a purpose, or function which has kept Freud alive. Freud is not theoretically dead yet. If we view a myth as a component of a community's social cohesion and a way of capturing events which have been chosen and perpetuated for reasons beyond the individual it is more empathetic than seeing myths as creations which are actively misleading. Freud did actively mislead us, as have many who have written about him but to call them liars would be too strong an accusation. History and mythology are subjective versions of events which bear the observers truths- how they have interpreted what they saw or experienced.

According to Robert Segal it was with the work of Freud, and subsequently Jung, that the subject matter of myth ceased to be about the external, physical world and became internalised to the subject of the unconscious. Segal claims that by building on this, adding, for example, the work of another psychoanalyst, W.D.Winnicott, myth becomes not only about the internal world of the unconscious but a transitional activity which allows the boundary between reality and illusion to be blurred comfortably.[38] Below, the use of the word myth reflects something of the need of the user and certainly, when used as a form of condescension, says much about the user and little about the myth.

Freud has been so shrouded by myth as to make it impossible to find a pre mythical Freud. The myths of Freud have become established in the traditions of psychoanalysis but are used in numerous disciplines and reflect how Freud touched upon them. Sulloway is not alone in exploring the significance of mythologizing Freud. Henri Ellenberger states:

> One of the difficulties of evaluating Freud's contribution to psychiatry is that psychoanalysis has grown up in a sphere of legend, with the result that an objective appraisal will not be possible before the true historical facts are separated from the legend.[39]

Ellenberger, writing in the nineteen sixties, still thought it possible to find "true historical facts"; an idea which must be regarded as illusory. He agrees that Freud is a legendary figure. Paul Roazen claims:

> Freud knew the power of the legend.[40]

A claim which is certainly borne out in Freud's contribution to his own mythology.

Mythologizing Freud is common place. In fact it is difficult to say anything about Freud without it becoming part of the biopic. Trying to discover the real Freud has been the task of many of his biographers. Ellenberger, Sulloway, Roazen and Webster have taken particular interest in trying to unravel him. They attempt to separate Freud from his work. With each attempt the biographer is left confused as there is no clear way of delineating them. Even with the knowledge that some of his theories were flawed Freud's awesome character is continually elevated. Even his most vehement critics fall into the trap of perpetuating the greatness of Freud the man, whilst knowing his theories were wrong[41]. It seems that mythologizing takes place regardless of one's stance on Freud. Any notion that there is a single myth of Freud must be dismissed. There are many and they vary from highly promotional to doom laden, with others still whose intentions may not be borne out. For example, Richard Webster compares Freud with the "self doubting" Jesus. His intention is not to promote Freud, as his own views on religion suggest that his motivation for using such a quote was one of condescension:

> Read sceptically the Gospels portray Jesus not as a messiah confident of his calling, but as a self doubting prophet whose tendency to submit to others is almost as great as his impulse to lead.[42]

Webster is not the first of Freud's biographers to comment on the mystique which surrounds Freud[43]. Numerous other biographers note[44] that there were followers who remained blind "enough" to his flaws to continue to build successfully on the mythology which had already been established by his family and himself. [45]

That a story has become wide-spread may give it power and credibility but it does not make it true. However, by virtue of the popularity of many stories about Freud they have become regarded as such. To use the word myth in the contemporary, derogatory way is not the only way. Stories about Freud and by Freud, like other myths, have been designed to serve a purpose. This purpose, or function, may change over time for the service of different groups.

THE CONSTRUCTION OF FREUD   33

Freud's biographers have shown repeatedly that he was economical with the truth. For example, Jeffrey Masson, regarded as one of Freud greatest critics, (originally a Freudian psychoanalyst), whilst working in the Freudian archives, discovered papers which endorsed Freud's original theory of sexual abuse:

> We know that his insistence (in 1896) that women were telling the truth about having been sexually abused in early childhood did not last, and that, by 1903, he had retracted this statement.[46]

If Masson is correct it took seven years before Freud retracted his findings. Seven years in the academy is a very long time. What took him so long? Freud had found that a number of his female patients had been sexually abused by either their fathers, or a close family friend, or relative. However, Victorian Vienna was not ready to hear this and Freud eventually denied this as fact and invented a theory which stated that all of the testimonies he had heard may be explained as fantasies or memories of fantasies. Masson's claim, that this theory "did not last", is off the mark if the dates above are correct. Seven years is not an insignificant time and one can only speculate as to what went on in the intervening period which made him retract his information.[47]

As we shall see below Freud was not adverse to actively distorting facts in order to cover his own back. However, he was also used to positing information which people found uncomfortable so what ever was going on at this time Freud made a decision which was somewhat extreme. However, that the original theories were still available for Masson to discover begs a whole lot of different questions. If Freud had really decided that these theories were untrue why were the originals still available in the archives fifty years after his death? Did he want them to be found at a time when they might be more accepted as true? Was this just another way for Freud to have fun with his biographers[48]? One thing is that if Freud had not intended this work to be found he would not have had any hesitation destroying it.

Another example of Freud's distortion of facts, was during the famous cocaine episode. He was conducting experiments into the anaesthetic properties of cocaine, which included using cocaine himself. Elizabeth Thornton argues that Freud's research from this period was flawed as his findings had been influenced by his altered state of consciousness.[49] Thornton is more critical of Freud than Webster but still leaves her reader with a sense that she, as others have, found him both awesome as well as abhorrent. The paradox of Freud is that those who despise him can also admire him at the same time.

The act of distorting facts was further exemplified by Freud when he destroyed all of his manuscripts, diaries, notes and correspondence, not once in his life but twice, the first time in 1885, and then again in 1907[50]. This was incredible in itself but added to this he confessed in a letter to his future wife, Martha, that:

> I am already looking forward to seeing them (the biographers) going astray.[51]

Such acts were clearly intended to distort history and were a way of covering his tracks. We will never know what it was that he was so frightened that people would discover about him. His disposal of correspondence, of things which he did not want people to find, makes what he did with his famous sexual abuse theory all the more intriguing. It is also incredible that when writing this he was a young man of twenty-eight, who already believed that he would have biographers (plural). Self-belief indeed.

Freud was correct in his prediction that there would be biographers (plural). He may, more accurately, have called them his co-mythologizers. Biographers, too numerous to list, have been unable to resist perpetuating old, or creating new myths. As previously noted, Ernest Jones had to have permission from, and a great deal of editing by, Freud's daughter Anna, before he could publish his biography[52]. Anna Freud played a significant role in mythologizing her father. When editing Jones' biography she is said to have corrected the punctuation of the quotations of her father and removed large sections of text but never acknowledged it as having been taken out or "lost". That Jones complied with this indicates his respect for the Freud family, although it is also probable that without such changes he would not have been permitted to publish and remain friends with the family. The phenomena of either embroidering or omitting information, is not peculiar to Freud or his biographers. It is almost par for the course in any historiography.

When researching we see what we are looking for, not what we are *not* looking for.

Although Richard Webster is still regarded by contemporary psychoanalysts as one of Freud's severest critics (his 1995 book was received as a major attack upon psychoanalysis)[53] he claims:

> ... it might well be said that the incorrect theory elaborated by Freud has been infinitely preferable to no theory at all, and in the vast desert of twentieth-century rationalism it is scarcely surprising that many have seen, in the drop of imaginative water which is contained in Freud's theories, a veritable oasis of truth.

In this Webster implies that whilst Freud made mistakes it is better to have tried and failed than not to have tried at all. This attitude is not borne out by Webster as he continues in his attempt to topple Freud. The toppling of Freud has proved a more difficult task for the critics than they expected. Webster is saying one thing and doing another. Many of Freud's critics condemn his work but have admiration for the man, although, arguably, there is little differentiation between the work and the man.

Webster talks of Freud as a "messiah"[54], which has different connotations to "guru", the title which Storr bestows on Freud. It is interesting to speculate about what Freud's own preference would have been and although commentators continually do speculate we will never really know what Freud actually thought. His written words are only one aspect of his communication, for example, his sense of humour, his acute Jewish wit was such that when quoting his words now we lose his sense of irony.[55] For example, Webster states:

> Freud himself consciously identified with Moses, and the prophetic and messianic dimensions of his character have been noted again and again even by those who have written sympathetically about psychoanalysis.[56]

Freud did compare himself to Moses and also to Hannibal and St Paul among others. And this may be good enough reason to accuse him of making a concerted effort to cultivate himself as a messiah[57] but he may just have been having fun. That he is accused of intentionally being messianic does not take into account the fact that there was an audience willing to receive him and his message. This willing audience were clearly people whose specific needs were met by such an attitude. The making of a messiah is not a solo pursuit: he could not have become a messiah in isolation[58]. Such claims are made as if the Freud we think we know has arisen in a vacuum. He was never an isolated character, as he some times claimed himself: this was/is fantasy a part of the ever increasing mythology.

Webster also makes a judgement about the psychoanalytic community by stating that even those who are sympathetic to psychoanalysis use these religious, heroic analogies, noting that it is not only critics from outside who make these comparisons. As illustrated in the prologue, it seems that few, if any, either insiders or outsiders, are asking why these comparisons have been made. May it not be that they are the most accurate? Others have tried to use political analogies but these are less convincing[59].The ways and frequency with which religious analogies have been used has added to the resistance of the psychoanalytic community to anything religious. Their difficulties in reappraising religion arise from their hallowed founder's views. Freud's views on religion set a framework for his followers which confines them to continue to view it as negative and until recently even the most forward thinking of them has avoided theoretical engagement with the subject.

Webster notes Freud:

> attempts to use reason in a "magical" rather than in a scientific manner—to use reason, that is to say, not in order to provide a genuine solution to an intellectual problem, but in order to provide a defence against the forces which we fear, and against aspects of our own nature which arouse society.[60]

Freud was willing to step outside of the rigid paradigm of science. He challenged the boundaries of science which Webster finds inconceivable, even although many early scientists were themselves alchemists and as such using approaches that today could be called creative or as Webster would have it "magical". Freud's "magpie" approach to knowledge is difficult for many to concede. He was an original interdisciplinarian. As noted above, Freud was not adverse to complicating matters. However, he was a trained scientist and was very keen to keep his findings and ultimately psychoanalysis within the realm of science.

What does it mean for knowledge when we begin to prescribe how reason must be used? We may be in danger of a kind of ethnic cleansing by advocating such disciplinary hygiene. Does reason not cease to be such if its uses are prescribed—when it then takes the form of dogma? There is something in Webster's criticism about magic versus reason which echoes the continuing dilemma in psychoanalysis and psychodynamic psychotherapy and is part of the wider debate of science versus religion which finds solace in perpetuating either or thinking.

Freud has become a valuable commodity in the biographical industry: with each commentator there is an agenda which is peculiar to them. Each has a question which drives their work, the results of which make a significant contribution to the mythology of Freud including those who have invested in finding Freud's mistakes. For example, Webster claims that the case of Anna O became one of the most "important elements of the Freudian legend",[61] and goes so far as to say:

> to entertain any serious doubt about the diagnosis of Anna O would be to deal a devastating blow to the psychoanalytic church.[62]

Practising Freudians know that this case was a disaster and Webster only serves to create yet another myth by making this claim. Freud is often shown as dogmatic and one can see that this makes him a more interesting character. However, it would appear that for every negative claim about Freud there will be a counter claim just around the corner. So, contrary to the claim of his being dogmatic, some of his followers claim that he was willing to engage in discussions and with criticisms about his theories, but one can see how this makes a less dramatic story. As with finding a pure Freud there is little if any chance of finding a purist Freudian, which is what Webster implies. And it may be useful to remember that within all churches belief is peculiar to the believer. In the Freudian church this is no different. There are some who believe that Anna O was useful and others who see it for what it was, a product of an over emotional collaboration of Freud and Fleiss. The case of Anna O has been questioned again and again and shown to have been a complete misdiagnosis and most Freudians know this. Freud's relationship with Fleiss was complicated and from their letters[63] we can tell that there was more to it than a merely professional alliance.

We can see from the above that Freud was/is part of an ongoing process of construction. People with an interest in Freud are rarely dispassionate and never work in a vacuum. Each commentator adds to those layers of Freud's mythology which he and his family carefully set in motion. The following chapter turns to his legacy which illustrates the continuity of the myth building.

Notes

1. Renée Gicklhorn used the records from Pribor to confirm Sigmund's birth date as May 6th 1856.
2. This name "Schlomo" has been given to a Square in Israel in his memory.
3. For back up of this information I am indebted to Michael Molnar the archivist at the Freud museum London. Telephone conversation on 18/02/03, AM.
4. Wittels, F. (1924) *The Man, His Followers and His School*. Translated by Eden and Ceder Paul. London: George Allen and Unwin.
5. Scholem, G.G. (ed.) (1977) *Zohar: The Book of Splendour. Basic Readings from The Kabbalah*. London: Rider & Company.
6. Gay(1988) uses Amalia.
7. The difficulty with writing on Freud is that new material keeps being released Puner, H.W. (1947) make no mention of either Rebecca or Julius, nor does Webster (1995). Gay (1988) Mentions that Amalia was Jakob Freud's third wife but does not give the names of the first two. He mentions Julius, Freud's brother.
8. Wittels, F. (1924).
9. Sulloway (1979) p. 476. There are different versions of each of these stories. No one relates them in exactly the same words. Puner, H.W. (1947) *Sigmund Freud: His Life and Mind*. (Reprint with new material 1992). New Brunswick, USA/London, UK: Transaction. She excludes both Rebecca and Julius and claims that the "gypsy" was the midwife. There are numerous discrepancies in the books. But most are similar enough for the differences to have been over looked.
10. Ibid., p. 477.
11. Roazen, P. (1975) p. 54.

12 In our contemporary climate these tales would be taken with a pinch of salt.
13 Sulloway (1979) p. 477.
14 Roazen (1975) p. 49.
15 However, for someone who did not have a career in research his contribution to the field was rather significant. Today there are few who would argue against the notion that he did become one of the most influential scholars of the 20th century. Testimony to this is the fact that there are few, if any, disciplines in the academy which Freud's theories do not impinge upon. Not always in a positive sense but his presence is felt none the less. He may even be found in aquaculture!
16 Webster (1995) p. 100, see also Freud's letters to Jung and Thomas Szasz (1979) p. 155.
17 Freud may best be described as an atheistic Jew because his he belonged to a nation of Jews and he was ethnically a Jew.
18 Freud's Jewishness has been well documented by scholars both Jewish and gentile. Gay (1987) *Freud: The Godless Jew* is comprehensive. Bakan, D. (1958) *Sigmund Freud and the Jewish Mystical Tradition*. Princeton/New Jersey/Toronto/New York/London: D. Van Nostrand Company, Inc.
19 Bakan, D. (1958) *Sigmund Freud and the Jewish Mystical Tradition*. Princeton/New Jersey/Toronto/New York/London: D. Van Nostrand Company, Inc.
20 Ibid., pp. 50–51.
21 Sulloway (1979) p. 464.
22 The work of Wilhelm Stekel, Karl Kraus, and Weininger were all far more risky for their time than Freud's own work. Each of these men supported Freud in his work. Added to this was Reich, Roheim and Marcuse each of whom adopted Freud's views and developed them in a more radical way.
23 Szasz, T. (1979) *The Myth of Mental Illness*, p. 155.
24 Storr, A. (1996) *Feet of Clay: A Study of Gurus*. London: Harper Collins (Paperback edition 1997).
25 It is interesting that Freud and Jung are chosen to rest among other alleged gurus all whom are regarded as having had a negative effect on their followers. The thing which seems to distinguish him most from those other alleged gurus in Storr, is the fact that he was a loyal husband and father who appears not to have had any extra marital affairs. Although, there has been some talk of an affair with Minna, his sister in law who lived with them, it is so far only speculation. When would he have had time?

26 Wittels (1924) p. 18.
27 Ibid., p. 100.
28 Sachs, H. (1945) *Freud Master and Friend*. London: Imago Publishing Co. Ltd, p. 45.
29 Sachs passim.
30 Sulloway believed it was possible.
31 Ellenberger, H. (1970).
32 Sulloway (1979) p. 477. Quote from Schur, M. (1972) *Freud: Living and Dying*. The psychoanalytic library, London: Hogarth Press and The institute of psychoanalysis, New York: International University Press.
33 This includes medical science.
34 Jones, E. (1955) *Sigmund Freud. Life and work. Years of Maturity. Volume 2, 1901–1919*. London: Hogarth, p. 466.
35 Roazen (1975) pp. 132–3, quoting introductory lectures Vol 16, p. 445.
36 Robert Segal. Unpublished paper given at The University of Stirling on May 7th 2001 Segal argues that we continue to make "heroes" of people (undeserving though they may be) because we have the ability to suspend our disbelief and our belief so that they may fill a role which is absent in a secular culture.
37 Carlyle, T. *On Heroes Hero-Worship and the Heroic in History*. London: H.R. Allenson (India paper edition 1905).
38 Robert Segal (2001).
39 Ellenberger (1970) p. 16.
40 Roazen (1975) p. 17?
41 Richard Webster for example.
42 Webster (1995) p. 301.
43 Biographers such as Jones (Implicitly), Roazen, Grosskurth Sulloway.
44 Jones, Roazen, Sulloway and Wittels.
45 In his letters, particularly those to Jung and to Fleiss, there is evidence that Freud, in the process of elevating others, was in fact in the first instance elevating himself. The many sources which sought to mythologize Freud, did so because they had a need in themselves.
46 Masson, J. (1988) *Against therapy*. London: Harper Collins, 1993 edition, pp. 25–26, p. 45.
46 Ibid., p. 45.
47 What ever happened in those seven years perhaps we will never know but it is not an insubstantial time given Freud's normal rate of research. This is not to condone Freud in his retraction but it does beg questions about the intervening years.

48 As I shall expand in the text in a letter to Martha he, having burned his correspondence, comments that he is intending to lead his biographers "astray". That he was anticipating biographers (plural) is something worth noting and adds credence to the notion that if things are being "uncovered" now it is because Freud intended this to happen.
49 Thornton, E.M. (1986) *The Freudian Fallacy: Freud and Cocaine*. Paladin. UK. In: Webster (1995) p. 33.
50 Within this period the controversy about sexual abuse was taking place. It is therefore of greater interest that he did not destroy the information about this and left it to be "found".
51 Sulloway (1979) p. 7.
52 As note above others have also "lost" bits of Freud. Anna was very close to her father and would be intent on his being respectfully portrayed.
53 Marcus Bowman "The significance of psychoanalysis on modern thought". http://www.psychoanalysis.org.uk/bowman.htm. On 12/04/00 at 11.50.
54 Webster (1995) Also talks of Jung as messianic, p. 370-1, 376-7.
55 Murray Cuddihy, J. (1974) *The Ordeal of Civility: Freud, Marx, Levi-Strauss, and the Jewish Struggle with Modernity*. New York: Basic Books.
56 Webster (1995) p. 9. Szasz (1979) is also guilty of this in *The Myth of Psychotherapy*.
57 I often call myself a "Domestic Goddess" (Nigella Lawson the cookery writer has made use of this term) and only were you to be present would you identify the irony in my declaration. Was Freud being ironic? He was not adverse to having fun with people. See Michael Molnar's *The Diary of Sigmund Freud 1929-1939: A Record of the Final Decade* in which he shows Freud as a man with a significant sense of humour.
58 Szasz (1979) pp. 155-156.
59 Adam Phillips. Start the Week BBC Radio 4 with Andrew Marr. Phillips compared Freud's movement to a political movement but his argument did not encapsulate the subtlety which the religious comparison does.
60 Webster (1995).
61 Ibid., p.131.
62 Ibid., p.131.
63 Masson, J.M. (ed.) (1985) *The Complete Letters of Sigmund Freud to Wilhelm Fliess (1887-1904)*. Harvard: Belknap.

CHAPTER THREE (I)

Freud's Legacy

The perpetuation of the many myths of Freud relied on a community which grew up in response to his character and his work. The community began with a small group of friends, colleagues, meeting in his home at Berggasse 19, in central Vienna on a Wednesday evening. The original four members, Stekel, Adler, Kahane and Reitler, who became the first psychoanalysts after Freud, met up to discuss ideas. By 1908 this group had grown too big to continue to meet in Freud's home and the bigger group was named The Viennese Psychoanalytic Society. However, it continued to expand and move beyond Vienna, and subsequently became known as the Psychoanalytic Movement. Whilst this did not happen overnight it was fairly quickly established as a movement of some significance.

Phyllis Grosskurth, a biographer who falls into the critical camp, illustrates the degree of commitment which was necessary for the development of the movement.[1] For example, she notes that not only were there weekly meetings but once "the committee", a group whom Jones suggested should meet together to make sure that psychoanalysis developed in the way that Freud wanted it to, was established they went on specific trips to discuss the future of psychoanalysis. Of this group we shall hear more below. However, although it was intended as a secret group, many people seemed to know about it. Minutes of their actual meetings add to the correspondence between them and show evidence of their individual commitment both to Freud and the development of psychoanalysis.

The fact that it was called a movement at all is significant and there was a great deal of resistance to this term at the time. "Movement" implied a less than scientific group. Ernest Jones argued that movement was appropriate and cited others such as the:

> Tractarian movement, the Chartist movement . . . characterised by the ardent desire to promulgate . . . beliefs that are accounted exceedingly precious.[2]

As noted in the prologue, Jones was willing to admit "the minute element of truth" in the charge that psychoanalysis was a religion but that "the reality" was "far different". The socio-political context in which psychoanalysis was conceived held science in such high esteem that "movement" was deemed an inappropriate title for a new society advocating a new area of science. As was Freud's wish, there are today as many, if not more lay analysts in practice than people with a medical background. However, this was not the case in Freud's time. Most of his early followers were trained in medicine and as such, scientists. The four men who were the original Wednesday group were all physicians.

Those people who helped to put Freud into a position of power have been described as disciples and followers.[3] That the word disciple is deemed the most appropriate to describe the followers is often over looked. Unlike those gathered around Plato, they were not described by the secular term pupil. Nor has psychoanalysis been regarded as a school or an academy. Why? That the term "movement" was chosen to describe the collectivity of psychoanalysts and their practice was not without motivation, if not "reason".

In the main Grosskurth's interest is in those who were regarded as Freud's "Inner Circle".[4] But she distorts Freud by claiming that he only had "two real friendships". His greatest friend, in her view, was Eduard Silberstein with whom he had been a friend since childhood. And if Grosskurth is to be believed the only other person considered a friend was Wilhelm Fliess. In this narrow definition of what friendship is she is doing a great disservice to both Freud and his many other friends. Freud described many people as his friends, for example, Oskar Pfister, and Jung. The fact that friendships were terminated does not mean that he did not have them.

The friendships, which Grosskurth describes, each came to an unsatisfactory end. With Silberstein it was less public than with Fleiss. This said, with Silberstein, there was an event in which, having sent his wife to Freud for help (she was depressed), she fell down (or threw herself down) the stairs of Freud's apartment in Vienna and died. Thereafter Freud and Silberstein drifted apart, although later in Freud's life they did meet up again. After an intense period of communication Freud and Fliess parted company. It is believed the break occurred as a result of Fliess claiming that Freud had stolen his ideas on bisexuality. According to Grosskurth even those people who managed to gain Freud's friendship had difficulty in maintaining it. She claims that even when Freud and the committee returned from their trip to Hildesheim and Schiercke there was no sense that deep friendships had been forged, only a sense that the patriarch was pleased with his subjects.[5] With this notion of friendship, a contemporary idea of what friendship means, Grosskurth is adopting a similar stance to that of Storr who claims that gurus are unable to maintain friendships. Storr adds that being single minded, despotic, and isolated are also features common to gurus. The difficulty with Freud is that he is so volatile. From one day to the next and one text to the next we find characteristics which are inconsistent. However, it is this inconsistency which makes his character interesting and also responsible for his productivity. Freud was no angel and behaved in ways which are almost incomprehensible for one so concerned with the behaviour of others. He was at times insecure, single minded and, as he would claim himself, isolated but he was not all of these things all of the time and rarely all at the same time. There is a good deal of evidence to counter such claims.

Freud apparently admitted that he was a "fisher of men" a biblical quotation which Webster exploits, by claiming that Freud "fished" for young vulnerable, impressionable, easily indoctrinated men:

> the kind of intelligent, imaginative but also deeply insecure intellectuals who he felt worthy of his attention and who he intuitively felt would submit to his leadership.[6]

If this was the case, any notion of Freud's followers becoming a homogeneous movement is somewhat doubtful. They were a group by virtue of having allegiance to Freud. Many spent time vying for his attention and, as such, were in competition with each other.[7] Stekel, as noted in the prologue, claimed "I was the apostle of Freud who was my Christ!"[8] Stekel was obsessed by Freud, and when Freud became disenchanted with him he was devastated, and set about trying to win back his affections. Sadly, he never succeeded and Stekel, as many others in Freud's wake, committed suicide in 1940 the year after Freud died.[9] If it was the case, that the psychoanalytic movement was merely a collection of weak and vulnerable people, the chances of it surviving after the death of the founder would be remote. It is testimony to their strength that the movement continues to go from strength to strength.

Of this community there were members both devotional and disparaging. The vast amount of biographical material both sceptical and reverential, is indicative of attention which is arguably unparalleled in other areas of the secular academy. It is likened by Ellenberger to the followers of the schools of Greco-Roman antiquity.[10] The difference is that the schools which developed from, for example, Plato and Aristotle relied on critical analysis of the work which was isolated from the founder. To criticise Plato's thinking was not to criticise Plato. For Freud this appears not to be the case. When Freud's work was criticised he often, but not always, regarded it as personal. And today the followers of Freud still find it difficult to criticise his theories for fear of being disrespectful. Whether Freud's followers may be regarded as homogenous is doubtful; there are probably as many varieties of Freudianism as practitioners who say that they are Freudian, in the way that there is no such thing as a Hindu because there are too many variables in the practice of Hinduisms. However, this does not prevent a significant commitment to evangelising about Freudianism. Even those who criticise psychoanalysis feed the notion that any attention is better than none in the same way as the atheist gives credit to theism, albeit indirectly.

Of Freud's earliest followers, we hear much about Ferenczi, Adler and Jung. This is due in part to the fact that they took the risk of challenging Freud and were either "excommunicated" from the group or left. In fact, "Freud himself applied the term heretics to defectors"[11]. That such terms as "heretic" traditionally applied in a religious context, and "defector" more commonly used in an ideological context, are used to describe anyone who left the fold gives credence to the notion that what Freud created was definable as a society rather than a science.

Many of the heretics became famous in their own right, developing theories which deviated from Freud's psychoanalysis but none the less had relied on it as a foundation. Jung, the most famous of them all and arguably Freud's favourite, left the fold with bitterness and a drive to create his own approach with which he eventually outshone the others, known as Analytic Psychology.

From the above we can see that Freud's success was in large part because of his charismatic personality, rather than as a result of his scientific credibility. Despite the dubiety of the theories, his followers continued to work with and in some cases to build on these shaky premises. Freud was not the first and will not be the last person to have become famous in spite of his mistakes. Carl Rogers' (of whom we shall see more below) theories have been hugely successful in spite of "proof" of their failure.

Webster, although less vitriolic than Masson, still manages to create a significant tome by deconstructing Freud and Freudianism. However, even after managing to get an extensive book out of deconstructing Freud's work and concluding that Freud was wrong, he never the less finds it difficult to completely topple the man:

> In the largeness of his ambition at least, Freud may serve as an example to those theorists who come after him. For this reason, if for no other, any wholly negative assessment of his achievement would be mistaken.[12]

Interestingly, Webster's critique relies on that of which he is so critical, psychoanalytic theory. That psychoanalysis has been built on flawed premises, which Webster exposes, appears of no consequence when he uses it for his own ends. There is no view which is without Freud. Psychoanalysis has become a significant tool for the literary critic, which Webster claims to be. This tool has become such a part of their tacit currency that they are often unaware of how much they rely on it.

Freud is a slippery character: just when you think you have the measure of him, something else turns up. He is described as ambitious, and with an impulse to lead, both characteristics which need not be seen as negative, but often are when it suits the critic.

The aspects of Freud's personality of a positive nature such as "generosity" and "considerable moral courage" are to be found, even in Webster, as well as in his letters to his wife, to Oskar Pfister, and to his teachers. These qualities do not make as convincing a guru as those which paint a more despotic picture. As noted above the construction of Freud often takes the form of demonizing or deifying him: few people explore his frailty without interpreting it as active despotism. Even those early followers, such as Max Graf, regarded his own participation in the Wednesday group as akin to being part of a religious sect. He declared:

> There was the atmosphere of the foundation of a religion in that room.[13]

According to Webster, Graf left because he could not stand Freud's "dogmatism".[14]

Roazen on the other hand shows that some of Freud's followers really wanted to live in his shadow and compares them to the followers of Mahatma Gandhi.[15] And it is worth repeating Weisz who stated:

> The group's elitism and sense of exclusiveness, combined with an extreme mistrust of and hostility toward the outside world; an eschatological vision of reality which made adherence to the group an experience approaching religious conversion, and more important, an over exaggerated reverence for the founder which transcended the normal bounds of scientific authoritarianism.[16]

Weisz makes it clear that there was an outside world which Freud and his followers believed was hostile. There are advantages and disadvantages to being either inside or outside but to be both is not necessarily a vantage point: it could just mean that each position has been diluted. When insiders make the comparison of psychoanalysis with religion it is never complimentary.

Sulloway also compared the psychoanalytic movement to an organised religion:

> Few theories in science have spawned a following that can compare with the psychoanalytic movement in its cult-like manifestations, in its militancy, and in the aura of a religion that has permeated it.[17]

Again with Sulloway there is no sense that he views this as a good thing his use of the words "cult" and "militancy" are not exactly celebratory. Max Graf in addition to claiming that Freud was the head of the psychoanalytic church commented on Freud's dogmatism. Further, Wittels claims:

> He watches over this theory jealously, will not tolerate the smallest deviation from it, and fences it round with a palisade ...[18].

These claims are not just negative they are describing something other than science. The claims, "approaching religion" and the "aura of a religion" are fairly typical comments but as we shall see do not go far enough. However, for each negative claim it is possible to find a counter-claim. For example, Lou Andreas Salome testifies that he was always open to developing his theories with suggestions from others.[19]

Freud's being dogmatic about his theories was not the only way in which he echoed other belief systems:

> Freud the profoundly atheistic scientist and skeptical foe of the "illusions" fostered by religion, was himself in thrall to a particularly subtle form of theistic fantasy. It was the crypto-theological view which sustained his belief that he could find the key which would unlock the mysteries of human nature by studying the mechanism of the "spirit" or "soul" which supposedly controlled human behaviour.[20]

Freud's aim was to "scientize" the soul or "psyche" by reclaiming and renaming it as the "unconscious" and in this he was successful.

Freud's favoured disciple, Jung, whilst having a relationship with Freud which may best be described as like novitiate to mentor, none the less became critical of Freud's charismatic status and could see the danger of this being developed at the expense of scientific rigour. Jung states:

> In scientific terms the reasons for adopting his theories were, as I have tried to show are no better than the reasons which might be given for imitating his way of talking or taking his neurotic

habits. In both cases we are confronted not by reasoned decision but by an act of irrational submission to the power of Freud's personality and to the capacity he had for projecting himself, both in his life and in his writing, as a prophet, sage, and even redeemer[21].

This illustrates the power of Freud's character and reflects how impressionable some of those who followed him were. However, in the context of Jung's own relationship with Freud he may also have been making a point about those "disciples" who not only clung onto Freud's every word but also copied his mannerisms and speech as well as taking to smoking the same large cigars.

Freud's theories, contrary to his belief, were contingent on his own world, a world in which it was impossible to escape the influence of the Judaeo-Christian ethics, which he saw as illusory[22]. Freud and his work were born at a time when the repression imposed on society by the church was at its most vehement. It is no coincidence that whilst Freud set out to build a science of the mind he was determined that what had once been firmly in the realm of religion, the cure of souls, moved firmly to that of the pseudo-science of psychoanalysis.[23]

Thus, whilst Freud believed he was usurping the territory of religion, of which he was so disapproving, he simultaneously echoed their beliefs but by couching them in the language of his new science, deluding himself into believing he had created an entirely new science. Webster compares Freud's theories to St Augustine's Doctrine of Original Sin, and states that his theories of sexual development and human history were based on a:

> culturally orthodox belief, derived ultimately from Judaeo-Christian apocalyptic. [24]

An interpretation of Freud's motivation is that it was exactly those cultural mores, prescribed by Judaeo-Christian traditions, which prevented people from having fulfilled lives, and gave him fodder for his theories on repression. It became Freud's work to undo these problems which prescriptions from these traditions had caused, not as Webster suggests, to control them in the way that the church had tried to. Although Freud was undoubtedly a product of his time there was a good deal more which influenced him than religion. The rise of National Socialism is but one, albeit, significant example[25].

Freud believed psychoanalysis could be useful to everyone, however, not necessarily in the way which Webster suggests, as Augustine had, that all souls were in need of redemption:

> by enlarging the notion of disease and by applying it to those whom, in reality, were not ill at all.[26]

In Christianity the act of confessing sins to a priest, followed by a suitable penance, can lead to redemption and may cause relief. Similarly, the process of psychoanalysis also leads to relief by enabling the patient to understand their allegedly sinful urges. Christianity and psychoanalysis play a part in controlling or directing people's lives, but psychoanalysis, if it is an alternative means of redemption, relies on an authority on earth. Webster appears not to see either as having any positive attributes.[27]

That psychoanalysis might provide an opportunity to air one's difficulties without the fear of judgement is not acknowledged by Webster. In psychotherapy punishment abounds in the form of the self-punishment of the client, an issue which itself should be explored in the therapy. Acceptance and tolerance are sought-after outcomes of psychotherapy and counselling, each of which seems to have lost its significance in the actions of organised religion.

If as Webster believes, Freud's theories perpetuate the Christian view that evil souls need cleansing:

> Freud represents the "anal character" by the image of a man who, like the devil is given to hoarding, sadism and pedantry, and who like the devil is a secret lover of excrement[28].

Then psychoanalysis must also cultivate a similar process of, "demonological projection"[29], as in Christianity. However, in psychotherapy clients are not in the same position of abdicating their responsibility, are not expecting an outside force to correct their issues but come to understand that the corrections come from within[30]. Therefore, if there is a "demonological projection" it is internalised. Webster's work reflects a particular reading of Freud, through his own anthropological lens and his views are not necessarily borne out by practitioners who claim that their goal is to enable:

a) freeing of the impulses; b) the strengthening of the reality by use of ego functioning including its perceptions so that it appropriates more of the id and; c) the alteration of the contents of the super-ego so that it represents human rather than punitive moral standards. Psychoanalysis is a process of re-educating the ego.[31]

Most people in the west have a view of Freud. Rarely does one encounter indifference to Freud, and more often antagonism than acceptance. He has had an impressive amount of attention for someone who, as Webster testifies, got it wrong. Darwin and Marx who each arguably got it more right than Freud and made highly significant contributions to academic development have much less attention than Freud. Why should this be? Why does Sigmund Freud attract the attention, not necessarily in the positive sense, of so many, across disciplines? Let us turn to his movement to see if we may shed more light on such questions.

As we have seen above Freud had many followers. Some continued his work whilst he was alive and then after his death. Others began with Freud and then evolved their own theories. During his life, in the early stages of the development of psychoanalysis he gathered around him, at the suggestion of Ernest Jones, a group of men whom he trusted to develop the psychoanalytic movement in the way that he believed it should. This group have come to be called "The Secret Ring"[32]. In Grosskurth's book of this title she explores the politics of psychoanalysis in direct relation to a select few men, "the committee", who were the members of this group. They each were given a ring with some form of intaglio, by Freud, who also wore one, as a symbol of their allegiance to the movement. Surely if he had apostles this group qualifies. Ironically Stekel who makes the claim about being the apostle of Freud was least likely to be one and perhaps it was for this reason he so desired it.

To discuss Freud's legacy is difficult because, as mentioned above, he has touched so many disciplines that such a task could be a life's work. However, if we look at some of what Freud left to the industry of the psychodynamic branch of the talking cure it is more manageable. It is appropriate to use the word "industry" because the talking cure has become regarded by some as a commodity, viewed in the negative, as a symptom of the disenchantment of industrialised, capitalist, societies[33]. The notion that psychotherapy is rarely found in developing countries, where religious institutions and indigenous traditions still have a significant hold, is an area which requires further research[34]. When we categorise psychotherapy as a development of religiousness it becomes part of an even more extensive lineage.

What Freud created in psychoanalysis was a contemporary confessional, a zone in which the patient pays the person whom they choose to receive their testimony. This presupposes a belief that with the skill of the practitioner they will engage in a transformative process. The fact that this relationship is under contract is one of the issues leading to the accusation of the commodificaton of the self. A covenant is entered into in the form of a contract, often written, between the practitioner and the client. This creates an allegiance, not an alliance which presupposes equality[35], which secures confidentiality and commitment from each person. One could argue that there was also "currency" in the religious confession in the form of a tithe.

The idea that one can cure or at least gain relief from life's difficulties by talking about them within the company of a specialist is nothing new. Freud did not invent the talking cure. As Thomas Szasz and others have argued, the idea of catharsis was around much earlier than Freud or even Christianity:

> Plato recognized the crucial role of katharsis in the dual sense of purgation and purification in the cure of souls.[36]

However, it was later with Cicero that the power of the "talking cure" was acknowledged:

> Cicero (106–43 BC) provides what may be the earliest articulations of the idea that the person suffering from a sick soul cannot be his own healer but must entrust himself to the care of an expert: "the soul that is sick cannot rightly prescribe for itself, except by following the instruction of wise men" added to which Cicero recommends the use of healing words.[37]

FREUD'S LEGACY 53

This claim, by Cicero is still crucial for psychotherapy today. People who argue that psychotherapy is a twentieth century indulgence, peculiar to capitalist economies, need to look at the writings of Cicero in which the contemporary practitioner's role is given justification through an extensive genealogy. When one is, at the very least, in a state of disenchantment it is difficult, as Cicero notes, to get a perspective which is untainted by the state of disenchantment. Thus, in this state it is profitable to employ the listening skill of someone who experiences the person's testimony through a lens which is not (usually) disenchanted. Added to this, whilst the practitioner gains professional kudos from the task, the contract ensures that they will not use what they hear against you. The power dynamic within therapy is complex and does become more so with payment. This is an area for further exploration. What do we mean by "payment"?

Such complex dynamics were, long before Cicero, endemic in religious traditions across the globe, and being employed both in the hierarchy between priesthood and laity as well as within the priesthood itself. The Platonic idea of katharsis was developed by Cicero, with talking becoming recognised as a form of purgation and purification. This was further exploited by the Christian church with confession which Freud proceeded to usurp.

Freud never knew his own legacy, and indeed even scholars of Freud can only speculate about its extent. What may be said is that his belief in the kathartic value of talking without being punished by an external force, as was the expectation with confession, is a significant aspect of his legacy. However, as Storr notes we are indebted to Freud for other things as well. For example:

> increased tolerance, contributed to the technique of psychotherapy, and revolutionized the way we think about our behaviour. Twentieth century man is greatly indebted to Freud.

The process of psychotherapy is one of mentoring. The therapist, either overtly or covertly, demonstrates different ways to view the events of which the client has spoken, and by example teaches them to be less judgmental. Not making overt judgements, for example, demonstrates a model in which the client sees that it is possible not to judge themselves and others. There are hopes for this process which go beyond the individual. For example, one hoped for epiphenomenon is that if individuals become more accepting and less judgemental of themselves then they will apply this knowledge with the consequence that society will come to behave with more tolerance. The Delphic Oracle's adage of "know thyself" is present in contemporary psychotherapy.

Although it is often said that Freud was ahead of his time, in some other ways the time was right for Freud. The increasing secularity of society and continued decline in numbers attending churches[38] created a gap which Freud's meta-psychology was ripe to fill. He offered something which churches no longer could, delineated times of refuge in which there was the opportunity to get to "know thyself". He offered a place where guilt about things deemed sinful by the church (and upheld by society) could be explored without fear of retribution[39]. This is still the case for psychotherapy and counselling today, although retribution appears to have taken up a new position, internalised within each individual[40].

For Freud the model of a human being was as a receptacle of both good and evil forces. In this belief his influence was undoubtedly the Judeo Christian model. Freud has been accused of perpetuating the same kind of control as that of the churches,[41] control of morality and sinful urges. Another view would be that of Eric Fromm, who, in comparing psychoanalysis and religion states:

> The question is not religion or not but which kind of religion, whether it is one furthering man's development, the unfolding of his specifically human powers, or one paralysing them.[42]

Freud's version of the talking cure intended to further the development of humans, not as seemed the case with the church, to cause psychic paralysis. However, to control what happens with the original prescription is difficult to police. For example, the ways in which Jesus' teachings are used is almost unrecognisable in churches today and the same may be said of Freud's work. Freud argued that the church served to infantalize its followers by creating the illusion of a father who was ultimately responsible for everything. This illusion continues to allow people to abdicate responsibility for their actions in the name of God. Whilst Freud believed that psychoanalysis was a way of accepting responsibility for one's actions there are practitioners who by exploiting their position also keep clients in a state of dependency and in so doing perpetuate infantalization. An attempt to gauge Freud's legacy requires looking at his direct descendents as well as those who claim no lineage to Freud. So, let us now turn to psychodynamic traditions and those who have come to be regarded as his immediate disciples.

In creating psychoanalysis Freud gave rise to a myriad of traditions which allowed those coming after him the reward, although many would dispute this, of developing a position of their own either as a response to Freud or in reaction against him. For example, Carl Rogers and his followers, whose works we shall explore below, whilst denying their links to Freud still owe a debt to him in so far as Rogers developed his work as a reaction against the Freudian model, which he perceived as outdated and hierarchical. Rogers and his followers' distaste for this model was that psychoanalysis had come to symbolise the establishment where hierarchy, expertise, aloofness, interpretation and anything which was attached to tradition, and therefore the past, was expected. Freud's ideas on the unconscious were actively excluded from this new model from Rogers and his emphasis was on issues in the here and now. However, he could not have created this without Freud.

Those who stayed with Freud had to embrace traditions which have come to be known as the Psychodynamic traditions, the most important of these is a continued belief in Freud's ideas on the dynamic nature of the unconscious. There are many practitioners who use this idea but there are a variety of names for their practices. Within this group there is also a hierarchy. For example, practitioners who are called "classical" psychoanalysts are regarded as purist Freudians. They are as mythical as the figure of Freud himself. The idea that there is someone out there who practices, to the letter, what Freud himself did is fantasy. No one knows what Freud actually did. Beyond the "classical" Freudian there are practitioners who call themselves psychodynamic psychotherapists, and psychodynamic counsellors, analytical psychologists and within each of these groups there are sub groups. Their parallels with those of the Christian church with its different denominations are uncanny. Each group and how they name themselves is influenced by what is in vogue and each has its own place in the wider psychodynamic scheme. Added to this the psychodynamic scheme has a place within a wider psychotherapeutic community with practices such as psychodrama and art therapy.

My intention is to describe what it means to be one of these psychodynamic practitioners, by giving an overview of the techniques and skills which they employ. I will also illustrate some areas of contention for the contemporary practitioner. This, I do in an attempt at drawing attention to the aspects of what practitioners do which may be described as religious.

In the description above of Freud's background, his work and the people with whom he began, the Freudian community, it is clear that despite the flaws in his theories those who surrounded him, both admirers and critics were often in awe of him. Even the critics whilst condemning his theories are unable to dismiss him completely. Freud offered an alternative to the cure of souls. His was an allegedly secular practice claiming to relieve the suffering of everyday living, giving hope to people who were disenchanted and socially anchorless. Some believe that his alternative cure of souls was just another form of moral, and therefore, social control.[43] This is an interesting view, given that Freud is more commonly regarded as someone who was always on about sex and as such was going against the overt morality of his day. Freud's Vienna, whilst appearing on the surface to be a city of high morals was not all that it appeared. Janik and Toulmin in *Wittgenstein's Vienna*[44], the same Vienna in which Freud was at work, show us a city of quite contrary standards.[45]

As we know, Freud's theory and practice provided the foundation for the movement of psychoanalysis and subsequently what has come to be known as psychodynamic psychotherapy, but that psychoanalysis was named a movement has been discussed above. Movement was not a word adopted by the philosophical or scientific community, they preferred the word school. As we have noted, the Platonists or the Stoics are described as schools not movements. In the beginning psychoanalysts were Freud's fellow medical men, scientists who would not have subscribed to the notion that they themselves were ill and would have to under-go treatment in order to practice medicine: which was the case if they were to practice psychoanalysis. The idea that the would-be Freudian analyst had to undergo analysis before being regarded as able to treat others is itself indicative of a process which was alien to science. To become part of a movement with this kind of initiation is common in religious groups and therefore it is all the more surprising that Freud should make this process one of the requirements of becoming a psychoanalyst.

This has another parallel with religion in so far as such prescription presupposes that all are ill and in need of healing in the same way as the church has assumed that all are sinners in need of healing and must be healed before they can heal anyone else. In both religion and psychoanalysis there is the belief that the practitioner will have a clean slate themselves before curing others of their ills. It is also worth noting that in psychoanalysis there is no eye contact which is interesting when in science seeing is believing. All social cues are removed in the same way as in confession. This is not new to healing: in the Ancient Near East it was a prerequisite to avert your eyes from the Goddess before seeking advice. If Freud had been analysing another group I expect he would have noted that it was an odd choice of training for a career in science and to name the group a movement would have sent his alarm bells ringing. However, Freud's proximity to psychoanalysis caused him, and as we shall see, his followers, to be so blinded by their position as to create and perpetuate the very thing of which he was so overtly critical. It is not difficult to imagine that the psychoanalysis of psychoanalysis could uncover this repression. But as yet there is little sign of it being treated.

The psychoanalytic movement has a membership which is as diverse as any religious movement. Its rapid spread beyond Vienna and Europe to the United States of America and as far east as Japan, resulted in a multitude of cultural influences. There is a wonderful photograph, taken in the nineteen thirties of the Japanese Psychoanalytic Society[46] which is of a rather earnest looking group some of whose members also came to Vienna for their own psychoanalysis—that prerequisite for practice. It is, however, unsafe to presuppose that, with such cultural diversity it was possible, even if desirable, to have a homogeneous group who practiced a single thing called psychoanalysis. In fact quite the contrary, their petty squabbles are parallel to sectarian relations between religious groups which serve to unduly magnify their differences, ignoring how much they have in common. There is still confusion today within the psychotherapeutic community about what certain practitioners should do and what they call themselves.

Traditionally the term psychodynamic has been used by therapists or analysts, whose practice reflect all or some of Freud's prerequisites for practitioners and at the very least it reflects belief in the existence of a dynamic unconscious[47]. More recently there has been a trend for some therapists to call themselves counsellors instead of therapists.[48] This may appear to be a superficial distinction but on further examination there is more to it. The relationship in psychodynamic therapy between client and practitioner, is as previously mentioned, regarded as hierarchical. Counselling, the term adopted by Carl Rogers, on the other hand is believed to describe a more egalitarian relationship between practitioner and client. This term has, for the moment, become more politically correct.

The choice therefore of therapist or counsellor is influenced by a climate where political correctness has become paramount, and pressure from other practitioners who regard themselves as more aligned to this political climate has had a significant impact[49]. The main criticism of using the term therapist is that it reflects an outdated model which is patriarchal and imperialistic. For example, person-centred practitioners, along with other humanistic counsellors, have regarded their own practice as egalitarian and therefore without the overt power imbalance of psychodynamic therapy[50]. Some sensitive psychodynamic practitioners, in an attempt to become politically correct, have adopted "counsellor". This is not the only source of tension between the psychodynamic and person-centred traditions. There is further evidence of tension as some psychodynamic practitioners have borrowed "empathy" one of the main tenets of person-centred counselling. Bateman and Holmes argue that:

> This emphasis on empathy may have arisen to counterbalance the rather rigid interpretive technique of some ego psychologists, but it also represents a shift from conflict to deficit as a central theoretical theme.[51]

This in some way echoes the conflict of the Reformation in the 16th century where each denomination was striving for status by making the claim that they had something different to offer. The psychodynamic tradition and the person-centred tradition do have different things to offer and it appears that if one adopts the techniques employed by the other it is regarded as a form of trespassing. Although the term counsellor is regarded by some as more client friendly those who use it are, paradoxically, often equated with superficiality and a lack of qualifications and thus somewhat light weight compared to psychotherapists. So whilst therapist can signal tradition, and be criticized for this, counsellor has a down side which is to do with a perceived lack of depth. The religious parallel here is with the gravitas of the Catholic priest and the informality of, for example, the Baptist minister[52]. The first relies on and relishes their depth of tradition whereas the other has rejected them and regards himself as reformed. An area we have yet to explore is the "apostolic succession" of those maintaining the strict tradition of the master. Those closest to the founder, regardless of how tenuous, still hold more credibility than those more recent in the genealogy.

Depth psychology has historically held the senior position but must be exposed for what it is, a powerful metaphor, illusory. There could be a whole debate about what is meant by depth and the way that it has been exploited because implied in depth is the counter which is superficial—if not deep it follows that one must be shallow. Cumulative traditions are a fundamental part of a depth claim for a psychotherapist but for person-centred practitioners it is equated with an old model, a framework held in place by people who claim to be experts and their need for control. This could be one reason for adopting the term counsellor which whilst politically expedient, could also be saying something about the beginning of a power amnesty. These controversies[53] are influenced by current trends and reflect how easily swayed professionals are, to be in fashion even when it comes to health. The dynamic nature of practice is not new as from Freud's commentators we can gauge the extent to which he was influenced by the social climate of his time. For example, his desire to be recognised as a scientist was tied to his desire to for professional status. Freud's mistakes were often to do with his timing. He on more than one occasion released information that his contemporaries were not ready to hear and he was subsequently condemned by them. Contemporary counsellors and psychotherapists are no less subject to desire for recognition and status than their respective founders were.

The word psychodynamic means that the psyche or soul is involved in an ever changing process. It is a hive of activity which is constantly in dialogue with internal (intra) relationships and external (inter) relationships. Both psychodynamic therapy and psychodynamic counselling use a model of human development which, whilst sharing a foundation with psychoanalysis, holds less dogmatically to all that Freud originally prescribed as essential. Michael Jacobs gives an example of a psychodynamic model:

> ... in which there is perceived to be a constantly moving set of relationships (dynamics) between different aspects of the personality, formed of past and present relationships between the growing individual and significant others, and therefore consciously and unconsciously influencing relationships within the internal world of the individual as well as the external world of the person and objects.[54]

In other words those inter/intra relationships and dialogues mentioned above.

There are many variations in practice ranging from those who either regard themselves as, or, and perhaps more importantly, are regarded by others, as at one extreme psychoanalysts or classical Freudians, and at the other counsellors. The reality is that there is no such bipolarity and it is a fantasy that so called classical practitioners adhere rigidly to Freud's particular theoretical framework with its procedures and techniques, whilst others adopt a somewhat eclectic or politically expedient, integrative approach.[55] The eclectic/integrative debate is another area of contention, where to be eclectic is believed to be unstructured, one might say unchurched, and as such, unsafe in ones practice. The Integrative practitioner appears to be more acceptable as they rely on a strong foundation of one approach with skills or techniques not traditionally associated with that approach being borrowed and integrated. This is all a matter of political manoeuvring. This may be seen in the same vein as the notion of being religious and having a commitment to a recognised, tangible tradition, whereas being "spiritual" which is regarded as "airy fairy", "New Agey" or "pick"n"mix". Such distinctions may appear arbitrary but are none the less a continuing source of debate. This debate echoes those within religious traditions whose factions are vying for supremacy.

On the matter of safe practice there is little evidence to suggest that one practitioner is anymore unsafe than another because of their chosen approach. It is more a matter of the integrity of the practitioner which makes them safe or unsafe. However, it is likely that such accusations are fear based. For example, it is unsettling if you find that your devoted Christian friend also hangs out at the Buddhist temple. The synthesising of religious traditions is common practice but theory and practice are different genres and have different motivations. Reading about Buddhism is not the same as being a Buddhist. If one is choosing a therapist or counsellor there is more at stake than simply scientific procedure. Clients will make life choices which reflect the process which they have chosen to do their exploration. Practitioners have also made a choice which have affected their lives. Ultimately there is something significant at stake for each person in the room. With Freud's model it is easy to blame events in the past for the discontent of the present because one of the tenets of psychodynamic therapy is that the past is always in the present. In a tradition where the past is occluded, as in the person-centred approach, the culture is one which is optimistic and forward looking. Each model affects the outcomes of the client. In becoming a Buddhist one reflects the tenets of a specific Buddhism in the same way as a Rogerian (for all he would have objected to this title) or a Freudian reflect the traditions of their chosen belief system.

Certain traditions claim that Freud has nothing to do with what they do. For example, practitioners of Cognitive Behavioural Therapy describe their relationship with patients/clients[56] as an "educational alliance" in which they are also concerned with the present and the future but not the past. One could argue that the evidence of the past in the present lies just beneath the surface and one does not have to dig too deeply to find the influence of Freud. Freud believed that there was considerable evidence that the past is always influencing the present and therefore those claiming to work in the here and now cannot avoid the past in the present. Cognitive Behavioural Therapists are unwilling to relate to the unconscious even though it has been acknowledged as a dynamic region of the psyche for a very long time. Ellenberger's work is testimony to this history. However, Freud's development of a theory about its dynamics has had the most wide spread and lasting impact. Cognitive Behavioural Therapists may deny Freud's impact in a way which echoes the denial by The

Free Presbyterian Church of Scotland of its relationship with Roman Catholicism. That one relied on the other as a platform from which to depart has been actively excluded from their understanding of their position.

As is now common knowledge, Freud ensured that the components of the unconscious or psyche, which have been translated as the; ego, the id and superego[57], formed his very own direct descendents of that other "Trinity", father son and holy ghost, and were acknowledged as constantly in motion, dynamic. The unconscious is equated with the psyche and is responsible for giving us the name, psychoanalysis. For some the psyche is equated with the soul, however, for others, secular in outlook, the preference has been to equate it with the mind. Whatever people choose to call it, they believe that within it there are components, which are constantly active. This is relevant in so far as it relies on belief and not proof. There is no hard evidence that the psyche exists or has those components which Freud led us to believe. Proof appears not to be an issue for those who have relinquished themselves to believe. For example, psychoanalysts have suspended their disbelief and their commitment to the Freudian model relies entirely on faith in what Freud proposed, which was not empirical science but a faith driven model. For this reason critics see Freud as a believer in things unseen, a man of faith in that which cannot be demonstrated. Freud chose to study the unseen and to be unseen himself in the process, hiding behind the patient in what he claimed was for the efficacy of psychoanalysis. Freud's model works (or not) but as with religion its credibility is maintained by assertion, authority and the excommunication of unbelievers and heretics.

In Freud's "Trinity" the assertion is that the ego acts as a mediator between the desires of the untamed id, and the social conscience, which the super ego is attuned to. Although these parts are intangible and as such indefinable, there are a variety arguments posited for and against their existence which serve to maintain a life for Freud's ideas. Even now, sixty five years after his death, the faithful maintain that this tripartite struggle continues. However, the so called heretics who question the existence of the unconscious ask, if it does exist in what does it consist? Freud had various arguments for its existence, one is that there are many times in every day speech where we make it apparent that we experience different aspects of the self. For example, when someone simply says that they are not quite themselves today, one may infer from this that on another day they have another way of being which gives them a different sense of their self[58]. The implications of this are that any notion of a, single core self as a fixed entity is redundant. The arguments against its existence are of the "you cannot see it therefore, it must not exist" variety. The post modern view of the self as socially constructed and constantly dynamic, if "it" is anything at all, has its roots in very much earlier religious traditions: one need look no further than the teachings of the Buddha (arguably a Hindu himself). Lest we forget Freud's own tradition, we need only look at his emphasis on the significance of dreams. In this he continued a tradition of his ancient Jewish forebears of whose long acquaintance with dreams he was well aware.

The inference from the first argument is that there is more than one aspect of oneself with which a person can identify, and as such experience times when there is inner conflict/tension. (When all is harmonious there is less to talk about). Such tension is attributed to what psychodynamic practitioners have referred to as splitting[59]. Statements such as those above, where it is evident that someone is experiencing some kind of inner division, or conflict, is confirmation enough for the psychodynamic practitioner. They believe that each of us is capable of an inner dialogue, and that it is possible to acknowledge and express these tensions which having such an experience may cause. In so doing we can come to understand and manage those experiences more usefully. What Freud did with this tension was to claim that it was internal. Before Freud such struggles were attributed to outside forces such as spirits or the devil or a poor relationship with one's God/s. The implications of this have been highly significant as people can no longer abdicate responsibility for their behaviour. It may be that a chemical imbalance in the brain causes someone to behave in an anti social manner but this is no longer attributed to an unseen external influence.

The tension between one part of the self and another has been the concern of healers for millennia. A person's inner conflict may be attributed to a sick soul, psyche, mind, unconscious or self, which ever term is used such disturbance is not new. For example, in the Old and New Testaments or in the recent past one need only read the literature/novels of the pre psychoanalytic period to find numerous accounts of inner conflict and divided selves. For example, Mary Shelly's *Frankenstein*, James Hogg's *Confessions of a Justified Sinner* and Stevenson's famous *Dr Jekyll and Mr Hyde* are each novels where the doppelganger and the idea of internal conflict is explored[60]. Freud's was not a new account: he was adopting and expanding notions which were already well and truly established and illustrated. Whilst Hogg and Stevenson attribute their characters' conflict to the devil's intervention, psychotherapy treats it without personifying it. In the same way as many people have used Freud as a position from which to depart, Freud's Trinity as internal was a departure from the external Christian Trinity. However, his theories none the less continue to reflect the Judaeo Christian tradition within which he was so immersed. Freud's attempts to usurp the work of the Church were successful in so far as church numbers declined and the numbers seeking psychotherapy continue to rise.

The existence of a hierarchy in psychotherapy and counselling, and within the psychodynamic approach itself, is akin to those of other institutional hierarchies where past traditions are still relied upon for current status and where such things as proximity to the founder and strict adherence to the founder's word give power and influence to those concerned. As mentioned above, there is an "apostolic succession" in which power is often disproportionate to the talent of the practitioner. For example, those people who worked with Freud directly have been, and still are, held in higher regard than practitioners who had no contact with Freud. Jung, despite their split, and Anna Freud, certainly gained more status through their intimate contact with Freud.

Thus there is a genealogy of power in psychotherapy and psychoanalysis still has the lion's share of it, although psychoanalysis is not only a treatment for disenchanted individuals but has been adopted as a theoretical model used for the analysis of social groups, institutions, and literature. However, as a treatment it still ranks highly not because it is better or more efficacious than other therapies but because daily sessions with a highly trained analyst over a long period of time are deemed necessary[61]. Many of Freud's clients had four or five hourly sessions each week. This means that there is a significant time commitment which incurs high costs and which maintains the status of psychoanalysis by surrounding it with an air of exclusivity. Each of these factors, until recently, rendered psychoanalysis inaccessible to all but the financially well off with time on their hands.[62]

There has been an attempt by some to introduce the notion of pro-rata payment a sort of tithe, so that people on low incomes can have analysis, but, as we can gauge from the above, payment is not the only prerequisite for this kind of therapy.

As noted, psychoanalysis has received some of its status by proxy in that it has maintained an alliance with the medical profession, which itself is regarded with disproportionate status. This belongs to the same process, as mentioned above, when the status of the practitioner is increased by virtue of contact with the founder, or someone who knew the founder and so on. Added to this is the social, political and historical context which influences which therapy is in vogue. It is not difficult to find psychotherapists who disagree with any notion of a hierarchy: as insiders they seem blinded by their position. One need look no further than the locations used by psychoanalysts: they are not to be found in areas of financial deprivation. Freud may have inherited the disenchanted church goer but he did not entertain those powerless individuals for whom the church had, in its infancy, been designed to embrace. There is little evidence of a philanthropic Freud. He considered himself to have lacked privilege and concerned himself with how to maintain a decent standard of living for himself and his family. (By the time Freud was forty two, in a letter to Jung, he claimed he was beyond sex as he already had six children and did not want any more). The template which Freud left was not one in which the practitioner would follow a vocation of benevolence and compassion but more an exclusive service where the client/patient should consider themselves lucky to get a place. (It is rare to meet a financially challenged psychoanalyst). The Cardinal need not struggle in the way that the parish priest does.

Some of the arguments used to justify the high cost of psychoanalysis are to do with professionalism[63]. This sets a dangerous precedent which implies that professionalism relies on high charges. The therapeutic community has a huge voluntary sector, which is unpaid, and would be offended at this assumption i.e. that payment equates with professionalism, when they give their hours for free. If one's professionalism is the reason for high charges the implications of this for practitioners of other approaches, who charge less is that they are viewed as less professional. Again parallels may be drawn with the training of clergy who in having a university training, may be compared with those with seminary formation or the lay preacher. None is a guarantee to becoming a good pastor. Morality is not something which one may train for in an institution and yet the belief that professionalizing the psychotherapeutic clergy as a way of ensuring moral, conscientious conduct during practice is ever increasing. This expectation, of high moral standards for practitioners, itself should indicate that psychotherapy is more vocational or at least aligned to vocations where the same standards are prescribed and where it is still shocking when people in such vocations transgress these standards.

The current debate about professionalizing psychotherapy raises issues about what it takes to be professional. Not what it means to be a good practitioner. To be qualified appears to be about hours, to have completed a certain amount of hours of study and practice after which one may be issued with a qualification. However, both Freud and Rogers believed that the amount of hours one has completed does not necessarily reflect ones competence, it only shows accounts of hours and not work. In other words people have often done the hours but have not done the work. So that the lengthy, expensive, training of the analyst combined with their own therapy which is also used as justification for high fees[64] tells us little about the competence of the practitioner. People who become analysts must begin from a position of financial strength which does not equate with a desire to become great analysts. Nor does it exclude the notion that one can, in such circumstances. The danger with professionalizing anything is that it can become an exercise in credentialism. In psychotherapy people collect pieces of paper which permit them to practice, but such pieces of paper do not tell us of their moral integrity, only of their ability to do hours. When engaging one soul to another, whether with psychotherapist or priest, there is no way of policing the encounter without transgressing the prerequisite of confidentiality which is one of their criteria for practice.

Pieces of paper which prove a qualification are really part of a wide but covert issue which is more sectarian in nature. Who has the truth? For example, it is often the case that the psychoanalyst will work in a medical type environment, such as a hospital or clinic.

Environments such as these add to the kudos of the approach. The public-private dichotomy is at work within the psychoanalytic community. Until recently psychotherapy and counselling have not been made available on the NHS. However, it appears that some GP practices have begun to employ counsellors to take some of the listening work away from GPs. This is done on the basis of economics, arguing that it is economically more viable to employ a counsellor for this job than to take up the time of an expensive GP. The motivation for this has echoes of the system in the USA where psychotherapy is employed as a commodity to save a more expensive one and is dominated by what insurance companies are willing to pay. But from all of this may be seen, with a little scrape at the surface of psychotherapy, what underlies this is a more fundamental belief about answers, the answers to those big, meaning of life questions which religion once claimed to have (and still may). All of this raises the question of what good practitioners do and how they become the kind of people with whom we associate moral conduct which is above the perceived average.

In addition, Psychodynamic psychotherapy has created a further exclusivity zone by recommending that it is only suitable for those who can understand, and therefore engage in the process of interpretation[65]. Thus it presupposes a psychoanalytic knowledge. For someone without this kind of intelligence, i.e. access to the theory/literature of psychoanalysis, it is not recommended. If it is only suitable for the educated middle classes psychotherapy is flawed, as Freud intended it for the masses[66]. Perhaps it is still the case that only the middle and upper classes have the luxury of being neurotic. The above gives some idea of the social, economic, and political workings of the profession but we must be wary of any notion of psychotherapy operating in a vacuum.[67] It would be foolish to argue that psychoanalysis was once available to the financially limited it has always been a middle class pursuit. However, within the middle classes, and certainly in Freud's time, there were powerless groups, people who had money but no voice. As noted above Freud's benevolence only ran to those who could afford it. However, as with early Christianity which began as a religion for the powerless and only later became a religion of choice for the powerful who could afford it, Freud's so called neurotic middle class women may also be seen as powerless in so far as they had been silenced until Freud heard their testimonies, testimonies that could not be told elsewhere without judgement.

Whilst Freud's ideas have determined the practice of the Freudian analyst, other practitioners using a psychodynamic approach have chosen to emphasize some of his tenets more than others. Post-Freudians, such as C.G. Jung, M. Klein, and W.D.Winnicott also regarded as major psychodynamic theorists, developed their own theories but not without building on Freud's. Each relied, as Freud had, on a belief in the dynamic nature of the unconscious. However, each departed from Freud's descriptive terms, the id, ego, and super-ego. Jung instead coined terms such as anima, animus, and developed ideas of a collective unconscious and archetypes. Whilst Klein, developed ideas such as internal objects, Winnicott had ideas of the true self and the false self, and the significance of transitional objects. These denominations are not without conflict as each makes claims about the necessity of their developments and therefore implies their subsequent superiority.

Freud's impact on psychotherapy is immeasurable. His legacy to post Freudians and psychodynamic practitioners has been a wide body of theory upon which to draw and build their own practice. The effect of Freud's work and the work of those who developed from him means that it is difficult to categorize practitioners as they consciously, and unconsciously adopt practices which no longer belong exclusively to one framework. The notion of a post Freudian era is as unlikely as the idea of a post Christian era. The passion for the original may have been diverted but is by no means lost. The synthesis of different traditions of psychotherapy make it more difficult to detect what was once regarded as exclusive to a particular tradition, as the language of each has become part of our everyday communication. For example, I have heard a Gestalt therapist talking about "challenging empathically", being empathic to the needs of the client[68] drawing directly on Rogers's theory and in this they depart from the tenets of their founder Fritz Perls. Gestalt is still one of the most confrontational of the talking cures but confrontation may now be viewed as empathetic.

Ideologies and their language are in practice dynamic: it is in theory that they are dogmatised. Theory and practice, orthodoxy and orthopraxy are different genres but are often expected to be the same. What people say they do and what they actually do are often at odds.

For example, we may see it as ironic that Freud's protestations about religion did not prevent him from establishing one of his own. However, as with psychotherapists there is always a position which we cannot see by virtue of our standing in it. Freud could not see his own position any more than anyone else.[69]

Psychodynamic theory came about, in part, due to a feeling of disenchantment with purist, dogmatic, approaches to Freud's theories, namely strict adherence to his pillars or cornerstones. In addition to this, there was pressure from other traditions which objected to the psychoanalytic notions of remaining aloof, distant and expertise which was expected in Freud's day but is much less acceptable today. To be more human centred is seen by many as a necessary and welcome development. As noted above, the world which Freud and his contemporaries inherited and inhabited was almost certainly a world in which the concepts of unconditional love, empathy, and congruence would never have been named as part of something which was deemed a scientific endeavour. In fact psychoanalysis had already been criticised for not being objective enough. It was difficult to make a place for these attitudes in the scientific domain of psychoanalysis. Sandor Ferenczi did see the worth in such concepts but was condemned by Freud for being too intimate with his patients. Psychodynamic practitioners today can be more like the practitioner that Ferenczi wanted to be.

Freud's talent was not so much in having original scientific ideas, but in assimilating the ideas of others and using them to create his own theoretical model, and in so doing, convincing the world that he had developed a new branch of the science of psychology.[70] His ideas were drawn from a variety of sources, some scientific, such as the idea of a unitary life force or libido theory. It is unclear how scientific the language, which Freud employed to describe his work was[71]. For some, the translations are regarded as missing his real point, although we are left in no doubt as to where he believed his work belonged.[72] Adam Phillips, himself a psychotherapist, in a recent publication claims Freud's work not as science but as literature and by doing so keeps psychoanalysis at a safe distance from religion.[73]

Whilst Freud was often accused of being dogmatic,[74] contemporary therapists working in the psychodynamic tradition do so because Freud's work has been developed and has not remained static. Many continue to interpret Freud's ideas and use them as guidelines rather than seeing them as doctrines, not open to interpretation or development. Development of Freud's work has probably been easier since his death as in his correspondence there is evidence of the difficulties which arose when he was challenged. He, at times, fought his corner like a terrier and his opposition to change was clear. However, Freud relied on the comments of his fellow scientists to make his discoveries. For example, he relied on feedback from members of the B'nai B'rith, a Jewish society to which he gave many of his academic papers. He remained a member throughout his life and was also an honorary member of Kadimah a Zionist organisation[75]. Freud claimed to be indebted to the B'nai B'rith for their continued support. The contemporary practitioner with a faith tradition has more to contend with. Freud's rejection of religion has made it almost impossible to practice religion and be a secular psychoanalysis or psychotherapist. There are however, individual practitioners who feel safe enough to make claims about their spirituality[76]. That is not to say that people do not say that they are for example, Christian or Jewish but this is qualified by "not practicing".

Without contraries there would have been little progress and Carl Jung, although set up by Freud to be the first "apostle", turned out to be Freud's biggest competitor. He was Freud's choice of successor because as a gentile he was believed to be the most prudent next in line to lead the movement. He in fact became Freud's most famous opponent. The reasons for their split are more complicated than the documentation would have us believe[77] but that Jung saw religion as a necessary aspect of the human condition was completely contrary to Freud who believed it was an illusion which caused more damage than good. Jung's overt embracing of things religious is why he has such a small part to play in this work. Freud on the other hand claimed to be an atheist whilst covertly giving rise to a powerful religious movement. Jung would also have denied that what he created could also be compared to a religious movement, preferring to see it as an ideology. Before their famous break Freud and Jung had given each other years of intellectual stimulation and their irreconcilable differences had a devastating effect on them both.

Whilst much of the documentation about this split is about differences in theory there may have been something else which is omitted. Freud and Jung gave each other mutual analysis, the contents of which were confidential. Jung's wife Emma, who is believed to have been jealous of their relationship, wrote to Freud stating that she was concerned about Jung's health. Jung found a letter in Freud's hand addressed to Emma and asked her why Freud was writing to her. We may only hypothesise about his response, but psychoanalysis and medicine are each bound by secrecy and the idea that Freud was discussing Jung with Emma without his consent would have been regarded as a breach of trust by Jung. The break up of their friendship was significantly detrimental to their health: Freud was, according to Anna Freud, depressed and Jung had a breakdown from which he took about five years to recover[78].

Freud was prone to dramatic splits and as with Jung his parting from Fleiss was also a very public affair. Adler and Stekel are also examples of men who challenged Freud and lost. The loss for each appears as more of a crisis of faith in that the effect was much more personal than a professional disagreement. Freud believed their actions to be heretical, an indication that his own investment was beyond professional. Followers who made the break from Freud did so because their integrity required them to and many are regarded as having created ground breaking work of their own. As noted above, the movement functioned in such a way as to mean that those brave enough to go it alone were described by Freud as heretics, and were in effect, excommunicated from the Freudian camp[79].

Jung's approach, known as analytical psychology, sits easily under the umbrella of psychodynamic therapy, but is often referred to as analysis which adds to the confusion of who is doing what. Some contemporary Jungian analysts call themselves analytical psychotherapists.[80] Jung's choice of name, like Freud's, gave his ideas a scientific edge which in many ways has lulled his followers into a false sense of security. As noted, Jung, unlike Freud, believed in religiousness as an important aspect of psychotherapy:

> Jung also viewed the unconscious as encompassing spiritual and transcendental areas of meaning.[81]

Recently Jung and subsequently Jungian therapy has been much criticized. Richard Noll's biography *The Aryan Christ* [82] posits the idea that Jung and his ideas were sympathetic to Nazism and whether one believes in his hypotheses or not it has affected the dinner party status of Jungian therapy. The ideas discussed above about the influence of political correctness have left Jungians in a weak position, (for the moment). The Jungians will not be back in vogue until another condemning biography of Freud is published, when the emphasis will shift. The notion that each therapy can function in isolation is discredited by the media influence which can swing the tide of popularity in just one article. However, for the faithful such media intervention is negligible.

Methods and techniques employed by analytical psychologists, psychodynamic practitioners and psychoanalysts are an attempt to work out what the unconscious is trying to communicate, which they believe appear in a variety of ways, for example, through symbols arising from free association, dreams, fantasies, and parapraxes, slips of the tongue or pen. The client brings these into therapy, where the practitioner will interpret and make inferences about their meanings. There is a current argument, which states that the interpretations which therapists make are barely related to the client and that the alleged findings only belong within the imagination of the therapist.[83] These therapists are so entrenched in their theories and traditions that their work consists in looking for theoretical assumptions which fit with what the client is saying, or even how they can fit what is being said into a theory. For example, the idea being that if you are in Jungian therapy you will have Jungian dreams and likewise in psychoanalysis Freud's framework is used. In Ellenberger the exploration of the ancestry of psychotherapy shows that in all traditions there is a framework which is applied in healing which relies on suspension of belief and faith in the efficacy of the treatment. This efficacy also relies on a presupposition of the community's belief in and upholding of the traditions espoused by the founder.

Other techniques involve identifying resistances and defences such as projection, where one would attribute to others characteristics which are difficult to accept in oneself or denial, when there is a complete lack of awareness and preparedness to take responsibility. This abdication of responsibility may be identified in the movement's denial of what their function really is. Transference and counter-transference are both regarded as valuable therapeutic tools of the psychodynamic trade, which has not always been the case. In the past the assumption has been that transference belonged only to the client, and counter transference something that only the therapist engaged in. It is now acknowledged that each person in the room can transfer or counter.[84]

The prescribed ways of being in the psychodynamic tradition have historically included notions such as practitioners act as a blank screen for the client. Although now shown to be impossible, this fantasy has been desired by empiricists[85]. The client may project any deeply held assumptions or fantasies on to the therapist who, unlike the ancient tradition of the priest who actually has a screen[86], just has to act as a blank screen. This act is adopted in an attempt to prevent the therapist overtly reacting to the patient, thereby allowing the patient free reign or rein if Freud's notion of the id as an untamed wild animal is adhered to. The issue of whether any human may be regarded, as a blank screen is contentious because at the very least blank screens still evoke a response. I expect that there are few contemporary practitioners who still believe this but would sit on the fence if asked to declare their beliefs about it, a form of "methodological agnosticism" that poor relation of Berger's "methodological atheism"[87]. This phenomenon is discussed by Carrette who very kindly calls it "disciplinary amnesia"[88]. Such generosity overlooks the possibility of this as an activity rather than, as Carrette would have it, an unconscious oversight. The psychoanalysis of such action would show that it is at least an activity in forgetting as there is no remembering without first forgetting.

Freudians also use the techniques described above but differ from the psychodynamic practitioner in their choice of environment and the manner in which the therapy is conducted. As in Catholic confession, Freudians also create a space in which the patient can be anonymous. They are renowned for having their patients/clients lying on a couch with the analyst seated behind and out of sight. This is in part intended to alleviate the discomfort of eye contact both for the client and the therapist.[89] For Freudians this is part of a ritual intended to create an environment in which the client can focus on those things, which freely come to mind. Repressed emotions will be transferred and the process of allowing feelings an opportunity to come to consciousness and be interpreted, can in turn lead to understanding, and subsequently, to some kind of management of them.

The absence of eye contact as a tool for altering the state of consciousness of someone in distress, as noted above, is not new.

Religious traditions have encouraged it for a long time: the Catholic Church is but one example. Losing eye contact does mean the loss of a significant social cue: there are very few social occasions where one does not rely on eye contact. Although this has become synonymous with Freudian analysis it was not designed this way. Freud disliked spending so much time being looked at and by default discovered the increased efficacy of analysis when he was out of sight. Freud claimed that patients could more freely associate, without normal social cues, a significant part of the psychoanalytic process. Psychoanalysis relies on an altered state of consciousness, which is easier to achieve without eye contact.

The therapeutic encounter is rich in ritual which ever tradition is being practiced. However, the Freudians are more overt in this than others. The rituals of Freudian analysis have been particularly criticized by feminists such as Luce Irigary, herself a continental psychoanalyst, as a set up which can be dis-empowering to the client, particularly if the client is female[90]. She argues that the connotations of a woman lying in this submissive posture are entirely different to those of a male.[91] She also presupposes that lying down is experienced as a more vulnerable position than sitting which may not always be the case. Also that one's vulnerability may be further induced by the denial of eye contact is not always the case. Case studies have shown that eye contact is at times difficult for the client. It is but one of the cues which body language betrays and gives the client an opportunity to work without suggestion. The analytic experience is an encounter which has been designed intentionally as a space and time which is devoid of normal social cues for the purpose of inducing a state which would not otherwise be induced. As noted, the removal of eye contact in psychoanalysis is for the purpose of creating an environment which is conducive to free association. Psychotherapy continues in the tradition of healers of the soul who have prescribed altered states of consciousness as part of the cure. Psychotherapy is not the secular practice that we are led to believe, one is not doing the shopping or having a drink down the pub but is setting aside specific time in a specific place with a specific person to engage in a task of inner exploration which relies on an altered state of consciousness.

In addition, following the time honoured relationship between healer and patient, in psychoanalysis and psychodynamic psychotherapy there is much that is actively withheld by the practitioner. Withholding is believed to be an important part of the process to induce transference. We do not ask personal questions of our therapist any more than we would our priest or minister or other religious practitioners. Outsiders regard this so called technique as exploitative and argue that it gives the practitioner more power than the client. This is a reductionistic notion of power and how it works, as within the dynamics of psychotherapy it is more complex than this view assumes. Psychodynamic practitioners, using a more integrative approach, do so to create a more empowering environment for the client[92], one which is less aloof than psychoanalysts are alleged to be. It may be of interest to note that Anna Freud knitted when she was analysing, something which Luce Irigaray saw as a positive thing. This is an indication of the highly subjective nature of the relationship between client and therapist and that clearly, one man's meat is another man's poison.

The efficacy of working in such a detached way is always under question by those who believe that it only serves to create and perpetuate hierarchy. Its real effect on the transference and countertransference has yet to be fully documented. In many ways all therapeutic relationships are role playing and one has to question whether the overt nature of this role is ultimately less destructive than those in other therapies who believe themselves to be less exploitative, and by virtue of this belief are perhaps experiencing self deception. Setting up a relationship which is from the outset a role playing activity is perhaps a safer way to begin rather than to lull one's self and one's client into a false sense of security.[93] If one realises that the space and time are sacred and that an altered state of consciousness is induced for therapeutic effect and that the activities which take place in the therapy session are peculiar to that space and that time it is easier to accept the religious parallels. The therapy room may, like many locations that were once only used for sacred activities, also be used for so called secular activities. However, this does not impinge on the sacredness of the space. The process required for this transformation is merely the suspension of belief or disbelief. The idea that certain spaces at certain times are believed to be efficacious has been part of religious traditions even before they were so called. For example, the mythology of the Ancient Near East is rich with ideas about specific places which were believed to be sacred[94]. We need not go so far as the Ancient Near East: in our own back yard there are many such geographical features. For example, the confluence of two rivers may be regarded as sacred and many wells are still used for healing. Both are pre Christian beliefs which have been assimilated into the Christian tradition and are testimony to that amnesia referred to above as they are not acknowledged as pagan.

There is no such thing as a pure Freudian any more than a pure Hindu or a pure Christian. Accusations about purism arise in a specific context which is against fundamentalism. Christian Fundamentalism was a term originally used in the 1920's by anti-modernist religious groups who were against change. If classical Freudians are the fundamentalist faction of psychodynamic therapy which, in the current climate of anti-fundamentalism, can only be a bad thing, they are bound to be used as convenient scapegoats.[95] Although there are serious question marks over whether such a thing actually exist other than in theory, "they" who ever they are, are still referred to in a derogatory way and are condemned for not moving with the times. It seems from this that one of the "fundamental"[96] outcomes of therapy, that of becoming more tolerant, is easier in theory than in practice. Tolerance of other ways of practice appears not to be a strong point for therapists.[97] Their talk is similar to inter faith dialogue in so far as their action does not echo what they say.

Psychodynamic therapists operate on the basis that they have expert knowledge, and that the client's state prevents them from seeing themselves with clarity; that clients' difficulties have their roots in childhood experiences. Also, that there is true motivation behind the actions of the client of which the client is not aware; and that the client will employ a range of survival techniques, such as defences to avoid what they really feel. Thus, by implication, the feelings that the client identifies are not the real ones. However, the therapist has access to those feelings of the client which are real and their expertise will help to uncover and make sense of them.[98]

This has led to criticism of the psychodynamic approach and accusations of the omnipotence of therapists. It raises concern about their detachment and whether this is necessary to the therapeutic process, or as critics have alluded to it, is it just a power game? Masson, for example, points out that the hierarchy of patient as inferior to the therapist is akin to the relationship one might have with a priest or with royalty.[99] Therapists are permitted to ask any questions but the client/patient is not. Therapists may approach clients. However, the client may not first approach the therapist. The therapist decides on the amount and frequency of time that they will allow the patient to spend with them. This is a relationship which may begin with reverence from the client/patient to the practitioner but often ends in reverse with the therapist revering the client/patient. During the process of arriving at such a reversal the client/patient will have been through many turbulent feelings about the therapist. This process echoes that of the priest and the novitiate where the novitiate, after much struggle, ends up in a position of strength equal to the mentor.

The psychodynamic practitioner is responsible for creating separateness. This is achieved by particular ritualistic behaviour and is, according to critics such as Masson, "essential for power"[100]. Masson gives an example of a friend whose therapist's office was three floors up but the reception was on the ground floor. Rather than call down to him she came all the way down to collect him and they walked all the way back up in silence thereby creating an intimidating atmosphere in which to begin exposing one's innermost fears. Were it not for the vulnerability of the client this could be seen as farcical.[101] There is another way in which this may be viewed, and that is, that the client enters into a space which loses its profanity by virtue of this act. Masson's judgement about this, without having been present, is perhaps distorted and it may be possible that it was an example of basic good manners. Masson, although an analyst himself, has become more critical than most of the process and he does not accept that there are other ways in which the relationship dynamics may be viewed. His is an entirely secular reading of therapy. He fails to see that there are as many therapies as there are practitioners in the same way as for example, there are as many Christianities as there are practitioners.

In therapy space and time are allocated for the purpose of worship that is, the worship of the self, by the self, for the self. Paul Vitz[102] has written disparagingly of what psychology has done, claiming that it has created a "cult of self worship" a culture of "selfism". However, he also seems to say that psychotherapy offers very little that is different to the great religions. His work is from an entirely Christian perspective, but he seems not to realise that if psychology is nothing more than a religion then he must praise psychology in the way that he praises Christianity. If Freud and Feuerbach were correct and religion is a mere projection of man, what does it matter whether the worship is inside or outside if ultimately the end is for the self? Vitz is among many who take issue with psychotherapy. Feminists take issue with the patriarchal framework within which it works and are therefore immediately suspicious of any assumptions and attitudes which come from it[103]. Irigary, mentioned above, is but one. However, Masson argues that even the feminists have not gone far enough in their condemnation. Their objections lie with those very things which make therapy other worldly. The way in which space and time are used is rendered hierarchical, as is the fact that there is no everyday conversation and the client/patient is not expected to question the practitioner. They realise that the psychotherapeutic relationship is comparable with that of a novitiate and their mentor but choose to see this as entirely negative. Psychotherapy is a conversion process where one intentionally enters a place and a relationship with the expectation that one will change, and not have the same views as when first having sought therapy. No one forces you into therapy, you make a decision and you do the work.

There have been many themes within this chapter which have parallels with religions: professional training, hierarchy, power, construction, sacred space, time and ritual to name a few but the parallels run more deeply than these.

All of the above exemplifies a tradition which functions as if it exists in a vacuum and yet it has been entirely constructed as part of a wider system which has particular use for such traditions. For example, in our culture to hear voices in ones head would be worthy of medication whilst another culture may regard this as wisdom. The cure of souls depends on what the wider group believe an unwell soul to be: mental health and how this is achieved is decided by the dominant culture. Mental illness is not fixed what was once regarded as madness may no longer be so viewed.[104] If mental illness and its cure are constructed then so are the institutions, the ways of training, the buildings and the way that they are used right down to the furniture, couch or chairs, tissues or not: each of these has arisen from expectations of the dominant culture and as such constructed for a particular purpose. This purpose may not be obvious. However, our social, economic and political institutions are still immersed in Judeo-

Christian traditions such that even the most ardent atheist cannot deny knowledge of Biblical prescriptions and even the Lord's Prayer. Our architecture also reflects this and skylines are testimony to this Christian legacy and yet the denial of such influence as intrinsic to who we are, is ongoing in psychotherapy. The words, gestures and expert knowledge of the psychodynamic practitioner echo those of a religious paradigm. In our own culture this, even with such cultural and therefore religious diversity, is a Christian model, which itself was based on the model of the Roman civic forum. The structure of the psychodynamic tradition relies on adherence to the work of the "high priest" Freud who saw himself as responsible for relieving the suffering of the masses. Psychodynamic psychotherapy still relies on Freud to justify its existence as an elite church albeit with different orders. Freud's determination to control what psychoanalysis was and would become, by choosing those who would do as he wanted as his successors, has been adhered to. He chose people who would not risk heresy and thus excommunication and so his tradition is maintained. The front runners in psychoanalysis and psychodynamic psychotherapy today still reflect Freud's resistance to things religious. Below is an exploration of the strategies which each has developed to avoid acknowledging their activity as religious.

CHAPTER THREE (II)

Contemporary Psychodynamic Psychotherapy

So, where does psychoanalysis and, therefore, subsequent psychodynamic psychotherapy belong? As we shall see, about this there is little consensus.

> Those who consider themselves to be serious actors in psychoanalytic affairs continue to disagree about the nature of the psychoanalytic enterprise.[105]

Although there is no consensus about where psychoanalysis and indeed psychotherapy belong there is consensus about where it does not belong. This gives us a starting point for elimination. The biggest area of resistance within psychoanalysis and psychotherapy is to the metaphysical. With so much disagreement about what psychoanalysis is, it would naturally follow that it would be difficult to locate. To which discipline does it really belong? The majority of psychoanalysts would still claim that it has a place in the sciences. However, the ambiguous nature of the psychoanalytic and psychotherapeutic enterprise has been, since its conception, and continues to be the subject of debate. Both insiders and outsiders engage in this debate. However, the reason for psychoanalysts' resistance to the metaphysical stems from Freud, whose criticism of religion is well known. To criticise religion has been part of what it is to be a Freudian. To accommodate religion requires criticism of Freud. Adam Phillips claims:

When Freud insisted that psychoanalysis had nothing to do with ethical inquiry, was not in the business of moral-world making or of providing a new *Weltanschauung*, he was trying to dissociate himself from the Judaism of his forefathers, and trying to dissociate psychoanalysis from any connection with religion (or mysticism). If psychoanalysis had been compatible with traditional religious belief it would lose its scientific credibility and its apparent originality. But one is only absolutely original, of course, until one is found out.[106]

In this Phillips implies that psychoanalysis has now been "found out". Freud's need to be recognised as a scientist led him to deny things which psychoanalysis was concerned with which did not fit a scientific paradigm. For example, his universalising all things religious as psychological disorder has, as we shall see, had significant repercussions. This stance, although no longer necessary, is difficult to reverse without appearing to reject Freud. Denying religion and the mystical has caused untold damage throughout the history of psychoanalysis, given their own adage "the past is always in the present". Such denial continues to cause difficulties for contemporary psychotherapists. That their founder was determined to dissociate himself and his work from any form of religion or mysticism remains problematic. That psychoanalysis has nothing to do with "ethical enquiry" or "moral-world making" is of course untrue as, in Freud's own words, it is in the business of alleviating suffering. Orbach claims it was Freud's intention that:

> psychoanalysis as a clinical practice is about transforming hysteria into ordinary human misery.[107]

What could be more moral world-making than this? Suffering, in the shape of "ordinary human misery", is a reaction to those issues arising from ethics and morals prescribed by the cultures which we inhabit. Freud was aware that psychoanalysis had the potential to transform human suffering, and believed that everyone could benefit from it. Psychoanalysis was not exclusively for the ill, rather Freud believed that the human condition was one of inherent sickness which was just a matter of degree. Orbach's stress on the benefits of "clinical practice" comes more from her own need to maintain the professionalism of psychoanalytic psychotherapy (which is how she describes her own practice) and she implies that the transformation which psychoanalysis or psychotherapy can facilitate is only available in a clinical setting. This has been shown not to be the case because free association, one of the main tools of psychoanalysis, has different areas of application. The "Freudian pair"[108] may be exclusive to the psychotherapy encounter but the act of free association can happen at any time with therapeutic effects. The point about Orbach perpetuating the clinical aspect of psychoanalysis is itself moral-world making, in that, it is clinging to and promoting their alleged scientific status in an attempt to keep them securely out with the metaphysical realm. Both Orbach and Phillips draw different conclusions from Freud's beliefs. Phillips that psychoanalysis has been "found out" and is not the science which Freud advocated. Orbach on the other hand in stressing "clinical practice" maintains the scientific facade. If psychoanalysis has been "found out "what have they been found to be? Phillips, Orbach, Bollas and Coltart each have tried to relocate psychoanalysis without, as yet, any real satisfaction.

The dissociation from, and condemnation of, religious beliefs has been harmful to psychotherapy and a change of attitude by many practitioners will be necessary before religion becomes acceptable. The harm caused is that of the continued denial and repression of religion, a state which psychoanalysts claim is psychopathological. The attitude within the psychotherapeutic community towards religion cannot be generalised but there still exists a good deal of suspicion based on Freud's early claims. The continued denial of the common ground of psychotherapy with religion, and the resistance to engage with the mystical aspects of their work is only now beginning to be addressed and the over emphasis of scientific aspects of their work is under question. The potential loss of the scientific status of psychoanalysis and subsequently of psychodynamic psychotherapies continues to cause tension.

Today the suspicion of religion held by practitioners is largely to do with religious institutions, rather than Freud's original presupposition of religious belief as pathological. However, as we shall see, Freud's views remain an underlying motivation for the resistance of contemporary psychotherapists to things religious. It would appear from the most recent literature and from conversations with practitioners that some find the notion of spirituality accessible and are beginning to make space for this. That organised religion is still met with resistance is not only to do with Freud's views but echoes the wave of resistance in contemporary attitudes towards organised religion generally and Christianity specifically. It is often implied that to be religious is to be un-evolved, a belief not lost on Freudians. Psychoanalysis and psychotherapy did not evolve in a vacuum and are products of their social, political, and economic environments and as such are tacitly informed by each.

That the psychotherapeutic community has been dogmatic in its views about religion is not surprising and yet the idea of dogmatism itself would be abhorrent to them. It has been their raison d'être to question orthodoxy and dogma. In fact they have been described as anti culture in their persistence to counter these dominant cultures which they regard as the source of many patients' problems. Freud, although using religious analogies, albeit ironically, appeared unaware that he was creating a creed which people would come to adhere to in a similar way to those creeds upon which they came to him to be released from. However, he was a very clever man, and in this view I think he is underestimated. Phillips has this to say:

> Despite Freud's disclaimers, psychoanalysis has always been about what it means to get bogged down in tradition, whether personal, familial, religious or intellectual[109].

Psychoanalysts need to look at the traditions in which they have become "bogged down". By virtue of being "bogged down" psychotherapists are blind to things which others with distance can see. Psychotherapists spend their time helping to sort out other people's difficulties and believing that they can see them with a kind of clarity which the client cannot. It is part of the human condition that, however much we desire it, we will never see ourselves as others do.

Fisher and Greenberg have written on the ambiguity and polarisation of thought within the psychoanalytic tradition. One of the most revisited questions is where psychoanalysis should be located. This continues because practitioners are human beings first and need to know that they belong. Freud until recently held enough power to keep the waters muddied. Freud's prescription that psychoanalysis should belong to the psychological sciences kept his followers committed to his ideal. In his famous recording of 1939, already mentioned above, he states this unequivocally. This has made it difficult for Freudians to debate without seeming to topple Freud. However, the notion of what is scientific and the change in this since Freud (not least because of him) needs exploration beyond this project.[110] The psychotherapist let alone the Freudian cannot function without the psychoanalytic model as Freud had to. Psychoanalysis has become such an integral part of academic enquiry as well as common currency that we forget that it is there.

Psychoanalysis and psychotherapy are now regarded as multidisciplinary and given this, it is ironic that its scientific aspects would have held such status for so long. There are contemporary practitioners beginning to challenge, and therefore, deconstruct the scientific myth. For example, Adam Phillips asks:

Why is so much science needed?[111]

He not only challenges their scientific status, but seeks to relocate psychoanalysis, for example:

In the language schools that are called psychoanalytic training institutions there are forlorn attempts to purify the dialect of the tribe, but psychoanalytic writing (and practice) of every persuasion still sounds a bit like religion, a bit like metaphysics, a bit like anthropology, a bit like science. And a bit like what was still in the earlier days of psychoanalysis, literature.[112]

As Phillips states, science has been one aspect of the psychoanalytic exercise and yet its power is still wielded today. To make a happy synthesis of all of these bits would be no mean feat and as yet has not been possible. As Phillips states, the training analyst is undergoing a process of learning a new language. Psychoanalysis however, as he points out, uses many. The language of psychoanalysis is therefore a hybrid, (a notion which I explore below). Psychoanalysis has not historically, as one may expect, borrowed its language exclusively from any one discipline. For example, given its claim as science, one might assume that its language would be dominated by this. This is not the case. However, it does borrow a good deal from the humanities, and in particular from religion. When the training analyst is qualified they go forth and train their patients in their chosen language. This language can develop into different dialects ranging from Freudian to Lacanian. Such hybridisation is not, yet, welcome in psychoanalysis, although widely practised. Hybrids are often frowned upon. For example, someone who adopts a mid-Atlantic drawl, a hybrid of British and American English, is regarded with disdain and somewhat fraudulent. The issue which underlies this is ultimately to do with purism, a not too distant relation of fundamentalism which with its modern usage is politically incorrect and as such undesirable. We seem unable to see that our wholesale condemnation of fundamentalism is itself an act of fundamentalism.

Whilst I am on the terrain of fundamentalism, it is apparent from various contemporary texts that this multidisciplinary subject appears to be relatively at home with all but its religious aspects. Psychoanalytic and psychodynamic practitioners have had to untangle their own beliefs from those prescribed by Freud. Freud was not only an atheist but held an anti religious stance, famously regarding it as a pathological state, an "obsessional neurosis"[113] which ought to be cured. Today psychoanalysis exists in a very different cultural context to that of its founder. This point must be taken into account for the sake of its development.

At a recent seminar on "Psychoanalysis and Creativity" it was evident from the participants' confusion that psychoanalysis, as Orbach states, has yet to find a home. Robin Holloway, a composer, Christopher Bollas a psychoanalyst, Susan Hillier an artist, and Blake Morrison a writer, were engaged in a debate about what free association means within each of their fields. None was willing to situate psychoanalysis. Holloway argued that psychoanalysis could not privilege free association, as it is what we all do every day. He, in struggling to locate psychoanalysis, stated, "the art or science or whatever psychoanalysis is . . ."[114]. Bollas countered Holloway on the exclusive type of free association in psychoanalysis by arguing that the "Freudian Pair" engage in a type of free association which differs from that of everyday life. Each had a view of what psychoanalysis and free association meant, which was peculiar to the individual, a fact which makes its location more difficult to find. Perhaps the answer lies in echoing the subject. In so far as psychoanalysis and psychotherapy are multidisciplinary it may be useful to allow multi-homes and cease trying to pin it down.

It has taken a long time for Freudians to challenge Freud's views on religion and to counter them will take even longer. The tradition that psychoanalysis has become has relied on its followers having a particular, almost evangelical, relationship to Freud, and the psychoanalytic movement. Those practitioners, who have begun to explore the positive aspects of religion, still do so with some trepidation, because implied in their challenge must be a rejection of Freud's views. This behaviour by practitioners is similar to that of disciples. If they were scientists there would be no problem with such a challenge, in fact on the contrary it would be expected.

Freud's anti religious views could not prevent his movement developing in a certain direction, as Phillips states:

> Psychoanalysis is the only religion in which you are not allowed to believe in God.[115]

In this he is of course incorrect. For example, Buddhism has no God and is still regarded by most as a religion (although some prefer to call it a philosophy). As discussed in the Introduction to this work religion has been defined by many scholars in many ways. However, in applying Wittgenstein's idea of family resemblance it is easy to see the features, or family connections between religion and psychotherapy. The paradox of psychoanalysis or psychotherapy as religion is that each has become that which it sought to usurp. Freud's condemnation of religion was protestation too much. If as Phillips states:

> psychoanalysis is the only religion in which you are not allowed to believe in God.

This is a step in the right direction. Whilst Phillips is not yet welcoming this attribute his statement gives little away about what he feels if psychoanalysis is such a religion. Freud and his followers are as overtly religiously faithful to their atheism as they are covertly religiously faithful to their Freudianism.

If one of Freud's patients had come to him with those attitudes which he himself displayed towards religion, Freud's notes would make interesting reading. We know little really, although there is much conjecture, about his early religious life and although brought up in a family of Jews his early care, as noted, was with a Catholic nanny. Freud claimed to be a non-practising Jew and yet he sought out a Jewish wife and his children were brought up as Jews and none married a gentile. Freud argued that he was culturally a Jew, a distinction which is difficult to imagine without assuming that he was a Zionist[116]. Such a separation between culture and religion is impossible to make, even if desirable. For example, those of us born and living in the west whether claiming to be atheists or not can, as noted above, recite the Lord's Prayer and could not fail to be impressed by skylines punctuated by Christian architecture.

From this we can at best hypothesise that the messages to Freud about religion were mixed and in his adulthood he was still confused by them. It would be reductionist to claim that Freud's attitude to religion arose merely from his desperation for success in the sciences: rather the real source of Freud's disdain for religion will remain obscure. Freud's views of other disciplines, for example, those named in Phillips above, were not granted the same disdain and yet are equally un-scientific, in that all rely on subjectivity, the arch-enemy of science. Freud was often inspired by literature, in particular poetry. However, this inspiration did not lead him to believe that psychoanalysis itself belonged to the arts. Some practitioners, in an attempt to acknowledge the ambiguity of psychoanalysis and psychotherapy, have had little difficulty in comparing themselves with the arts. For example:

> These days, when we are not being told that psychoanalysis is not a science, we are, perhaps unsurprisingly, being told that it is an art.[117]

Whilst Phillips himself is not comparing what he does to art he is aware that there is such comparison being made elsewhere. Phillips and Sulloway, among others, claim that Freud himself was confused as to what he was and where he belonged. Freud during one of his many times of doubt, as noted, declared himself an "adventurer", and a "conquistador", denying that he was a man of science at all. However, written evidence points to the fact that Freud's personal confusion about what he was never prevented him from continuing to claim psychoanalysis as a science.

Metaphysics, anthropology and literature have continued to have more credibility in the psychotherapeutic community, than has religion. More often than not when comparison with religion is risked the connotations are negative. For example, Phillips states:

> But when psychoanalysts spend too much time with each other, they start believing in psychoanalysis. They begin to talk knowingly, like members of a religious cult[118].

Lest we are lulled into a sense of Phillips as happy with psychoanalysis as religion his use of the word "cult" illustrates that he sees this as negative and shows he believes that it can be dangerous for psychoanalysts to show such belief and this is important because psychoanalysis survives as a pseudo-science by this kind of denial. The fact that prior to their getting together this particular group had not already invested in and committed to the belief system of psychoanalysis is over looked. Phillips' comparison of analysts to members of a religious cult is clearly not intended to be flattering rather it marginalizes them with its mocking, condescending tone. Cults are a whole area worthy of study but suffice it to say that when cult is used as an analogy it is rarely as a positive example[119]. According to Phillips, that psychoanalysis should be regarded as a cult was one of Freud's fears, a fear, which could be argued, has been transferred to his followers:

> It was important to Freud that psychoanalysis should not become a cult of the irrational.[120]

Phillips although unhappy with the idea of psychoanalysis as either science or art none the less believes that it should be:

> Located somewhere between literature and science, psychoanalysis can begin to look like a legitimate and intelligible social practice—not so much a mystery for initiates but a skill that can be learned, with real rules and a body of knowledge.[121]

Psychoanalysis and psychotherapy are a "mystery for initiates" and it is this which they need to emphasise and develop. In addition Phillips fear of association with religion is implied in his denial of the mystery and his claim of "rules" and a secure "body of knowledge" sounds somewhat institutional and dogmatic. Elsewhere Phillips suggests that psychoanalysis would be better placed in the field of phenomenology[122]. Ironically Phillips' resistance results in demonstrating those qualities which he is determined to argue out of psychoanalysis. Christopher Bollas, a contemporary of Phillips, appears to embrace the mystery of psychoanalysis as the title of his book; *The Mystery of Things* would lead us to believe. He seems not to see mystery as an obstacle, which Phillips claims it could be. Bollas regards mystery as where the riches of the psychoanalytic encounter lie and sees it as essential to the transformative process[123]. However, his attitude to religion and the spiritual is not included in his embrace of mystery.

Orbach, like Phillips, in an attempt to demystify psychotherapy, claims:

Psychoanalytic practice has roots in neurology, psychiatry, psychology and philosophy, but a home in none.[124]

Also like Phillips she is flexible about the home of psychoanalysis and psychotherapy as elsewhere she claims it as an art form comparing it to sculpture.[125] In fact each author who tries to define where psychoanalysis and psychotherapy belong, as part of this process, seem to change their minds. Echoing the nature of that which they are trying to define, a subject which has many homes and which is indefinable due to its subjective, dynamic nature. Each is selective in their reading of Freud as to where the roots of psychoanalysis were. Phillips is less fearful of the subjective areas. Orbach in emphasising the clinical locates it more firmly in the medical sciences.

Neither Orbach nor Phillips could be regarded as practitioners who embrace religion. However, there are other contemporary practitioners and theorists who appear more willing to move beyond suspicion, the most enduring legacy of Freud, and investigate more fully the relationship which psychoanalysis and psychotherapy have with religion. Not seeing it as threatening, they are more able to accept that there is much about psychoanalysis and the language it uses to describe both the movement and what they do, which overlaps with religion. This applies to the institutional structure of psychoanalysis, which parallels that of many religious institutions, as well as the actual process of therapy which when deconstructed shows a similar process to that of religious conversion. Neville Symington is one such practitioner. Symington's *The Blind Man Sees* lists the criteria which he believes founders of religions go through. They are as follows, "blindness; awakening; struggle; enlightenment; gathering of followers; the founding of an institution."[126] It is not difficult to see this process in Freud although not necessarily in the order Symington posits. He makes a distinction between revealed religion and natural religion, concluding that psychoanalysis is indeed a natural religion but has yet to accept this[127]. His belief is that a natural religion has:

> the implicit view that the meaning of life is to be found in a reality which is beyond the tangible[128].

Although he is correct in naming psychoanalysis as a natural religion, if it is to be religion at all, his comparison does not account for the commitment and conformity shown by Freud's followers which are more indicative of a revealed tradition. Symington in acknowledging that psychoanalysis would be richer by accepting this is taking the risk that others have not. Psychoanalysis whilst being in the business of conversion, or as Symington prefers to call it "awakening"[129], has not yet experienced its own awakening.

As noted, although psychoanalysis has been described as a science since its conception it has had to struggle to maintain this place. For Freud the difficulties were peculiar to him, his time and place. Freud had enough credibility as a man of the medical sciences to make his unorthodox ideas appear scientific enough to be accepted by many as orthodox. However, his own suggestion that lay people could just as effectively become psychoanalysts, as could medical practitioners, opened psychoanalysis up to further criticism from the scientific world. This was a significant shift for psychoanalysis and its practitioners now bridge many disciplines out with medicine. There is, none the less, still a hierarchy which is supported by our cultural views of medicine. Whilst many non medical, contemporary, psychoanalysts regard what they do as science, for others, as demonstrated above, the boundaries have become unclear. As is often the case, the discrepancy between theory and practice is evident in psychotherapy. In theory there are those who resist any notion of psychoanalysis as anything other than science. However, in conversation with practitioners, it appears that there is much more acceptance of its mystery than theory would lead us to believe.

In Freud's time it was *de rigueur* if one was a scientist to reject, or at least to be seen to reject, that which was regarded as the opposition, religion. Thus Freud, as a modernist, was not exceptional in his response to religion, and his original followers accepted that this was indeed the case, and have perpetuated this idea in his name. (Those such as Carl Jung who questioned this were dismissed) Their determination was given impetus by their need to please the founder and honour his beliefs as well as their own need to be regarded with the status which science could afford them. Part of this legacy has been that there have been followers who, like Freud, have resisted looking at the whole process, selecting areas which would fit their particular needs, and in so doing omitting aspects which do not sit comfortably with the scientific.

Freud's anti-religiousness did not prevent him from using its signifiers. He often used religious language when other languages proved inadequate. So what did this mean? Like religion psychoanalysis has become so much a part of our implicit culture that one would be pushed to realise just how often we call upon its language in order to criticise it. Was this the case for Freud? Was it that religion (both Jewish and Christian) was such an implicit part of his culture that it was inevitable that he would borrow from it, not only to condemn it but to best describe what he regarded as its cure—psychoanalysis . Freud's critics suffer a similar dilemma in that they often use psychoanalytic language and method in an effort to unseat Freud. Richard Webster (1996) is a good example of the pot calling the kettle black!

Given Freud's idea that those things which we resist most are the things which we want the most it is difficult to believe that he regarded his reliance on religious language as simply ironic. It is true that when Freud used religious language it was often with condescension or irony. However, there were times when Freud used it in a complimentary way. For example, in his correspondence with Jung he describes himself as Moses and Jung as Joshua.[130] Given his relationship with Jung at this time such comparison was intended as flattery. In this he is willing to override his abhorrence of religion in favour of considering his own status as comparable to that of a messianic figure such as Moses. Freud's rejection of religion lived in parallel to his borrowing from it which adds to the confusion for his followers.

It would be foolish not to note that in psychoanalysis and psychodynamic psychotherapy, there is a continuing scientific debate which relies on their resistance to being allied to religion. Science and religion have long since been held with the same polarity as day and night and yet it is their reliance on this polarity which makes the other significantly different. Their dissonance only exists in the light of the other. It appears that if psychoanalysis and psychotherapy do not fit neatly into the scientific model, implied in this is that they must belong to another model. If this other model is the arts then implied in this is the notion that psychoanalysis and psychotherapy are anti science and as such regarded as subjective. Not necessarily an accurate appraisal, just an opportunity to note that there is a deficiency in the paradigms which are currently available and that without proof and objectivity it is difficult to hold a place in a scientific paradigm. The question of proof frequently arises in psychoanalysis as the nature of the psychotherapeutic encounter means that anecdotal information is what is available and does not count as it is too subjective, i.e. not repeatable.

The fight to be recognised as science is still apparent but some are less strident than others. For example, the most striking change is in becoming open to the mysterious aspects of their work and Bollas is one example. Although not yet prepared to celebrate this, the fact that their resistance to it is softening is significant. It at least signals that psychoanalysis and psychotherapies are willing to challenge and revise ideas which where fundamental to their founder. It is a sign of maturity that psychotherapists are taking these steps.

Christopher Bollas in his exploration of the mystery of psychoanalysis is less fearful of subjectivity than many. Note he does not call it mystical! Bollas approaches mystery by drawing upon literary sources. Shakespeare, for example:

> . . . so we"ll live,
> And pray, and sing, and tell old tales, and laugh

At gilded butterflies, and hear poor rogues
Talk of court news; and we"ll talk with them too –
Who loses and who wins, who's in, who's out –
And take upon's the mystery of things
As if we were God's spies . . .
        (King Lear, Act V, Scene 3)[131]

Is his inference that psychoanalysts are God's spies?

Although Bollas is interested in the mystery of things he does not talk of religion, in fact the absence of religion from the index of his book is glaringly obvious. Rather he makes a suggestion about spirit which is interesting, but, serves to highlight the absence of religion in his work:

> In another essay I suggest that under special circumstances the term "spirit" should be introduced into psychoanalysis, even though there would be many objections to a term laden with pre-psychoanalytic meanings. If, however, we understand spirit as the expressive movement of an individual's idiom through the course of his or her life, we may say that each of us is a spirit, and that we have spiritual effects upon others—who will indeed carry us as such within themselves, and we in turn will be inhabited by the spirits of others. Spirit is not the same as an internal representation although it does, I think, come very close to what we mean by an internal object: something deeper, more complex, beyond representation, yet there.[132]

Here Bollas is sneaking religion in by the back door. His need to qualify his use of the word "spirit", by permitting its use only "under special circumstances", illustrates the degree of resistance which he anticipates from the psychoanalytic community to anything related to religion. It seems absurd that this should be regarded as a significant step but Bollas clearly believes that he taking a risk here.

Nina Coltart compares psychoanalysis to Buddhism and is open to the influence of world religions on psychoanalysis and psychotherapy. She appears to have worked through her own resistance to the idea that psychoanalysis itself has parallels with religious traditions. However, as we shall see, she still has her blind spots.

She cites an early psychoanalyst, Wilfred Bion as one of her mentors who was an advocate of faith:

> A term that would express approximately what I need to express is "faith"—faith that there is an ultimate reality and truth—the unknown, unknowable, "formless infinite". This must be believed of every object of which the personality can be aware ... [133]

Bion's use of faith is qualified:

> To return to the act of faith. I found that Bion *uses* this phrase and by it intends to signify the most highly desirable stance of the psychoanalyst. He says that the act of faith is peculiar to scientific procedure and must be distinguished from the religious meaning with which it is invested in common usage[134].

In reading Bion's own words one would be forgiven if one had believed him to be a theologian. Scientists need to know what the unknowable is and it is their constant pursuit to find this out. Bion in advocating that psychoanalysts learn "sitting with the not knowing"[135] is inviting them to do something alien to most scientists. However, psychoanalysts are not scientist and Bion's idea has been adopted and has proved to be a valuable analytic tool. Like the priest the psychoanalyst has no choice but to accept the mystery of things. Interestingly, as is most often the case, when trying to describe the influential characters in psychotherapy religious analogies are sought. Coltart herself describes Bion:

> probably a mystic and a genius[136].

Freud also took risks by challenging the notion of what constituted science at the time:

> People did not believe in my facts and thought my theories unsavoury ... resistance was strong ... in the end I succeeded[137]

Contemporary practitioners must do the same and take risks—leaps of faith.

As noted in chapter one Freud was a product of his time and his past. He, as we all are, was driven not only by his individual circumstances but by the social, political, economic, and psychological climate of his time and his theories reflect his attitudes, born of these cumulative traditions. The difference in values between those of Freud's time and those of now are responsible for some of the tension in psychoanalytic circles today. Freud's beliefs have to be seen as a reflection of, or a backlash to, his own climate. To make the necessary challenges to Freud theorists must let go of him enough to criticise effectively the very thing which has been their main source of inspiration—Freud.

The negative views which Freud had of religion litter his correspondence and his theories. As noted above his followers have continued in this vain. The current examples of psychoanalytic and psychodynamic writings in which there is a softening of previously held dogmatic attitudes towards religion, are in tune with post modern beliefs which attempt to counter dogmatism. Views held by psychoanalysts and psychodynamic psychotherapists about religion have until recently, in the main, echoed those of their founder. However, the field is further complicated by accusations from outsiders that psychotherapy itself is nothing more than a pseudo religion which serves to put the insider on the defensive and in so doing battle all the more to be anything other than religious. Such accusations of being pseudo religious pose similar difficulties to those arising from being accused of being pseudo scientific. These accusations, this condescension, has exacerbated the existing resistance to religion, in giving psychotherapies a greater incentive to be anything other than associated with religion.

Freud and his contemporaries have left today's psychoanalysts and psychodynamic psychotherapists in a difficult position. With tensions to resolve, or if not resolve, to manage, which must show on the one hand their allegiance to Freud, i.e. by showing that their own beliefs in some way reflect his , whilst at the same time evolving to accommodate contemporary cultures. Freud, a product of modernity, a man at home with grand theories, meta-narratives, and a belief that science would overcome the questions which religion had failed to answer, is still present in psychoanalysis today. Contemporary psychodynamic practitioners have, in some way, to develop or interpret those theories of Freud, born of and as such steeped in modernity, in such a way as to reflect the current cultural climate in which psychotherapies exist. This at times entails a hybridisation of ideas from each era, which is problematic. To make matters worse in a post modern age, it is even inaccurate to use the word "era" as if they are describable, or definable.

Whether psychoanalysis can or wants to claim a place in science is still an issue for theorists today. Those intent on arguing that psychoanalysis is best placed in science must find ways of expanding the notion of what science is[138] to make a viable claim. This requires being seen to be abreast of contemporary thought. "Being seen to be" is a key issue, in that Freud's own need was "being seen to be"— as opposed to producing the proof requested of him, and continues to be requested of his followers today. For example, Mearns and Thorne, both person-centred practitioners, in the 1980's invited psychodynamic practitioners to produce proof of their findings.[139] (They are no doubt still waiting).

The proof required to secure a place in science is not available from a subject where the interaction of two human beings is not reproducible or objective. Finding ways of extending the boundaries of what is scientific to ways which accommodate the subjectivity of the encounter whilst acknowledging the techniques as reproducible, are key aspects of the psychodynamic enterprise. For example, Stephen Frosh claims that psychoanalysis is scientific on the one hand, but acknowledges that it also " . . . involves a shift in feeling". Frosh claims that the unconventionality of psychoanalysis may serve to illuminate science rather than work against it as is often argued:

> Psychoanalysis is "a specialist science, a branch of psychology" dealing, it is true, with the "mental field" but in so doing extending the reach of science, rather than betraying it.[140]

Rather than accept that psychoanalysis is not a science he continues to "extend" what constitutes science by claiming that the very core of much science, "objectivity", is a form of "blindness":

> Given the emphasis on objectivity which is characteristic of science as it is usually conceived, on separating out the personal investment of the researcher from the collection and interpretation of data, the transformative aspect of psychoanalysis is deeply

problematic. It reverses all the usual argument by stating that scientific understanding of the psychoanalytic variety is not possible *without* personal investment and that "objectivity" is really a kind of blindness.[141]

In Freud's life he shifted significantly in his attitude to his work:

Once Freud had promised himself a new science, it was interrogated and interrogated itself, for the truth claims it could make on behalf of its method. But towards the end of his life ... Freud was making very unscientific statements about the kinds of reconstructions of the past that would work in analysis. "Constructions in Analysis", he wrote in a paper of that title, making a significant concession to the fictive nature of the project, "can be inaccurate but sufficient".[142]

If, as is often the case, the contemporary practitioner uses the same argument which Freud used they may find it useful to acknowledge that the above shows that he was a man given to contraries. Freud's own ambiguity about where he belonged has been demonstrated above[143]. If the contemporary theorist is able to adopt a position like this it opens up their options.

This said Frosh[144] does regard dreams as proof enough, as they "show"[145] the existence and dynamism of the unconscious. He claims they show a subjective truth peculiar to each individual but none the less available to all. Until now it has been part of the scientific tradition to separate the act of cognition from that of feeling. Frosh states that there is a place for each. The idea that this was not the case is a complete anathema. How could one exist without the other? I have yet to encounter an example of how one can have cognition without accompanying feelings and vice versa. The idea that cognition and feelings can be separated has been directly influenced by the tradition of valuing rational thought over our emotions. (This belongs to a tradition of politicizing which seeks to attribute gender to each. For example, reason is masculine and emotion is feminine.) Frosh is forward thinking but he still clings to the notion of being a scientist and like Freud seeks to change how science may be defined rather than accept that a paradigm already exists where psychotherapy could have a home.

The clarity which Freud sought the need for things to be either/or, a prerequisite of the modernist, no longer has a viable place in contemporary culture, which undervalues the dualities of the past in favour of acceptance of ambiguity. This marks a change in attitude toward the value of objectivity and subjectivity. Subjectivity was of little positive value to the modernist but is essential in a post modern society. Freud's buying into a paradigm of objectivity posed difficulties even for him, for example, aspiring to the notion of practitioner as a blank screen while at the same time claiming that what really mattered was the relationship between client and practitioner. The personality of the practitioner, although impossible to leave out of the equation was, what he desired. Today this is much less the case.

> The idea of analytic neutrality is increasingly challenged or subject to redefinition.[146]

Ideas about objective knowledge, are increasingly viewed with suspicion: the "objective knower"[147] is no longer in vogue.

Acknowledging the value of subjectivity has been happening elsewhere in the academy, and is now adopted by some theorists of psychotherapy. The place of the self and the influence of this on the academic project is now accepted by many post modern scholars of religion and psychotherapy. And dogmatism, valued by modernity, is being eroded by a call for fluidity and reflexivity where reflexivity is a bi-product of subjectivity. This, however, does not indicate an end to modernity, (only modernity requires beginnings, middles and ends) it does however indicate that there are new values which challenge the old. As noted, psychoanalysts are fond of saying the past is always in the present therefore the continued presence of modernity should not be surprising in this so called post modern development.[148]

As noted above, for Freud the objectivity of the practitioner was not in question. He advocated that the practitioner remain distant and aloof, in the name of professionalism, and in an attempt to engender transference between patient and practitioner. The notion of the practitioner as a blank screen upon which the patient could transfer their issues is increasingly under question, as is the belief that withholding is necessary for the success of the relationship.

Sandor Ferenzci disagreed with Freud on these issues. Ferenzci brought to his work a human touch. He used himself as a subject which allowed him to interact with his clients in a more natural way than the acting of other Freudians. For this he was punished. Freud disapproved of Ferenzci's way of working and they eventually parted company over this. The difference between Freud and Ferenzci is captured below:

> By being Freud, of course, Freud was very "present" in the analytic treatment; despite the reticence of his technique his patients were treated in a space which he had invented. Not surprisingly it soon became a contention among the early analysts how much they make their particular presence felt. Beginning with the work of Freud's greatest follower, Sandor Ferenzci, the issue of the analyst's self-disclosure in the treatment, the possible "mutuality" of the psychoanalytic process, became the focus of intense debate. The Independent group in Britain, and certain "intersubsectivist" American analysts, have sustained the legacy of Ferenzci's pioneering work, which sees the supposed authority of the analyst as part of the problem, and what the analyst wants in the treatment as integral to the process, and so something that has to be made available for discussion.[149]

The authority of the analyst remains an area which other traditions find difficult to accept. The person-centred tradition regards its practice as more egalitarian than that of psychodynamic psychotherapy. It is difficult to know whether Ferenzci, in moving towards a subjectivist position, was the only one at the time, or if other practitioners were also practising in this way but not yet writing about its importance.

Ferenzci's interest in subjectivity caused his exile from Freud's inner circle, which in turn made him appear as a bad boy of psychoanalysis. As noted above, his influence is still apparent in psychoanalysis today particularly in the USA. Ferenczi was ahead of his time, and the approach which he adopted is now being described in contemporary literature:

> Doubtless the clinical impracticality of holding the position of objective knower as well as the influence of post modern

epistemologies have led to the intersubjective and relational revisions in contemporary psychoanalytic thought.[150]

Ferenzci pre-empted what are now regarded as post modern values, values which contemporary practitioners believe have actually caused this change rather than being symptomatic and symbiotic. In particular his ideas on mutuality within the relationship have been developed. Today there are British psychoanalysts who, whilst not declaring an allegiance to Ferenzci, have adopted his use of the self in practice. That is to say, rather than actively denying their influence in the relationship, they are aware that there are two dynamic people each of whom has an effect on the other. Christopher Bollas uses the term the "Freudian pair"[151]. Whilst this term sounds exclusive to Freudians it may be regarded as a generic term for the acknowledgement of the work of two individuals in the room each impacting on the other.

The current attitude to objectivity by Frosh is, as we have seen, that it is a form of "blindness"[152]. He also argues that one should remain open to each position:

> To become disinvested in any one position in this way, is close to the goal of mental freedom which Freud strove to formulate[153].

However, such disinvesting may also have contributed to the increase in the hybridization of frameworks and the subsequent relaxation of purism. Current ideas on the place of subjectivity are more than just disinvesting and more actively ignoring the use of the self. Disinvesting signifies a healthy choice to detach from an outdated model. It is no longer appropriate to invest in only one area but to remain open to all possibilities. Frosh makes the point that Freud had a goal of mental freedom and yet freedom for Freud was still in some way bound, in that Freud's will was to formulate and the very idea of formulation is a form of dogmatism, which is no longer desirable. Dogmatism runs counter to the notion of freedom. The freedom to remain open to other positions is allied to post modern epistemologies where there is no place for the fixed[154]. Those old fantasies of the psychoanalyst or psychotherapist as an objective knower or an aloof, blank screen actively withholding from the client are now, largely, accepted as exactly the fantasies that they always were. The impracticality of working in such a way along with the fact that it would run counter to current epistemologies, advocating intersubjectivity, would signify an inability to evolve one's practice.[155]

This said even when ideas are out dated they can still have a good deal of power. For example, the notion that it is possible or desirable to separate cognition and feeling belongs to a climate of either/or thinking and seeks to perpetuate the notion of exclusivity. It does not encourage inter-subjective ideas, which are currently desirable. Such ideas, whilst accepted in theory have a long way to go before practitioners reflect this fluidity by letting go of their need to belong to one realm or another. The discomfort of having a foot in two camps is difficult to come to terms with and perhaps a new paradigm which could begin to embody both, one which is somewhat hermaphroditic, to accommodate the wide ranging ideas from patriarchal to post feminist would be preferable to joining the religious one which already exists.

It is encouraging that Adam Phillips asks "Why is so much science needed?"[156] Freud was a maverick scientist who needed to exploit the status of science to make psychoanalysis known. He did this from his medical platform but he was a modernist not a particularist. He read widely and had little difficulty in combining theories from differing disciplines. In this he may be described as eclectic, a term which, ironically, has contemporary therapists up in arms. Phillips' question has been a long time coming and is a useful one which he answers in part by claiming that psychoanalysis should have phenomenological status, which reduces the burden of the scientific question.

> Psychoanalysis is, in fact, a phenomenology of processes—repression, repetition, transference, memory, dreams—that cannot begin without forgetting. There are in other words two ghosts in the machine: the unconscious, and the capacity to forget.[157]

Phillips is right to declare psychoanalysis as a phenomenology because phenomena are notoriously difficult to pin down in that you cannot easily put them in a wheel barrow. The phenomenon of psychoanalysis is much greater than the sum of its parts would suggest. As Phillips notes that psychoanalysis, and this may be applied to psychotherapies as well, is comprised of processes. So that when we talk of the encounter it is a dynamic process which is constantly in motion. As Phillips states, we do have both the unconscious and our capacity to forget but there is more to the encounter than this. The transformative nature of the relationship is as un-pin-downable as the unconscious or the memory, if indeed we can separate them. Different approaches have different ways of describing this transformation but seem to agree that the quality of the relationship is what matters. Both Freud and Rogers claimed there is something inexplicable that happens in the relationship which is not to do with skill or technique: an X factor which seems to make change happen. Recent psychodynamic researchers have named this "moments of meeting", and in the person-centred approach Mearns and Thorne have called it "relational depth"[158]. Clients themselves name it as an "epiphany" or "revelation" and at times "spiritual"[159].

Theorists today have to contend with tension arising from maintaining an allegiance to the founder and his work, and the need to develop and revise those theories of his, which as products of his time are clearly out of date. Attempting to remain in line with the dominant culture is no mean feat. The values of modernity are ever present, even when a characteristic presence is created by their absence[160]. New ideas are born of a need to counter the old, but without the old there would have been no need for this counter. Adam Phillips, like Freud, may be regarded as a modernist as he is also a multidisciplinarian[161]. He has not constrained himself by staying within the bounds of science but draws from philosophy, literature, politics amongst others. However, whilst this affords Phillips the opportunity to be expansive it also makes him a maverick and, as such, psychoanalysts are both in awe and suspicious of his work. Phillips displays his belief in Freud and others whose ideas were fashioned by grand theories and a need to universalize. In fact although he mirrors them he also needs their mistakes to develop his own ideas on things such as contingency, openness, and fluidity, all of which may be regarded as backlashes to the constraints of modernity.

As noted above, the scientific question is revisited again and again by psychotherapists. Is psychoanalysis science or not? The question itself is a product of binary thinking which although open to question appears to be inevitable. What really is their need to have their work acknowledged as science? For many it appears to be more concern at being placed in the alternative camp, than to do with a real concern to be scientific, because if not scientific what is left are the arts or religion and neither seems acceptable. Although Susie Orbach compares what she does as a psychotherapist to sculpting and poetry, a comparison which is uncommon[162], her claim of being a "clinician" and her continued use of medical language reserves her a scientific position.

Whilst to be allied to the arts would be bad enough it seems that any religious connection raises even more resistance. This has its basis in Freud and an out dated notion of what religion is or can be. In contemporary culture there exists the widest possible definitions of religions that there ever has been. Institutionalised religion, whilst still in decline, is not representative of people's loss of belief or faith. In fact in some parts of the USA there has been an upsurge in fundamentalist Christianity. In the UK people appear to be choosing spiritualities which cover such a wide spectrum of devotional activities as to render it almost impossible to define[163]. However, spirituality has become a useful term to bridge the gap between institutionalized religion and secularism.

Phillips returns to Freud again and again whom he uses as a way of reiterating that the relationship which psychoanalysis has with religion has its roots with Freud:

> Despite the horror of the history that is contemporaneous with his invention of psychoanalysis, evil is simply not a word Freud was given to using. But it was, of course, essential to his post-enlightenment project to find a way of talking about the unacceptable without allying it to the supernatural.[164]

Freud did all manner of things to evade being allied with the supernatural. Freud's medical background deluded his followers and himself into seeing psychoanalysis as a science as opposed to the illusion which it was. The illusion which Freud claimed religion was is a closer ally to his own creation than he could see or was willing to acknowledge. His need to be at the forefront of his profession meant his rejecting religion and other allied subjects, otherwise risk being regarded as the dubious scientist which he had become: or worse as supernatural. Freud's psychoanalysis was not to be associated with the unexplainable, such as theology. And it has taken the likes of Symington, Phillips, Bollas and Coltart a long time since Freud's death to begin to explore their relationship with religion in a way which is more than superficial.

Freud's awareness of people's suffering and his determination that psychoanalysis was a way of alleviating this was of course an opportunity for him to usurp what had traditionally been the task of the church. He was aware that suffering was often caused by persecution and that religion had played a large part in this persecution. It is clear from Freud's work that he felt that evil was a human predisposition and not something unexplainable. It is what humans do as a result of their personal histories. He was not prepared to write it off as something beyond our control. He was fearful of the unaccountability which claiming that something belongs to the supernatural, would create.

Whilst Phillips hypothesizes on Freud's discomfort with the supernatural he like Freud, freely draws upon the language of the supernatural or religion when other language fails. For example, in a passage describing an experience of Marcel Proust he states:

> secular epiphanies like this reveal the past but one's personal history is an elusive God[165].

Whilst making sure we know about the secularity of his stance he goes on to use "epiphanies" and God as it seems that secular language cannot convey his meaning. Of course from the point of view of the atheistic all language is secular, man-made, a projection of ourselves. Whether we attribute sacred or profane qualities to something is up to us. Phillips makes a distinction between the sacred and the profane because it is what he needs to do for his own clarity for belonging.

In a golden age when all had a religious aspect there were degrees of sacredness but one would have been hard pushed to find the purely secular. The secular is commonly used to refer to that which is profane, *pro fanum* (outside the temple) and as such need not be applied to those many spiritualities which have no temple. It is increasingly mis/used to describe anything which is not only not institutionally religious but which is actively not religious. People actively ascribe secularity to things as Phillips frequently does. The need for this must surely belong to a school of protesting too much. In his explanation of Proust Phillips states:

> But from a Freudian point of view, discussion of coincidence is inevitably tainted with notions of the paranormal, or the kind of mystical animism that psychoanalysts tend to pathologize.[166]

In acknowledging their need to pathologize Phillips is opening the way for other psychoanalysts and psychotherapists to sit with the unknown. Bollas and Coltart already appear to be at home with Bion's notion of "not knowing". He claimed that it was important for the patient that the practitioner tolerated not knowing and that psychotherapy required an act of faith:

> It may be wondered at what state of mind is welcome if desires and memories are not. A term that would express approximately what I need to express is "faith"—faith that there is an unknown, unknowable, "formless infinite". This must be believed of every object of which the personality can be aware . . .[167]

Psychotherapists have to let go of their need to know and sitting in a state of suspension. Coleridge talked of the "willing suspension of disbelief"[168], a concept which has been essential to the construction of the Freudian Empire. Freud said something similar with regard to the activity of listening[169] and claimed that listening is diluted if one is hanging on to the last words of the patient/client resulting in attention being in one place rather than suspension. If a practitioner is unable to suspend their need to know they are not actually engaging in the process of analysis or free association, as their thoughts both conscious and unconscious are otherwise engaged. The state of not knowing may be described, had it not been for Freud's anti supernatural stance, as an altered state of consciousness, akin to meditation.

Phillips not only echoes Coltart's parallels between psychoanalysis and Buddhism, but draws his own parallels between psychoanalysis and Christianity. He states that psychoanalysis and religion are in the business of turning pain into meaning. According to Theodore Zeldin "a life without pain is a life without meaning"[170]. Implied in this is the notion that the more pain one experiences the more meaningful the life. The type of pain which Zeldin and psychotherapist speak of is metaphorical, and as such is not comparable with physical pain which is of a different quality. People experiencing psychological pain are often unable to identify it as such. They are in such a state of "bad faith" that they would never believe themselves to be suffering. (On this basis are they suffering if they have found a way of blocking out, or splitting off, as psychoanalysis would have it?)

As with religions, psychotherapies and counselling have found differing ways of dealing with suffering. Each uses a normative model of what a good life is and thereafter prescribes how this may best be achieved. The pre reformation "Good Life" was a world apart from the notion of the post reformation "Good Life" The first one was of contemplation and meditation and the second of productivity and reproduction. Phillips argues that psychoanalysis is committed to a notion of Eden albeit that this commitment is not prescribed overtly.

The above demonstrates the confusion which Freud's attitudes to both religion and science have caused for contemporary practitioners. In the following chapter we shall see that this has not been peculiar to Freud.

Notes

1. Grosskurth (1991) p. 22.
2. Gay (1988) p. 175.
3. Ellenberger (1970).
4. Grosskurth, P. (1991). Her whole text is devoted to them.
5. Grosskurth (1991) p. 22.
6. Webster (1995) p. 305.
7. Grosskurth (1991).
8. Webster (1995) p. 305, quoting Gay (1988) p. 179.
9. There does not appear to have been a reconciliation between the two, and there is only speculation that Stekel's death was influenced the death of Freud.
10. Ellenberger (1970) p. 550.
11. Storr (1996) p. 117.

12 Webster (1995) p. 508.
13 Webster (1995) p. 305. Quoting Sachs p. 57 but has no full reference to which Sachs, either in the notes or the bibliography. Sachs, H. (1945) *Freud: Master and Friend*. London: Imago (First published by Harvard University Press, Cambridge 1944).
14 Ibid., p. 305.
15 Ibid., p. 307.
16 Ibid., p. 308.
17 loc. cit.
18 Ibid., p. 309.
19 Livingstone, A. (1984) *Salome*. MT/Kisco/New York: Moyer Bell Ltd. Salome claimed that he was always open to suggestions.
20 Webster, p. 179.
21 Webster, p. 308.
22 *Future of an Illusion*. In this text Freud explores religion as illusion.
23 Ellenberger (1970).
24 Webster, p. 311.
25 Janik and Toulmin (1973) *Wittgenstein's Vienna* does more justice to the impact, on intellectuals in Vienna, of National Socialism than can be shown here.
26 Ibid., p. 313.
27 Ibid., p. 324.
28 Ibid., p. 325.
29 Ibid., p. 325.
30 Jacobs (1988) describes the text book client. People do in fact abdicate responsibility in that they hope the therapist will have the answers.
31 Nelson-Jones, R. (1995) *The Theory and Practice of Counselling*, p. 172. London: Cassells, 2nd edition.
32 Grosskurth (1991).
33 This is an under explored aspect of psychotherapy and counselling. Alex Howard has written on it in his book *Challenges to Counselling and Psychotherapy*. MacMillan Press Ltd. (1996) In this text he has a chapter on "Counselling PLC", in: Carrette, J.R. & King, R. (2005) *Selling Spirituality The Silent Take Over of Religion*. London: Routledge.
34 In a paper given at University of Abertay an academic from Quatar explored the development of counselling or rather the difficulties of setting up a counselling service in a country dominated by Islam. She demonstrated that there were layers of resistance arising from the cultural expectation that, in difficult times the answers are to be found in the Quran.

35 One of the ongoing debates between person-centred and psychodynamic practitioners is about equality. In the psychodynamic tradition they believe that equality is illusory where as in person-centred traditions it is mandatory. I realize that equality is a complex issue but for now that someone is in a state of emotional distress and the other one is not implies inequality of states already exists. This is of course countered to some extent by the payment to the practitioner. More research in this area would be useful but is not within the limitations of this current project.
36 Szasz, T. (1979) *The Myth of Psychotherapy*. Oxford: Oxford University Press, p. 13.
37 Ibid., p. 13.
38 Webster (1995) claims that the decline of the church was one of the main reasons for Freud's success.
39 The idea of there being something out there which is responsible for punishment is replaced n psychotherapy with an internal judge. The judge is not eliminated by the absence of an external judge.
40 As a practitioner I have experience of the ways in which clients demonstrate their internalised retribution in all manner of psychic and physical punishments. These range from internal dialogues to self mutilation.
41 Webster (1995).
42 Fromm, E. (1951) *Psychoanalysis and Religion*. London: Victor Gollancz Ltd., p. 34.
43 Webster 1995.
44 Janik, A. & Toulmin, S. (1996 edition).
45 Freud and Wittgenstein were not friends but were of an over lapping intelligensia which included literary, philosophical, medical and artistic minds of the time.
46 Molnar, M. (ed.) (1992) *The Diary of Sigmund Freud: The Final Decade 1929–1939*. New York: Scribner, p. 115.
47 Freud did not discover the unconscious as Ellenberger's work shows. He did however posit the idea of its dynamic nature.
48 Feltham, C. (ed.) (1999) *Controversies in Psychotherapy and Counselling*. London: Sage.
49 What one calls oneself has a different impact depending on the situation. A point which supports the idea that the way a word is used and in which context determines its meaning.
50 Feltham (ed.) (1999) Chapter 24 by Thorne. *Psychotherapy and counselling are Indistinguishable*.
51 Bateman, A. & Holmes, J. (1995) *Introduction to Psychoanalysis, Contemporary Theory and Practice*. London/New York: Routledge, p. 169.

52 Each of these traditions has different expectations of their clergy and the training for each determines this. However, I am aware that whether it be Catholic or Baptist the individual practitioner has some scope for their personality to inspire their practice.
53 Ibid.
54 Jacobs (1988) p. 7.
55 I have spoken to many practitioners who believe it is less acceptable to have an eclectic approach. I am grateful to Marilyn Nicholl for giving me a detailed explanation of why this is cause for debate.
56 What each practitioner chooses to call the people that they see professionally is not without significance as patient sounds more medical than client, a term use in other non healing professions. For example, the law.
57 Bettelheim, B. (1982) *Freud and Man's Soul*. London: Penguin, p. 53. Discusses how distorted Freud's meaning became because of the inadequate translations.
58 For further information/debate on the non existence of the unconscious see Feltham (1999).
59 This notion of splitting was explored most fully by the early Freudians, Klein, and Fairbairn.
60 All three novels grapple with notions of good and evil within among other themes.
61 In the same way as one might argue that a Rolls Royce is necessary when a Mini Metro would do.
62 Today the Portland Clinic in London offer psychotherapy on a sliding scale which means that it is more available in financial terms, however, the time factor still remains a boundary to this exclusive zone. Freud advocated free psychoanalysis for those who could not afford it but this was not borne out in his practice. However, other Freudians did take up this mission and began clinics which although not free did charge on a pro rata basis. For more on this see Elizabeth Ann Danto (2005) *Freud's Free Clinics: Psychoanalysis and Social Justice (1918–38)*. Columbia, USA.
63 This current debate is about professionalism versus credentialism. Freud and Rogers believed that you could have all the qualifications in the world and you could still be a poor practitioner.
64 The talking cure as an industry has been explored by Howard (1996) and Carrette & King (2005).
65 Jacobs, M. (1988) *Psychodynamic Counselling in Action*. In which he has a table of client suitability, p. 53.
66 Ibid., p. 53.

67 Its "middleclassness" appears to be one of the most common accusations of this approach.
68 In conversation with a Gestalt practitioner whilst on retreat at Dhanakosa. He practices in a FE college in Greenwich.
69 The author has the privilege of taking up positions as both an insider psychotherapist and outsider religious studies scholar. Each influences what is observed.
70 Freud Museum, Maresfield Gardens, London has a video with the voice of Freud where he makes this claim.
71 Bettelheim (1982) explains that the German language has a variety of terms where as in English science is a cover all.
72 Many authors have shown that Freud's work sits more comfortably in religion than in science, see Webster, Weiss, Sulloway etc. Bettelheim argues that Freud did not try to make his work scientific but that translators of his works have.
73 Phillips, A. In a prepublication review in the Guardian 9/12/2000 of *Promises Promises*.
74 Wittels (1924).
75 Bakan, D. (1958) *Sigmund Freud and the Jewish Mystical Tradition* Princeton/New Jersey/Toronto/New York/London: D.Van Nostrand Company Inc., p. 49.
76 At the beginning of this project I interviewed practitioners and there were some who spoke of their spirituality most often without connection to a particular religious tradition.
77 McGuire includes Emma Jung's correspondence with Freud in which she asks Freud not to tell Jung. This is a breach of trust which began in 1911 whilst Freud and Jung were still "mutually" analysing each other. Jung is believed to have discovered this correspondence and was extremely unhappy about it. Whilst their break is believed to be purely about theoretical disagreements, it is my contention that this was an additional factor which has yet to be explored. It is interesting to note the changes which Freud makes in his address to Jung. Jung is consistent and always referred to Freud as Dear Professor Freud. Freud changed the way he addressed Jung. He began with Dear Colleague, then it became Dear Friend and Colleague then moved to Dear Friend, Dear Dr Jung then Dear Dr and in the end Dear Mr President.
78 Webster (1995) p. 390.
79 Many of whom committed suicide: it may have been as many as 8 from his close followers. Was there a correlation between those who committed suicide and Judaism?

80 Susie Orbach (1999) *The Impossibility of Sex*. London: Penguin. prefers this term. What therapists chose to call themselves is not insignificant.
81 McLeod (1993) p. 28. Jung's overt religiousness has meant that he is not considered essential to this project.
83 This book has been vehemently criticised for its exaggerations by Sonu Shamdasani himself a critic of Jung.
83 Feltham, C. (1999) *Controversies in Counselling and Psychotherapy*. London: Sage, Chapter by E.M. Thornton. This is the same Thornton who writes critically about Freud's cocaine episode.
84 This is further evidence of the power amnesty mentioned earlier where the client and therapist are each regarded as having fallibility.
85 Notions of blank canvases and screens are of course seriously under question. Noam Chomsky in an article in the Guardian 20th January 2001 bucked "the empiricist tenet of the blank slate".
86 In the Catholic Church in some parts of Spain men actually confess on their knees in front of the priest with their head bowed.
87 Berger. P (1967)*The Sacred Canopy* Argues for methodological atheism where one brackets off religion.
88 Carrette, J.R. in Jonte-Pace, D. & Parsons, W.B. (2001) *Religion and Psychology;Mapping the Terrain. Contemporary Dialogues Future Prospects*. London: Routledge, p. 123.
89 Freud himself could not tolerate having people looking at him for the length of time their analysis took, and so devised a way of minimising eye contact. He found that this was also useful for clients and their ability for free association was increased.
90 This argument is too general and easily falls when a vulnerable man has similar difficulties.
91 Irigaray, L. (1993) *Sexes and Genealogies*. NY: Columbia University Press. Translated by Gillian C. Gill.
92 Jacobs, M. (1986) *The Presenting Past*. Milton Keynes: Open University Press.
93 Masson, J. (1993) explores this covert abuse of power in more depth.
94 Wyatt, N. (2001) *Space and Time in the Religious life of the Ancient Near East*. Sheffield, England: Sheffield Academic Press.
95 There are times more in the past than now when to believe fundamentally in something was a sign of good character and perhaps even honour. So is fundamentalism always a bad thing? Or is it the case that the political climate is determining the climate for all else?
96 In today's climate this word is more often associated with a form of bigotry.

97 For more on this issue of tolerance and of compassion as outcomes in therapy see Epstein, M. (1998) *Going to pieces without falling apart: a Buddhist perspective on wholeness.* London: Thorsons.

98 There is some debate about whether or not it matters about the truth of the client's narrative. There has been an upsurge in a movement which believes that therapy is responsible for the manufacture of "False Memory Syndrome". This group believes that therapists plants seeds of doubt which they then cultivate, creating memories, which in fact do not exist. Notions of truth and falsity are complex but there are always value judgements about the goodness of truth versus the badness of falsity. Which ought to be questioned elsewhere.

99 Masson, J.M. (1988).

100 Ibid., p. 14.

101 Loc. cit.

102 Vitz, P.C. (1977) *Psychology as Religion: The Cult of Self Worship.* England: Lion Publishing.

103 Masson, J.M. (1988) *Against Therapy.* London: Harper Collins (Paperback edition 1993). In conversation with feminist scholars of religion and of psychotherapy I have encountered a good deal of criticism for being pro-Freud and been invited to justify my views on Freud.

104 An example of how madness and the treatments for it have evolved would be that of Vivian Elliot the wife of T.S. Elliot. He had her "sectioned" for what would now be regarded as PMT. This was less than 100 years ago.

105 Fisher, S. & Greenberg, R.P. (1996) *Freud Scientifically Reappraised: Testing the Theories and Therapy.* New York/Chichester/Brisbane/Toronto/Singapore: Wiley and Sons, Inc., p. 1.

106 Phillips, A. (1994) *On Flirtation.* London: Faber & Faber, p. 138.

107 Orbach, S. (1999) *Towards Emotional Literacy.* London: Women's Press, p. 231.

108 Bollas, C. (2002) *Ideas in Psychoanalysis: Free Association.* Cambridge, England: Icon Books.

109 Phillips (1994) *On Flirtation,* p. 139.

110 There have been many comparisons of religion and physics and more recently between nuclear physics and spirituality.

111 Phillips (1994) *On Flirtation.*

112 Phillips, A. (2000). *Promises Promises.* Faber & Faber, p. xiii.

113 Freud, S. (1912-13) *Totem and Taboo.* This text is devoted to the pathological state that he believes religion is.

114 The seminar, "Being Creative" was on the nature of "Free Association". 10/03/02, Brunel Gallery SOAS, London.
115 Phillips (1994).
116 Bakan, D. (1959) Bakan claims that Freud was an honorary member of a Zionist group. But it does not follow that Freud was an active Zionist, p. 49.
117 Phillips (2000) p. 1.
118 Phillips, A. (1995) *Terrors and Experts*. Faber & Faber, p. xvi.
119 Eileen Barker (BASR conference SOAS 2000) gave a paper which was the result of many years researching cults and noted that those who are anti and antagonistic towards cults behave in ways which are far worse than those that they accuse and condemn.
120 Phillips (1995) p.18.
121 Ibid., p. 18.
122 Phillips (1994).
123 Bollas (2000).
124 Orbach, S. (1999) *Towards Emotional Literacy*. London: Women's Press, p. 227.
125 Orbach, S. (1999) *The Impossibility of Sex*. London: Penguin.
126 Symington, N. (2004) *The Blind Man Sees: Freud's Awakening and Other Essays*. London: Karnac, p. 2.
127 Ibid., p. 164.
128 loc. cit.
129 Ibid., p. 2.
130 McGuire (1991) [125 F], p. 133.
131 Bollas (1999) Pre contents page.
132 Ibid.
133 Ibid., p. 4.
134 Coltart, N. (1993) *Slouching Towards Bethlehem ... And Further Psychoanalytic Explorations*. London: Free Association Books, p. 4.
135 Ibid., p. 4.
136 Ibid., p. 4.
137 Transcript of recording of Freud (1938). London: Tavistock Clinic Library, 04/03/02.
138 Frosh in Elliott (1999) p. 5.
139 Mearns and Thorne (1988) *Person-centred Counselling in Action*. London: Sage.
140 Frosh in Elliott (1999) p. 13.
141 Ibid., p. 15.

142 Ibid., p. 73.
143 Sulloway (1979) p. 216 and p. 477.
144 Frosh in Elliott (1999) p. 14.
145 Ibid., p. 14.
146 Elliott (1999) pp. 128–129.
147 Ibid., p. 128.
148 Heelas, P. (ed.) (1995) *Detraditionalization* is a collection of essays exploring the notion of detraditionalization versus coexistence.
149 Elliot (1999) p. 146.
150 Ibid., p. 128.
151 Bollas (2002) p. 7.
152 Frosh, in Elliott (1999) p. 15.
153 Ibid., p. 7.
154 Phillips (1994) explores the idea of contingency.
155 Elliott (1999) p. 128.
156 Phillips (1994) p. 10.
157 Ibid., p. 29.
158 Mearns and Thorne (2000).
159 The clients to which I refer are my own and for purposes of confidentiality cannot be named.
160 Derrida, J. (1972) *The Margins of Philosophy*. Chicago: University of Chicago Press (Translation 1982). Has written on the changing quality of presence that is created by absence and that absence is not nothing.
161 Phillips did his first degree in English literature.
162 Orbach, S. (1999) *The Impossibility Of Sex*.
163 King, A.S. (1996) "Spirituality:Transformation and Metamorphosis". In: *Religion* (1996) 26: 343–351. Has a very good attempt at this.
164 Ibid., p. 59.
165 Phillips (1994) p. 15.
166 Phillips (1994) p. 17.
167 Bion, W. (1970) *Attention and Interpretation*. London: Tavistock, p. 31, in Coltart (1993).
168 Coleridge, S.T. *Biographia Literaria*. Chapter XIV.
169 Phillips (1994).
170 Zeldin, T. (1988) *Conversation: How Talk Can Change Your Life*. London: Harvill Press, quoting Dostoyevsky.

CHAPTER FOUR (I)

The Construction of Carl Rogers

As illustrated in the chapter on the construction of Freud biographies, although a useful source of information, are not always consistent. Carl Ransom Rogers (1902–1987) was born on January 8th in the Midwest of America. Some say he was born in the suburb of Oak Park, others that he moved there when he was five. Oak Park was an exclusive area of Chicago but was intentionally kept as a separate area (even voted against becoming part of Chicago). Rogers was aware that his parents wanted to control who their children associated with and Oak Park seemed safe enough. This was not to last and the Rogers family were removed to a farm on which the children would be kept away from associating with people whom his parents deemed the wrong type. Rogers was twelve by the time they moved to the farm which has been described as a hobby for his father who by now was a successful business man. His family may be described as upper middle class. His father with an engineering business, his mother worked in the home. He claimed that his parents were loving, but controlling and called them "masters of subtle emotional control"[1]. Rogers was very critical of his mother and in particular her strict commitment to a religious life. Drinking alcohol was not part of the Rogers' family life[2], nor did they engage in a great deal of the common entertainment of the time. Rogers described himself as a sickly child but appears to have been quite intelligent and bookish, but claims that because they moved around and he had attended different schools he was prevented from forging meaningful friendships. In his late adolescence and early adult life he developed an ulcer which, significantly, abated when he left the family but was to arise in times of family conflict.

As is the case with many siblings, each of the Rogers children viewed their up bringing differently[3]. Rogers was the fourth of six children. Their different views created conflict between them and as Carl Rogers began to write about his childhood experiences his siblings disagreed with his portrayal of their family life, claiming that he had been too harsh a critic and that their parents had provided them with a secure and loving up bringing. Rogers began his adult life believing that he would have a career in agriculture but changed from agriculture to history with the intention of studying the history of Christianity. He graduated in 1922. It was in 1920 whilst he attended a conference with a group of missionaries he realized that he did not want to be a farmer and the idea of a ministerial career was planted. It was not until 1922 when he went to China that he claimed:

My intellectual horizon was being stretched all the time[4].

During this trip Rogers developed a personal relationship to Christ which was unlike that of his parents. During this time he decided that he was called to the church.

Before this trip Rogers had proposed to Helen Elliot. At first she was reluctant because of his commitment to a Christian life. However, she did eventually accept and in 1924 their life-long marriage began. It seems that this commitment from Helen gave Rogers the necessary confidence to make the changes in his life which he had until then been unable to take. They set off for New York City, as Rogers had chosen to study for the ministry at Union Theological Seminary, a very liberal institution. Rogers' parents did not approve of his career choice. However, they did give the couple a substantial sum of money as a wedding gift. This allowed Rogers and his new wife to begin their married life not only without fear of poverty, but with a nest egg, which could last for their first three years.

It was at Union that Rogers was introduced to encounter groups, the use of which he was to become famous for himself[5]. During these encounter groups Rogers had an opportunity to explore his faith, with the result that he gave up the ministry and turned his attentions to psychology. He had already started attending some classes at

Columbia University which was just across Broadway from Union. Rogers' loss of faith is not something which we hear a great deal about and one could easily understand his choosing to go into the church as an option which avoided going into his father's business. Whatever the reason it did not take long before his faith was lost and his focus on psychology was established. He was bitter about his family's strict Protestantism and even as an old man referred to how unhappy this had made him. In his final years he began to acknowledge that he had actively ignored an important aspect of human existence, the mystical dimension. This aspect of Rogers' work has had a controversial impact on the development of person-centred counselling and in particular the work of Brian Thorne who is one of its foremost advocates in the United Kingdom. Elizabeth Sheerer when questioned about Rogers and his attitude to the spiritual replied:

> We learned early in the game not to talk about religion with Carl ... That was a taboo subject because it was uncomfortable for him ...[6]

We can see from this that Rogers' own attitude to religion has had a lasting effect on his followers.

The different changes in career must have given Rogers a somewhat bumpy start. However, in psychology it seems he found his vocation. From the biographies, including Rogers' autobiographical work, we get a sense of how driven Rogers had become. He was a prolific writer and a committed practitioner of counselling, a term which he popularised in an attempt to distance his work from that of other therapies because of his belief that they were either too prescriptive and or hierarchical. He believed that Freud's view of human nature was "too superficial".[7] Rogers claimed that he:

> soaked up the dynamic Freudian views of the staff, which included David Levy and Lawson Lowrey, and found them in great conflict with the rigorous, scientific, coldly objective, statistical point of view then prevalent at Teachers' College.[8]

He had also been introduced to Freud through Jessie Taft and Frederick Allen, both of whom were followers of Otto Rank. Rank had been in Freud's inner circle but as was often the case, on disagreeing with him, was excommunicated. Rogers' views on Freud and others, such as J.B.Watson the behaviourist, led him to develop his own form of therapy which he called counselling. This he called "client centred" counselling or therapy, but later the name was changed to person-centred counselling. One of the most fundamental beliefs held by Rogers was of the inherent goodness, which lies at the core of all human beings. This may not sound particularly revolutionary but in comparison with other therapies of his time, such as psychoanalysis, with its emphasis on exploring the dark and evil potential of human beings, it was revolutionary. He compared the human organism to other animals and concluded that we are as egalitarian as they are, given the right conditions. With such comparisons we can see that Rogers was willing to take risks. According to Thorne, Rogers described himself:

> As the adventurer who thirsts for new terrain to conquer and new problems to overcome.[9]

This sounds familiar.

Rogers remained committed to his belief in the goodness of human beings for his whole life, and much of his work was concerned with developing ways in which people may actually come to believe this of themselves. Sadly Rogers did not display this compassionate attitude toward his parents, whom he remained angry towards until his old age. Such anger would, from a psychodynamic interpretation, be enough to sustain his life long drive to invent theories and forms of practice designed to create conditions in which warmth and genuine kindness were paramount for the growth of the individual. As noted above, Rogers parents' strict religious beliefs, and the way in which these had impacted on his life, were a source of pain for Rogers, so much so that he still alluded to this in a speech which he gave on his eightieth birthday. With the criticism Rogers had made of his mother, whom he felt had been detached and lacking in real warmth, it should come as no surprise, that his theoretical assumptions developed in the way that they did, especially with parents as judgemental as his, who even when he was an adult caused him to react in such a way as to bring about his ulcer again. So much so that in 1922 on returning from China he had to have surgery. The kind of Christianity which Rogers had experienced on this trip was so far from that of his parents that he was in anticipation of their further reproach. They attempted to keep their son on a much more conservative Christian path. His choice of Union Seminary was the cause of much distress for his parents who tried to bribe him to change his mind.

Rogers remained married to Helen until she died in 1978, when he was in his seventies. He did nurse her but resented the fact that her immobility prevented him from travelling in the way that he loved. The period of Helen's illness was fraught with tensions for them. However, it appears that before she died they did manage to resolve this. One of Rogers' core theoretical ideals, unconditional positive regard, was very difficult for him to provide in this relationship at this stage.

Whilst Rogers was a great advocate of therapy (in his writing Rogers inter-changed therapy and counselling) for others, he was a reluctant client himself. If the biographers are correct it seems that he only sought help from colleagues a couple of times in his career. During his years in Chicago, in particular during 1948–49, Rogers had a client who proved overwhelming and after this period he is described as having a breakdown. It was at this time that he agreed to have therapy with Oliver Bown and which Rogers describes as his most difficult years[10]. In the main he, like Freud and others, looked after his own self-development. Later Natalie, his daughter, was concerned about his drinking and tried to encourage him to stop[11]. A problem with alcohol would be regarded in therapy as a sign that there were unresolved issues.

The moving about referred to above was an interesting part of the Rogers' family life, both in his childhood and after he married. Whenever life challenged Rogers he was inclined to move on without much attempt at a resolution. Perhaps he would have argued that the resolution came from the move. They did however move on with tension still lingering.

Rogers' career was very full and quite varied. It ranged from, a real concern with education, to working in encounter groups, at times with some of America's top scientists. He also did some work for the Government, a step contrary to his belief in openness, as it was for the secret service. In one ambitious project, his scientific application of his theories to a group of schizophrenics in Wisconsin his core conditions failed[12]. However, as with Freud, the failure of his work did not prevent his fame and notoriety. In his obituaries those studies, which had made him famous, were politely overlooked. Rogers also spent a great deal of time with individual clients many of whom have become famous case studies. The "Gloria" case is a particularly well used example.

Rogers' biographers claim:

> He was responsible for the spread of professional counselling and psychotherapy beyond psychiatry and psychoanalysis to all helping professions—psychology, social work, education, ministry, lay therapy and others.[13]

As with Freud there have been criticisms about Rogers' fidelity. For founders there is no allowance for the frailty which they advocate, celebrate and at times applaud in other humans. Rogers was open about his infidelity, both to Helen and then, after her death, to the public. It seems that it was not until Rogers was in his seventies that he openly began to seek out other relationships. If Cohen[14] is correct this was a very challenging time for Rogers and it seems he made rather a fool of himself. There was one woman in particular, Bernice, with whom he became besotted but who unfortunately did not return his affections. Helen was devastated by this but had no real power to do anything to change the situation. This does not mean that she passively accepted it. She attempted to talk him out of this and his other relationships, but to no avail. Rogers' followers are no less dedicated to him for his infidelity. Like Freud's followers it has taken some time for the new hierarchy to become established and it has taken two decades, since his death, for them to begin to really critically revise his theories. With this brief resume of Rogers' life we can see some parallels with Freud. Rogers was set apart from his siblings because he was ill, sickly but bookish; he rejected the religious tradition of his family; he rejected existing theories of the mind and he developed a completely new approach to the talking cure; and finally, his desire was to be recognised as a scientist. Unlike Freud who was in the medical sciences, Rogers was in the human sciences but none the less believed that his work could be measured. The legacy of this desire is evident in the work of his followers, to whom we shall now turn.

CHAPTER FOUR (II)

Person-Centred Theories and Practice

Like Freud, Carl Rogers' life and practice became committed to atheism and, as noted, his overt rejection of religion has created a legacy full of tension and dissonance for his followers.

Person-centred counselling may be seen as a Protestant reformation of psychoanalytic Catholicism. Rogers and his followers tried to pare away all the hierarchical attitudes, the ritual, and other ways of practice which Rogers regarded as unnecessary accessories. Little did he realise that his movement would suffer the same sort of developmental hiccups which had occurred with Freud and the psychoanalytic movement.

Carl Rogers, the founder of Person-centred counselling, also created a movement which functions as a religion. Like Freud he had rejected his own family's religious tradition and because of his disapproval of things religious would have been disapproving of the ways in which his approach has been developed. Rogers' intention was to create something of a diversion, a counter to the traditions of psychology and psychotherapy. This he did by dismissing those things which had been fundamental to psychoanalysis and psychodynamic psychotherapy. He saw psychotherapy as dependent on things which belonged to a bygone era, things which he thought superfluous—in this he echoed other movements which were antitradition. The traditions of psychoanalysis and its immediate descendents belonged to modernity, in so far as they relied on grand narratives and hoped for universals. Rogers excluded those elements which had been the foundation of psychoanalysis and psychotherapy. He rejected the importance of the past and was not concerned with the Freudian ideas of denial, repression, or the unconscious and its processes. His choice to ignore, or give credit to, the influence of the past and his intent on stressing the here and now were very different to his psychoanalytic contemporaries. He was not concerned about whether the unconscious existed but whether or not its existence was relevant for the work of the client in their present life. Person-centred practitioners' concern with the here and now, and not the past, has meant that dreams and other things which psychodynamic practitioners saw, and still see as indicators of unconscious communication, were and still are viewed with contempt. Rogers' school of thought may be compared to that of Janet and Adler, who believed that an empirical approach to psychotherapy was the way forward. Rogers was the first practitioner to tape his sessions and then transcribe them, a process which is used as justification that what they do is objective and therefore scientific.

Although, Rogers was a principal exponent of humanistic psychology between 1960–81 it is important to remember that the foremost experiences in his career were first the church, then psychoanalysis, then behavioural psychology and it was his disenchantment with these which led him to develop his own approach, which he originally named, Client Centred Therapy. In addition he was influenced by other theories popular in America during this period. For example, he had read the works of Alistair Hardy and William James[15] on religious experience. His first experiences with encounter groups, which have become synonymous with his name, were when he was a seminarian. The humanistic psychology movement has been distinguished from other branches of psychology because of its American roots: an interesting concept when the roots of most Americans are from else where. Thus the histories upon which the tradition draws must be more diverse than is acknowledged. The ideas cultivated in humanistic psychology were drawn from European philosophies such as existentialism, from which Rogers borrowed the idea of experiencing and being in the world. In addition to this he adopted from phenomenology, the idea of suspending ones judgements/beliefs or "bracketing off", or epoche, a concept taken from the work of Husserl. Here we can see more evidence of the presence of Europe in his work than is acknowledged.

Throughout his career Rogers believed in the notion of non-directive work. He was keen on "scientific rigour"[16] and claimed to have devised methods of measuring aspects of the therapeutic process. As noted above, he was the first person to make tape recordings and transcribe therapy sessions and to devise a model for gauging the levels of empathy which the practitioner would need to develop for effective practice. Applying this model meant that Rogers had created a measurable and therefore empirical way of studying the encounter. Freud had written his own accounts of sessions which relied entirely on his recall and so Rogers was offering something which he alleged was more scientific, evidence based. In his early career Rogers seemed not to take into account the influence that recording would have on his results. Nor did he acknowledge the influence of the therapist's presence on the encounter. He was not concerned with transference, which was a major tool for psychoanalysis and psychotherapy. It is claimed that person-centred therapy was developed in response to the wider American cultural norms of:

> distrust of experts and authority figures, emphasis on methods rather than theory, emphasis on individual's needs rather than shared goals, a lack of interest in the past and a valuing of independence and autonomy.[17]

Rogers saw therapy as a vehicle for social change, especially for minority groups. He believed that therapy could be egalitarian, and that clients would take charge of their own power not the therapist, which was the model that Rogers was determined to change. He was reacting against the old model of the perceived authority of the practitioner which had, until his work, been predominant. The person-centred approach is accused of being light on theory,[18] even though Rogers himself was a prolific writer. It is certainly the case that there has been less written about Rogers and his work than of Freud. This is due in part to his having less time in the market, but is also to do with his own prescriptions for the application of his theories. Whilst Freud can be found in almost any discipline, Rogers is more often found in the social sciences and education.

Rogers, like Freud, developed his own Trinity which he believed were *"necessary and sufficient"* conditions which could enable persons to change their "self–concept". Rogers believed that if the therapist could provide the following conditions, the client would feel safe and confident enough to flourish. These three necessary and sufficient elements are known as the core conditions. They are firstly, *empathy*, which in this context is when the therapist can "experience" what the client means from the client's frame of reference. (Bearing in mind that one can only ever infer what the client's frame of mind is). *Congruence* is also necessary, and requires that therapists are genuine, authentic, in their empathic responding, not simply role-playing. Finally he believed that acceptance, which means adopting a position of non-judgementalism otherwise known as *unconditional positive regard*, would create an environment in which the client could grow. Whether these core conditions are actually possible is open to debate. However, for Rogers, it was necessary to try to work towards providing these elements, in order for the client to move forward.

The goal of the therapist in this approach, as with all others, is to facilitate a process of change in the client, a conversion process where the result is that the client has a different world view from the one which he or she began with. If anyone goes through the therapeutic process and still has the same world views it has not worked! The facilitation of the person-centred counsellor is one of minimal intervention. The person-centred practitioner works from the theory that within each human being there is an "actualising tendency", a desire to reach a part of themselves without "conditions of worth", which are those layers of values adopted from "significant others", as we grow up, for example, parents, teachers, and other authority figures. In person-centred therapy the client works toward a self-concept which is more realistic/congruent. This may be achieved by virtue of experiencing the core conditions, mentioned above, which, if present, can create a safe environment in which the client can explore areas of his or her life where they feel dissatisfied or incongruent. They also believe that incongruence occurs because the person values themselves through adopted values, such as "I will love you if you are X". This can lead to beliefs such as, "I am only worthy of love if I am what others want me to be", which in turn can lead the person to "being for others"[19] in order to be loved. The notion of "Bad Faith", explored in Jean-Paul Sartre's *Being and Nothingness*, is a close relation to what Rogers described. In that people cannot distinguish between their own thoughts and values, and those adopted from others, and this leads to self deception and consequently behaviour which demonstrates their incongruence.

The techniques used by person-centred counsellors in the facilitation of their clients' goals are supposed to be few but this is only a belief arising from their comparison with the techniques used by psychodynamic practitioners. The person-centred counsellor uses as little active intervention as possible. One example, known as the minimal encourager, has gained them a reputation for what had been called nodding dog syndrome because when counsellors have newly completed their training they are often overly dependent on such prescribed behaviour. Attention is given to the body language of both practitioner and the client which, if in harmony, will often be mirrored. Person-centred counsellors are accused of trying too hard to mirror the body language of their clients. They do this in an attempt to create rapport but it can result in a counter effect. Unlike psychoanalysis the person-centred practitioner depends on eye contact sometimes to the detriment of the client who is often embarrassed and seeks to prevent eye contact. Further, unlike in psychodynamic therapy, the person-centred therapist does not make interpretations of what the client says they reflect back by paraphrasing the words of the client. Then they are supposed to check out with the client the accuracy of their understanding. The criticisms of such techniques are that it can sound patronising, or like parroting. Questioning the client is on a need to know basis only and was something which Freud had also found useful. Testing out questions, such as; I was wondering . . . ? Or it sounds like . . . ? These are tentative enquiries, which allow the client to stay within their own frame of reference. Questions which distract the client from their train of thought are to be avoided. The therapist should not ask questions which are for their own interest and therefore must stay alert to what is for the benefit of the client and what is not. This means that the self-awareness of the therapist, i.e. knowing when an issue belongs to them and not the client, is really important as it forces the therapist to constantly ask (inwardly) who the question is for. Questions which have the purpose of filling in data have the effect of arresting the flow and as such are unhelpful or counter productive to the process, although interesting to the therapist. This aspect of the process contradicts the notion, posited elsewhere, that the client is the expert in the encounter. If the practitioner has to hold back for the benefit of the client this is a form of control and presupposes some expertise. All of this behaviour is ritualistic and carried out in a space and time which requires that the client alter their state of consciousness. They speak to the practitioner in a fashion which they do not use in every day living.

In most psychotherapy and counselling, clients own the time allocated to them and as in psychoanalysis, they adhere as much as possible to the fifty minute hour. Part of the therapeutic process is for the client to take responsibility for themselves and so if they are late for their session, they will only have the time remaining in that hour. The therapy in person-centred counselling is not supposed to be directed by the practitioner but by the client, in so far as they go at their own pace, and not at the pace which the therapist feels they should. Clients are believed to have their own expertise. They know the issues and difficulties which they need to explore and may be trusted to do this when the time is right for them. The task of the therapist is to create a safe enough environment in which he or she facilitates this process. Supervision is an essential part of any practitioner's support system and is encouraged (by most approaches) as a way of monitoring relationships and helping practitioners to see more clearly his or her role in the therapeutic encounter. Practitioners are allocated an advisor with whom he or she discusses cases and their handling of them in an attempt to prevent malpractice. It is still left to the supervisee what they choose to bring up for discussion and therefore there is no way of knowing the whole story. Neither Freud nor Rogers had "supervision" in the way that it is expected today and each agreed that good therapy relies on the quality of the relationship between client and practitioner and not qualifications as such, to increase the qualifications of practitioners is not a guarantee of good practice. As with other forms of therapy there is no way of policing the morality of the practitioner and the client just takes a leap of faith.

In person-centred theory there is much talk about trust, for example, to trust in the process is a person-centred mantra. Trust in the client to go at their own pace: the counsellor should trust his or her intuition along with their felt sense or bodily sensations. Person-centred practitioners congratulate themselves on not being trapped by the hierarchical traditions which they accuse other therapies of relying on. This is of course illusory and has come to be problematic.

Person-centred counselling is not without traditions, it just understates their importance. That person-centred traditions remain covert or subversive is not the same as not having them[20] and does not mean that they are without influence or power. The notion that clients have expertise of their own issues makes the person-centred approach distinct from others where the expertise of the practitioner is celebrated. In today's world of political correctness the views held by this approach are highly acceptable. However, they are often accused of being naive and over simplistic, particularly on their views on the nature of human beings. Their continued belief in Rogers' idea of the inherent goodness of human beings has been criticized again and again as a Pollyanna model of therapy, an accusation which Rogers refuted and countered well with his comparisons with other animals, as noted above.

The possibility of actually carrying out the core conditions of empathy, congruence, and unconditional positive regard is much maligned by other approaches who regard this as somewhat utopian. Practitioners' claims of being congruent have at times been used as an excuse for behaviour which may otherwise be regarded as inappropriate. For example, Brian Thorne claimed to have felt incongruent with a client because he was denying his faith in the counselling relationship[21]. It is difficult, if not impossible, even if it were desirable, to leave any part of ones self outside of the therapy room, and yet this is underlying Thorne's claim. It is not possible for Thorne, or anyone one else, to detach themselves, from something as integral as one's faith. His need to have his faith overtly in the relationship begs different questions. His claim about his motivation would have best been explored in supervision[22]. In the succession of psychotherapy it can be problematic for the leaders to receive supervision. Supervising the supervisor is difficult because one's response to a superior is loaded with emotional charge. A response one can see arises not from reason but their respective positions in the hierarchy.

If applying Rogers' notion of necessary and sufficient conditions perhaps Thorne is just challenging the reality of their sufficiency. Thorne claimed not to be fully present with the client if he could not involve his faith[23]. This is interesting on different levels, as it runs contrary to the need to know philosophy which person-centred therapy advocates. It also acknowledges that there are parts to a person, a belief posited by Freud and which Rogers marginalised. Recently there has been work by person-centred theorists on compartmentalizing[24] but without any significant tribute to Freud and the unconscious.

There is some confusion about how to interpret congruence. Thorne's challenge to the doctrine of Rogers could throw open the flood gates to other challengers. If his faith becomes necessary as well as the core conditions the doctrine has been breached. Thorne has been open about his Christian commitment and has gone as far as to call himself a "reluctant prophet". He then goes on to prophesise in a less than reluctant way and thereafter refers to himself as a "counsellor/prophet"[25]. Each person present brings something into the therapy room, some of which he or she will be conscious of and some not. Thorne believes that he is losing something of himself without having his faith in the room. Imagine the chaos if every therapist wanted to have everything about themselves which they believed to be significant, consciously in the process. For example, ones politics, or eating philosophy or sexuality are all in the room but need not be made conscious. The client does not need to know this, unless her process would benefit from it and if the practitioner makes such a decision i.e. the client would benefit then they go against the alleged expertise of the client by making a decision on their behalf. This raises issues of power to make decisions, to withhold or not to withhold, in what is claimed to be an egalitarian relationship.

The difficulties which can arise from a prescribed set of criteria were further demonstrated by Thorne in his confession that, he was being fully congruent when he spent the night with a client. He argued that she would have been stuck or indeed regressed had he not taken this action[26]. This, one may only guess, had nothing to do with the fact that, in his own words:

> [S]he is commonly regarded as an attractive even beautiful woman and it was therefore not surprising that I quickly became aware of my own sexual responsiveness[27].

According to Thorne his action was for the benefit of the client, as if it was an act of benevolence or even altruism. Even if they both claim to have gained from the experience it is never deemed appropriate for a practitioner of any approach to transgress the sexual boundary. Codes of Ethics and practice[28] are clear, there should be no sexual contact either during or after the therapy has terminated. Easily stated, but difficult to execute because how does one define sexual contact?[29] Thorne may have argued for congruence here but he took this action at the expense of one of the other fundamentals of person-centred counselling, that the client is the expert, one may interpret as infantalising the client by taking responsibility for her. He claimed to know what was best for her. Yet another ethical prescription in this tradition particularly is that the practitioner is not responsible for clients but to them. The first allows the client to abdicate responsibility for themselves, the second allows them to take responsibility for themselves by making their own decisions. Thorne is not the only practitioner to transgress an ethical boundary, nor do I imagine he will be the last, but his actions have given us much to consider about the difficulties of interpreting the person-centred doctrine for behaviour in such a subjective encounter. Thorne claims that he is a maverick who has constantly struggled against this tide of dogmatism in an attempt to remain true to himself. At what cost to others?

Alex Howard, a critic of psychotherapy and counselling states:

> Counsellors quite often try to distance themselves both from judgement and advice giving, but to perceive, think and feel at all involves judgement and evaluation, and to counsel at all involves a judgement that the client has something to counsel about.[30]

Howard is very clear about the subjective nature of the work of counselling and Thorne has demonstrated the difficulties which arise when trying to adhere to a strict (dogmatic) theoretical framework. In addition practitioners have been willing to delude themselves into thinking that prescribed behaviour is possible. The naive illusion of objectivity and equality are still prevalent regardless of how often their futility is shown.

The theoretical assumptions of any approach must remain open to debate, in that, one-dimensional theory does not transfer easily, if at all, into three dimensional practice. The question of equality in the person-centred relationship is clearly very optimistic. It is argued by other traditions that by virtue of seeking help the client is always the more vulnerable person in the room. This is often the case, but not always, for example, the case of a client who for legal reasons (or at least in an attempt to manipulate the law) comes for counselling. There is a significant difference in coming for counselling and doing counselling. Someone may come for hours of therapy or counselling without doing the work. This is not as exceptional as one may think. Lawyers increasingly recommend counselling as a tactic for more lenient sentencing. So there are exceptions to the notion that the client is always the most vulnerable.

That it is part of the therapist's role to maintain professional boundaries also becomes questionable. The power imbalance may not be as clear as it appears. The therapist may keep the time and prescribe the location. However, one can see the complexity, in the many variations in relationships which may arise.What may at first look straight forward on paper can take on a host of other characteristics when put into practice. Statements which appear benign can disguise a more malign nature which ends up rendering them as dangerous as any of those explicit exploitations which person-centred counsellors accuse other traditions of. Each tradition may exploit and be exploited: the difference lies in whether or not these are overt or covert.

The raison d'être of the person-centred approach was as a backlash to those approaches which were dominant in Rogers' early career, and whose structure he believed to be too controlling and hierarchical. Rogers' goal was to create a model which was opposed to this and has thus appeared to be completely in opposition. However, it could be argued that he and his subsequent followers have lulled themselves and their clients into a false sense of security with their somewhat naive idealism. The core conditions may seem plausible when viewed in isolation, on paper. However, complications arise when an attempt is made to put them into practice where it is easy for one core condition to negate another, as the example from Brian Thorne demonstrates: congruence ends up usurping, countering, the notion that expertise belongs to the client. The disjunction between theory and practice is not peculiar to therapy. Orthodoxy and orthopraxy are different by virtue of their respective intentionalities, they are different genres a useful comparison is the book and the film of the book.

Carl Rogers knew that his work was out of kilter or at times at odds with the rest of society:

> Carl Rogers often used to comment that his way of being and working, ran counter to the mechanistic ethos of technological society, which thrives on efficiency, quick answers and the role of the expert.[31]

He believed that society could be improved if humans could change their way of being in the world. He proposed non-judgmentalism as a way of conflict resolution for individuals, institutions and ultimately global. He knew that the availability of so many technologies, designed to give quick fixes, was at odds with his person-centred approach which he believed provided an opportunity for people to slow down and take the necessary time to explore their difficult lives. He did not want to prescribe a way of being, and suggested that the individual find his or her own way. This has proved difficult for his discipleship. Rogers and Freud made similar claims, which implied that if people were doing what they were doing then they were not doing what they were doing. The Buddha actually got there a long time before either of these men: that people should be doing their own thing and not copying what someone else is doing.

Person-centred practitioners accuse psychodynamic practitioners of exploitation and elitism, due to the long periods of time which they recommend their clients commit to therapy[32]. Ironically, although Rogers wanted to counter the quick fix culture, his approach has come to be regarded by other therapies as just this. This is illustrative of the hierarchical nature of the therapeutic community where one approach believes it is better than another. For some time is equated with quality, as is depth, and quick fixes are regarded as superficial. This attitude to time and the way in which it is valued requires further exploration[33]. Theory does not exist in a vacuum any more than practice, although it is sometimes perceived this way by its adherents.

The debate over the benefits, or not, of lengthy and frequent therapy still continue to be unclear because of the complexities of measuring benefits. Whilst these approaches continue to differ on this subject, they do, as did Rogers and Freud, share the belief that the relationship is fundamental:

> Gradually I have come to the conclusion that one learning which applies to all of these is that of the quality of the personal relationship which matters most.[34]

If this is the case it is a wonder that each still invests in conflict which appears futile. What is their motivation for continuing to compete for supremacy? Yet there are other issues, relative to the beliefs of depth and superficiality, for example, the creation of dependency, and financial exploitation, which remain areas of contention. Once quality was equated with frequent visits over a long duration, now this is challenged. As noted above because someone attends many sessions it does not follow that they are doing more work. One person could conceivably do more work in one session than another may do in many. However, the value of time and depth are relative and are wrapped up in respective traditions. The psychodynamic approach may argue that it has a longer genealogy than the person-centred approach but the same argument that quality versus quantity may be applied here.

The significance of the above is that Rogers' movement, like Freud's, echoes a religious institution. So much so that, as noted, psychodynamic practitioners are compared to Roman Catholics, and person-centred practitioners have become the Protestant reformers. The psychodynamic tradition has all the pomp and circumstance, creating an illusion of depth and meaning whereas the person-centred, in actively removing the pomp, allowing less traditional baggage and consequently accused of lacking lustre. Practitioners of both psychodynamic and person-centred therapy seem blind to the fact that their values have been derived from religious traditions, but even when some do acknowledge the resemblance to religion it is often with irony. The fact that Freud and Rogers rejected their family's religion added to their determination that they were creating movements which were scientific but also, and perhaps more importantly, atheistic. Religion for both Freud and Rogers was problematic, something to be cured. And yet their respective movements could not have functioned without religious values or an ecclesiastical structure. Brian Thorne, mentioned above, was (at least a decade ago) tussling with the role of his own faith and how he could make more use of it in his work. Thorne has developed his ideas on how to include his faith and, as noted, now writes on his role as a "reluctant prophet", a reluctance which soon becomes almost imperceptive.[35]

The critics of person-centred therapy appear less concerned about its social role than about that of psychodynamic psychotherapy. In the main, person-centred therapy is regarded as somewhat benign compared to psychodynamic therapy. As an exception to this, Jeffrey Masson,[36] a major critic of all talking therapies, argues that one of the biggest areas of contention in person-centred counselling is their alleged genuineness. He believes that the therapist can only ever act out the core conditions and that this is a form of self deception which while it appears as benevolence, is actually malevolent in effect. Masson goes as far as calling Rogers a "benevolent despot"[37] and uses this amazing parallel:

> [T]o draw an inexact but illuminating analogy from political life benevolent despotism may make a better polity than a malign Hitlerian one but it remains a despotism and is built necessarily on the same bedrock.[38]

The deception to which Masson is reacting is that of the therapist's congruence. He believes that the therapist is never real because if they were real they would be exactly as they are in any other situation in life. Given that reality is entirely subjective and contingent on all else his view is somewhat simplistic and reductive. Masson implies that one way of being is more real than another, a view which does not accommodate the notion that we each have many realities.

Masson believes that therapy is at its most dangerous when bad faith is extreme. It could be argued that we are all acting all of the time and that this acting is itself genuine. Who dictates what acting or genuineness are? For example, when we are with friends, with family, with colleagues, with whom so ever we encounter, we change our way of being to accommodate the other person in some way, and in so doing may be accused of acting. Given that acting is such an integral part of who we are, it is surprising that it is so condemned. This goes back to congruence. We desire congruence because of its connotations of authenticity, truth, ultimately reflecting our desire for absolutes.

Whilst suspicion of experts has its roots in the 19th century, it is alive and kicking in contemporary theory and practice. Suspicion, fear, and intimidation are manifested in the criticism of psychodynamic practice. Psychodynamic practitioners have an extensive and old body of literature, history, training, medical contact, all of which they believe substantiates and validates their claims to superiority and authenticity, claims which person-centred practitioners use as justification for their criticisms.

The way in which the person-centred approach has denied their expertise has become problematic. According to Masson, this denial just means it is covert, and in this, more dangerous than others. Their expertise is in facilitating the client's growth with their use of core conditions and consists in their self awareness and their ability to draw upon very few overt techniques, as each is supposed to be worn like an invisible gown. This is an example of an approach saying one thing which sounds politically correct but doing something else which is not.[39]

Above, I have used Brian Thorne as an example of how openness can go wrong, but wonder, in reality, how openness is tested?[40] For example, how open could an ex prisoner who is now a practitioner be and still have a practice? When clients ask therapists questions how genuine are their replies? Brian Thorne arguably took this to the extreme. He used genuineness as an excuse to carry out what may, from the one dimensional view of the page, be described as an abuse of a client. Given Thorne's high profile in person-centred counselling, it is conceivable that others can and will use his example to justify their own wayward behaviour. Many followers are so in awe of their leader that they copy even their most undesirable habits as was demonstrated by Freud's followers smoking the same cigars as Freud.

When Rogers developed person-centred counselling his intention was to strip psychotherapy of those things which he believed unnecessary and, subsequently, in person-centred counselling rituals are believed to be minimal. Rogers prescribed a face to face encounter, where the chairs are facing each other and of equal height; this, designed to create an environment of equality in which practitioner and client may be fully together and present in the session. The time is set, as is the location and the way in which the room is laid out. The therapist keeps control of the time, and is responsible for the location and the layout of the room. From this position of perceived power the therapist tries to create an atmosphere which is conducive for the client's self-exploration. Given the above, any notion of equality between client and therapist must be questioned. It is superficial to think that such a veneer can create equality. The message is, we are equal but it is my room, my furniture, and my time that you the client require and are, at times, purchasing. Can equality be bought? Some would argue that it is the payment which levels the playing field in so far as each has something that the other needs: supply and demand bring equality to the relationship.

Being fully with the client requires that the therapist maintain eye contact, and be aware of their own body language as well as that of the client. Each therapist has their own rituals when meeting the client, for starting off and rounding off the session and will have an environment, which they perceive as conducive to self development. How the client perceives all of this will be specific to them at a given time and stage in the relationship. The above has illustrated some of what Rogers described and advocated for his followers: his attempts to distance his work from those patriarchal theories, of which he was so condescending. Below we shall see that Rogers was successful in his attempts to change the appearance of therapy. However, rather than eliminate those things to which he was reacting, he just gave them a different disguise. His theories and methods have become doctrinal and as such have created difficulties with parallel themes to those of Freud's followers. Let us now turn to what contemporary practitioners are doing with his work.

Notes

1 Cohen, D. (1997) *A Critical Biography of Carl Rogers*. London: Constable, p. 21.
2 Ibid., Cohen describes Rogers' daughters concern for her father's drink problems later in his life.
3 Cohen (1997) pp. 32–3.
4 Ibid., p. 37.
5 Kirschenbaum & Land Henderson (1990) *The Carl Rogers Reader*, p. xi.

6 Thorne (1992) pp. 22–23.
7 Kirschenbaum & Land Hendersn (1990) p. 407.
8 Rogers, C.R. (1967) *On Becoming a Person: A Therapists View of Psychotherapy*. London: Constable, p. 9.
9 Thorne (1992) p. 16.
10 Cohen (1997) p. 138.
11 Ibid., p. 223.
12 Ibid., p. 167.
13 Kirschenbaum & Henderson (1990) *The Carl Rogers Reader*, p. xi.
14 Cohen (1997).
15 Cohen (1997) p. 46.
16 Kirschenbaum & Henderson (1990) *The Carl Rogers Reader*, p. xi.
17 Macleod, J. (1993) *Introduction to Counselling*, p. 15.
18 Mearns & Thorne (1988) They argue that other approaches misunderstand the theory of this approach and as a result regard it as superficial.
19 Sartre, J.P. (2003) *Being and Nothingness*. London: Routledge Classics.
20 If something is subverted there is an argument for its having more power.
21 Mearns & Thorne (1988).
22 Supervision is increasingly part of the therapeutic contract. That the therapist themselves have somewhere to discuss issues which are raised by their work.
23 Mearns & Thorne (1988) It is worth noting that Thorne's approach to therapy has evolved and his most recent work reflects his ability to synthesise his faith. See Thorne (2004).
24 Professor Dave Mearns, University of Strathclyde.
25 Thorne, B. (1994) *The Counsellor as Prophet*. The Frank Lake Memorial Lecture. Clinical Theology Association. Lingdale Papers, 21.
26 Thorne, B. (1991) *The Spiritual Dimensions of Counselling and Psychotherapy*. London: Whurr.
27 Ibid., p. 89.
28 These are supplied by BAPC and BACP.
29 In a Recent paper Dr Jeremy Carrette has explored the difficulties that defining any relationship poses. Conference Paper. Department of Theology, Glasgow University. 27th April 2001.
30 Howard, A. (1996) *Challenges to Counselling and Psychotherapy*. London: Macmillan, p. 84.
31 Thorne (1991) p. 174.
32 Feltham, C. (1999) This work is illustrative of the contemporary debates.
33 Recently some therapists have been dabbling with the idea that "Time Limited" counselling is actually more beneficial than those therapies

PERSON-CENTRED THEORIES AND PRACTICE 137

where time is open ended. Colin Feltham (1999) argues that shorter term treatments are being imposed because of the financial requirements of health legislation. And so short term counselling has arrived due to economic factors, particularly in the USA where insurance companies foot the bill. Thus, emotional economies are controlled by financial economies.

34 Rogers & Steven (1967) *Person to Person*. USA: Real People Press, p. 89.
35 Thorne, B. (1994).
36 Masson (1988).
37 Ibid., p. 229.
38 Ibid., p. 229.
39 Bond, T. (1993) *Standards and Ethics in Counselling and Psychotherapy*. London: Sage.
40 Thorne took the risk in being very open about his actions and has paid the price for such confessions.

CHAPTER FIVE

Rogers' Legacy

Below is an exploration of how contemporary person-centred therapists have responded to Rogers. As with Freud, many of Rogers' followers are thinking people themselves and intent on building on the foundations which Rogers created: the death of the founder gives license for change. As we have noted, Rogers was adamant that the core conditions were necessary and sufficient, and that nothing else was required. Eugene Gendlin, a contemporary of Rogers, dabbled with the notion of adding what he called "focusing". He believed that this could enable the client to locate feelings which were on "the edge of their awareness". Brian Thorne also believes that "tenderness" could be added to Rogers' "Trinity". At a conference (in the University of Stirling, Scotland, 1990) three years after Rogers' death in 1987, the followers of Gendlin and his ideas on focusing were gathering strength and confidence and even purists such as Bozarth and Temaner Brodley, who had been vehemently against any additions, were not challenging them in the way that they previously had. Although the tension has not yet been fully resolved between experientialists and purists, it may be that in time the reactions caused by the loss of the founder and the need to hang on to the, albeit illusory, authenticity of the tradition, will abate. The position of top dog in the person-centred tradition has as yet to be established: in the UK Thorne is certainly still a contender. The most recent evidence of this came at the BAPC conference (The University of Strathclyde 1999) where he behaved, and was treated, as if he was the new messiah, father figure of the person-centred approach.

Thorne has noted that at the conference in Stirling the purists acted like parents accepting of experientialists;

> The purists seemed to adopt a parental role rather than a judgmental role as if they had come to accept that the Gendlin supporters, were, after all members of the same family.[1]

Implied in Thorne's observation is the notion of parents as non-judgmental, which is somewhat naïve given that person-centred counsellors spend their working lives trying to facilitate the repair of what they call conditions of worth, those conditions imposed upon people by their parents and significant others. The criticism of idealism, which is what the person-centred approach are accused of, seems appropriate in this regard. The division between purists and experientialists is described in terms of orthodoxy versus heresy: additions to Rogers' original work are regarded as "heretical"[2]. Freud also used this term to describe dissenters from his psychoanalysis.

So we have Rogers with an interesting history. He comes to psychotherapy through his rejection of the church, then as a revolt against the hierarchical structures of the psychoanalytic and behaviourist models, which dominated in his early career, he developed his own theory and practice. His scientific studies of therapy sessions and his claims to objectivity have raised questions about how one actually determines what good therapy is. There are also questions about expertise, as surely people will choose a therapist, at least in part, because of their skills expertise. Why would clients pay money to work with someone who denied their skill?

There is smugness at times bordering on arrogance within the person-centred tradition, which is due in part to the notion that they are somehow higher up the evolutionary chain. That letting go of attachment to egocentric things such as expertise, and relinquishing power, usurps the psychodynamics. The fact that the practitioner has the power to allow this is over looked. Covert power is further explored by Tim Bond[3] who claims that even the lay out of the therapy room communicates expectations. For example, the presence of a box of tissues whilst practical, even thoughtful, does not mean the therapist has an allergy or a cold, but implies that the therapist is looking after the client and in addition that it is okay, or even expected, that the client will be upset.

There are a number of issues around training, for example, how can it be effectively monitored or quality controlled? Tim Bond implies that therapy is a klondyke, a free for all. Many people who become attracted to the caring professions do so because they themselves need to be cared for. The wounded healer is more than evident. Training is an area of contention, as there are areas which are inadequately addressed. It seems there is little, if any, training which covers what to do if you become sexually attracted to a client or vice versa, other than the rule of abstinence and denial. Ethics, the area which Bond specialises in, has as yet only skimmed these issues, issues such as financial and emotional exploitation, which appear to be common complaints, have also had insufficient external research. All of this gives the appearance of a rather mundane, secular activity but as is often the case what you see is not what you get.

The person-centred approach, like the psychodynamic approach, arose from the psyche of someone who had rejected the religion of his father as well as his chosen tradition (which was much more evangelical that that of his parents). Rogers was, like Freud, determined to become scientific, a leader in the field of psychology. However, what actually happened was that he gathered around him, not colleagues who reject his findings and who function as equals alongside of him, but disciples who become dependent on his doctrines with faith and loyalty in him and his theories, which does not reflect a scientific community. As noted above, those who have, since Rogers' death, begun to develop his work have been accused of heresy, not because what they are doing is particularly controversial but because development is disrespectful to Rogers. The divisions in the person-centred approach are part of a process which happens with the death of a founder of a religious movement[4]. There are those purists, as Thorne described above, who are determined not to blemish the work of the founder and those who are willing to begin to challenge the doctrines and who in so doing become regarded by the former group as dissenters. Those adopting a more eclectic, post modern approach, such as Thorne who is using religious language and insights wherever he sees this as appropriate, may perhaps be described as being more congruent. The omission of religion has not meant that it has not existed but its noticeable absence has served to highlight the bad faith of psychotherapy. The psychodynamic and the person-centred approach have actively prevented an exploration of religiousness other than in the negative. Although such denial, an area so close to their hearts, is now beginning to surface, it may be too kind a description as it presupposes an unconscious motivation and not the activity which it has been.

Let us turn now to claims being made by contemporary practitioners of the person-centred approach: what they say that is new, in what ways they overlap and borrow from other traditions, and what their areas of disagreement are, both within their own tradition and with other traditions. This exposes the ways in which they see themselves as having developed and ways in which they have developed but do not articulate, particularly since the death of Carl Rogers. In addition this uncovers allusions to religion which, although present when the Rogers was alive, were excluded until very late in his life when he began to talk about the mystical. Their shutting out the mystical has had a lasting effect on contemporary practitioners of person-centred therapy and their attitudes to religion have followed a similar path to those of the psychodynamic tradition, in so far as they have been functioning in ways which, by virtue of their position as insiders, have prevented them from seeing the bigger picture. Rogers was the first therapist to publish a methodology for effective counselling[5] and was determined, like Freud, to be view as an empiricist. To have a structured method, which Rogers believed could be repeated, was the way to make a science of psychotherapy. He, like Freud, left behind a struggle in which his followers are still engaged.

There are different camps developing within the person-centred approach and the way in which they address the founder may be significant. For example, in Brazier the contributors refer to Rogers as Rogers[6] whilst Mearns and Thorne each refer to him as Carl[7]. This familiarity or intimacy gives them an advantage, in that having had direct contact with the founder has an influential effect on the reverence shown towards them and their work. Proximity to the founder is often a prerequisite for the next in line and the effects of this have yet to be fully recognised.

The current literature illustrates those developments which are forging new frontiers as in the title of Mearns and Thorne (2000). Some are brave and far reaching, others more tentative. For some there has been a change in attitude to religion. For example, Thorne, as noted, is most explicit about his. This development is more significant seen in the light of Rogers own rejection of religion. Thorne goes as far as to claim that God[8] is central to the therapeutic relationship. This is a major declaration from a person-centred practitioner because whilst Rogers acknowledged the spiritual and the mystical in his later work, he had previously spent a good deal of his life denying its existence. Thorne is here relocating religiousness, moving it from outside the periphery, making it the chiasmus of the therapeutic encounter. Rogers' work had this, however he and subsequent person-centred practitioners suffered from a need to ally themselves with the sciences and resisted or denied any notion of the religious for fear of not being taken seriously as scientists.

Since Rogers' death there have been many developments of his work some of which may have gone against his hopes but others which echo what he aspired to. Rogers was against any notion of Rogerianism[9], and yet this is what has happened. It is a common pattern and has occurred in other traditions: Marx was not a Marxist; Jesus was not a Christian; the Buddha was not a Buddhist; and Freud was not a Freudian. Rogerianism is what Rogers' followers have done and are still doing with his work. Rogers believed that if people were adopting his work as dogma then they were not doing what he had advocated, which was to develop their uniqueness. As noted, some developments of his work have already given rise to internal strife, causing tension between those who believe that Rogers would have wanted developments and those who think his work is not only being developed, but that his core ideas are being contaminated.

Although contemporary person-centred practitioners make claims which may only differ from Rogers in their emphasis and as such do not seem like a significant development, this is none the less a necessary part of the distancing process which often occurs after the death of the founder. Those people who begin to develop the original theories can create breakaway groups which function as denominations.

Carl Rogers believed that for the client to make any progress the therapist would have to be real in their presence. One of his famous core conditions is congruence. Congruence in this context means to be genuine or authentic and requires the practitioners to have an acute sense of them selves. The concept of authenticity is a complex,

ROGERS' LEGACY 143

and controversial claim, as it is difficult to quantify and/or substantiate. However, it is none the less regarded as a quality which is paramount to the success of the person-centred therapeutic encounter and is reminiscent of a "to thine own self be true" philosophy. Authenticity requires the practitioner to have a level of self awareness which takes time and effort to achieve, especially in a world which is driven by inauthenticity.[10] Rogers expected that the practitioner would develop this quality.

However, although today's practitioners are no less committed to the notion of authenticity than previous practitioners, they seek to expand it, as David Brazier states:

> In such an authentic mutual encounter, there may be moments in which the therapist almost relinquishes his professional role and encounters the client in every personal and profoundly human way. According to Yalom, such "critical incidents" often become turning points in therapy. He believes that they are seldom mentioned in the psychiatric literature out of shame, or out of fear of censorship; they are also seldom discussed with trainees because they do not fit the "doctrine" or because one is afraid of exaggerations.[11]

In this Brazier makes several claims, the first that the therapeutic encounter aims to be authentic and mutual whereas the original notion of authenticity was designed to apply to the practitioner. However, Brazier extends it to include the client. By using this particular example, Brazier raises another issue because Irvin Yalom, referred to in the quotation above, is a practitioner whose familiar discourse is that of psychiatry and therefore of the medical model. As such, he is associated with a hierarchical model which does not sit comfortably with the person-centred approach. The notion of authenticity was not something which Freud emphasised, or which until recently, psychodynamic practitioners were particularly concerned with[12]. These words from Yalom are indicative of "cross pollination", the beginnings of inter-denominational dialogue. To synthesise ideas from one tradition with another is a challenge to the work of the founder. Finally he raises the issue of censorship and acknowledges, albeit in inverted commas, that there is a "doctrine" which should be adhered to.

Yalom, as an integrative practitioner has borrowed (perhaps unconsciously) from the person-centred tradition, and in turn, the person-centred tradition have reappropriated a concept which they regard as their own anyway[13]. This may seem like a somewhat trivial observation. However, in the light of continuing arguments about the dangers of eclecticism[14] purism and contamination, this is a good example of the futility of such terms. Irvin Yalom is just as much at ease talking of authenticity as he is talking about transference and counter-transference, those essentials of the psychodynamic tradition.[15] Brazier has inadvertently given us an example of how a synthesis of ideas from different and apparently opposing traditions can be successful and even enlightening and not, as is often claimed, necessarily destructive and threatening: an interdenominational approach.

The claim that the therapeutic encounter is authentic and that authenticity is mutual is optimistic. Given that the encounter relies on the client being in a state of incongruence, (otherwise they would not be in therapy), it is unlikely that authenticity is mutual. It is possible that the client may be authentic in their incongruence but this is a somewhat advanced notion. The idea of authenticity as necessary is, it would seem, part of the myth building required by each tradition to create pockets of superiority, by introducing something which is exclusive to them and inaccessible to other traditions. My questions about this concept are not about whether it is possible for the person-centred practitioner to achieve this state of authenticity, but what do they gain from making such a claim, and why do they desire it? It appears to be a "will to truth" claim.

Mearns and Thorne[16] claim that authenticity is essential for therapy to work and are aware of the complexity of such a notion. However, what each person means by authentic is woolly. In the context of therapy it is a truth claim which implies that other therapists are engaged in an act, an untruthful parody, of a human encounter and that person-centred practitioners have the true way. If authenticity is about knowing thy self and about honesty Mearns and Thorne acknowledge how difficult these are to achieve. They note that whilst authenticity is an essential ingredient for healthy relating it is a difficult way of being in contemporary society:

authenticity (a prerequisite for mental health) becomes dangerous, and to trust others to be responsive, let alone empathic, can seem at best foolhardy and at worst psychologically lethal.[17]

This is their view of what it costs to be genuine or authentic out with the therapeutic encounter in our society today. They discuss how feelings per se, in today's world are an inappropriate currency, stating that business still holds firmly to a "Let's leave feelings out of this"[18] type of culture. This makes congruence or authenticity very difficult for people who live in the so called real world which itself has been socially, politically, and economically constructed. It thus begs the question of whose reality are we talking about. The therapeutic encounter is designed to be very different to everyday situations and is a space and time which allows the development of an altered state of consciousness which is different to every day life.

The idea that authenticity may be switched off and on, when in the real world or otherwise, surely means that it is a form of acting in the same way that person-centred practitioners say that psychodynamic practice is. The question is, what is the purpose of making such a claim? I have already suggested that the person-centred tradition is making a truth claim, the purpose of which is to set itself apart from other traditions. They do this in the same way as different church denominations do, to convince themselves that they have chosen the right way. Their authenticity claim sets them apart from other therapeutic traditions which in their view are not being authentic.

The claim of authenticity is but one of many which are difficult to prove. We are involved here in the world of human interaction and encounter within which there are likely to be as many variables as there are people engaging in this world. So this next claim, that "empathy dissolves alienation"[19] although also too general, is at least corroboration that practitioners of this approach have such faith, strong beliefs in its basic premises that its practitioners continue to make them. This claim is made by Greet Vanaerschot[20] and whilst there may be some truth to this claim in some cases the fact that the research was founded on Rogers' failed experiments where people believed to have schizophrenia did not respond to empathy, did not dissolve alienation, does not bode well for its universal application. This study, has been used by Vanaerschot with a fervour which does not belong in the sciences. If practitioners of the person-centred approach continue to make the claim of being scientists they cannot also build their own theories on material that is known to be flawed and not raise questions about their motivation for doing so. Scientists do not have a problem with rejecting flawed material, in fact they live for it even when, as they often are, standing on the shoulders of giants, they identify areas where there is room for improvement.

It may well be possible to dissolve alienation by sustained empathy, as Rogers suggested. However, empathy can also create a type of alienation. There are in fact few people, especially in the early stages of therapy, who can easily receive empathy. The therapist who is finely tuned will understand this and, without naming it, will accommodate the reaction by becoming different in the sessions. This leads to the fact that there are multiple ways of being empathic, so to make the claim that "empathy dissolves alienation" is too general and ideologically loaded. This said it almost does not matter whether empathy dissolves alienation or not. What matters here are the circumstances which warrant such a claim. It seems to me to be underpinned by a similar motivation to the authenticity claim, in that it also highlights a them and us dichotomy. That person-centred practitioners have empathy at the core of their practice sets them apart from other traditions which they believe do not use empathy in the same systematic way. But it says more than this because Vanaerschot is willing to use information which is known to be flawed and as such demonstrates blind faith by an unwillingness to reject the findings of the founder.

The therapeutic encounter, what ever the approach, is conducted[21] in an environment which is intentionally alien. This is one of the reasons for therapy's profitability in that it claims to be different from any of our other relationships. It is not just a chat, it is not friendship, it is not advice or guidance: therapy is more definable by what it is not than what it is.[22]

Brazier makes a similar claim that "therapy is an altruistic activity"[23]. To someone who is sceptical of the very existence of altruism this claim seems even more challenging than those of authenticity, and the ability to dissolve alienation. What does he mean by altruistic? Is it an act of unselfish regard or of devotion to the welfare of another?[24] Neither is deemed appropriate or desirable in the context of psychotherapy. In the person-centred tradition such intervention runs counter to beliefs such as the client's autonomy, that the practitioner is responsible *to* the client, not *for* the client[25]. Each is regarded as paramount both ethically and for the efficacy of the therapy.

The claim of altruism, unwittingly, flags a hierarchy of responsibility which attributes power to the practitioner. By virtue of claiming that altruism is within their power they are also making a claim that it is theirs to give. Even if this suggestion is only that the client can learn within the therapeutic encounter, to become altruistic he still implies that the therapist is acting as a mentor. Added to this is the issue of benevolence, the very idea of which has sent critics of psychotherapy such as Masson into raptures[26]. The process of therapy is one of a novitiate to a priest or Zen master to pupil, where a good deal is learned at a level which is beyond articulation.

Whether practitioners in the person-centred tradition like it or not mentoring is an active part of the therapeutic encounter their ideal of non-directiveness[27] is exactly that, an ideal. Clients often comment on how they can hear the therapist in them selves. They begin to adopt the language and the values which practitioners cannot prevent being present in the room. There are studies which claim that 80% of communication is non verbal[28]. If this is the case, or anything like this figure, then practitioners have even less control than they think about what they communicate to the client, at least until they learn that they are still communicating in the silences and in many other ways with their body language, breathing, even their smells.

In this tradition to overtly look after or direct a client is regarded as ultimately disempowering for the client who is encouraged to take responsibility for them selves. In this Brazier raises an issue about the authenticity of the tradition, as person-centred practitioners have condemned other traditions for disempowering clients through infantilising them, by creating relationships which rely on parenting and therefore dependency. What they say they do and what they do, appear from this to be at odds. There is conflict within the tradition on this as Brazier himself states:

> It seems that the authors cannot discard the belief that the therapist must intervene in some way, at some point, to set

the client in an appropriate direction. This presupposition can only lead to the conclusion that ignores one of the fundamental premises of the person-centred approach i.e. that it is the client who knows best what hurts, what direction to go, and that the client has vast resources for renewal.[29]

The above are indeed fundamental presuppositions of the person-centred tradition which Brazier contradicts in his claim about the altruistic nature of therapy. Many practitioners make claims about the way in which they regard the client as the expert and that the client is trusted to go at their own pace[30]. To make a declaration of therapy as altruistic, counters too many person centred conditions. The notion of any thing as altruistic is dubious and this may be said particularly of person-centred counselling[31]. Brazier's motivation for claiming that they are altruistic has connotations more reminiscent of a pastoral tradition than of a psychological tradition.

Why do they need altruism? What is the underlying motivation for this declaration? On further reading of Brazier's work it would seem to me that it is saying something of his own personal quest, as he begins to grapple with the place of the spiritual in the therapeutic encounter. Continual reference to the therapeutic encounter is to be expected in such writing and the repetition of it does promote it as exclusive or sacred.

Brazier's attitude to spirituality and religion has parallels with Rogers', prior to his death. He is tentatively engaging with the mystical part of the tradition by comparing his own tradition with spiritual traditions. Although he acknowledges the "wisdom of the world's spiritual traditions"[32] he does this in the context of such a comparison having "a certain novelty"[33]. He also notes that:

In passing, we should note that religious faith provides an example of a well developed version of such a repertoire[34].

"In passing"! In psychotherapy when something is mentioned prefixed by "in passing" the practitioner would be alerted that something is significant. Brazier, like other therapists, has little choice but to draw upon religious analogies. He believes himself to be open minded about religion yet he qualifies his comments in such a way as to make it clear that he remains at a distance from it.

Rather like someone commenting on how they do not mind gay people; "I even have gay friends", completely oblivious to the fact that in this "even" they are making a value judgement. The person-centred notion of unconditional positive regard appears to have its limits "even" for Brazier. He does however make a claim for the "enigmatic nature of the subject" in reference to his own work, which implies that he realises that there are still areas of mystery as yet to be explained.

Brazier is concerned with authenticity, altruism and discusses, albeit, "in passing" the similarities between the world's spiritual traditions and his own enigmatic tradition. However, he does so in ways which are so tentative as to induce suspicion about his motivation. There appears to be some of that fear which he referred to in the "Yalom" quotation above. In another paper Brazier is less tentative. He does take a leap and challenges the notion that the core conditions are necessary and sufficient and he argues that they are "not necessarily necessary but always sufficient"[35]. Such risks may seem minimal, of little consequence, but to challenge the very core of Rogers' doctrine is a significant rejection which makes a statement about Brazier as a contender for the leadership. There are different ways to stand on the shoulders of giants: one way is crushing.

Many practitioners are concerned with ways in which they can use person-centred practice in combination with other practices. For example, Expressive therapy is being developed by Natalie Rogers, Carl's daughter; psychodrama and body work; focusing; guiding out; multi-media approaches; family therapy; cross-cultural therapies. Whilst these changes may be regarded as developments they may also be regarded as heresy in that if Rogers' belief that the core conditions were necessary and sufficient then most of these developments in some way contradict this. Of course one could always argue that each is being done in a non directive way whilst still using the core conditions. However, given the above notions about what is perceived as directive, this is unlikely.[36]

Len Holdstock makes an interesting contribution to person-centred theory as he advocates a shift from what he calls the "individuocentric"[37] world (which was that of Rogers), to one in which individuals no longer regard themselves as separate from society but each is inextricably bound. He regards the individual and society as one body, which is a post modern concept, and in this it seems that Holdstock is something of a lone player for the person-centred tradition, which has functioned in a similar way to psychodynamic psychotherapy, in so far as they have maintained an illusion of isolation from political involvement.

Rogers regarded himself as a human scientist and argued for the scientific validity of his work, and his followers defend him in this with a sense of dogmatism which Rogers himself would have objected to, at least theoretically. Brazier compares Rogers' contribution to that of Einstein.[38] Finally an issue which is not peculiar to person-centred practitioners but which is an issue for therapists per se is eclecticism and whether this can be regarded as an identity crisis for the person-centred therapist. To practice in an eclectic way is frowned upon by most traditions, even though at some level practitioners realise that the notion of purism is only a fantasy. Practitioners can, at some level, perhaps a level beyond their consciousness, allow themselves to suspend their beliefs about purism. This suspension is indicative that facts are secondary to their relationship with Rogers and his community, a relationship beyond that which happens in science.

Mearns and Thorne (2000) have an entirely different tone to that of Brazier et al. They are willing and more confident in their challenges to outsiders and are clearly tired of the way in which their tradition is and has been perceived by other approaches. They claim that they have an extremely complex and superior approach which is not articulated in Brazier. Thus in these things at least, there have been significant developments which must in part come from an increase in confidence and a perhaps maturity which has taken time to establish.

Mearns and Thorne make the claim that there is "almost universal respect"[39] for Rogers. They may believe this to be the case within the tradition, although there is evidence of dissent within each text which I have drawn from. However, out with the tradition he and his approach are not without critics. Masson, mentioned earlier, is but one and they themselves highlight areas of criticism as did Brazier. Their motivation for making this claim seems to be somewhat evangelical. Rogers is dead, so he does not need to have universal respect to validate him. Although in Rogers' name this acts as a reminder that they have him to be thankful for.

Mearns and Thorne are at times inconsistent. For example, they talk of universal respect for Rogers on the one hand, and of the harsh criticisms made of their tradition on the other as if they are separate:

[There is the . . .] denigratory and scurrilous myth that person-centred therapists merely nod, and reflect the last words of their client and can only be trusted with the concerns of middle class clients.[40]

In the same way as the Protestants stripped away the ritual associated with Catholicism Rogers did the same with person-centred therapy in an attempted backlash against the psychoanalytic tradition. He saw the rituals of psychoanalysis as unnecessary props which he felt did little for the client but much to maintain a patriarchal tradition which should be jettisoned. Person-centred practitioners are still expected to work with far fewer props than psychodynamic practitioners. This said those practitioners who want to use additions, such as expressive therapy, may be accused of using different props.

Mearns and Thorne are ready and up to the challenge of what they have described as the "superficiality myth"[41], which has arisen, in part, as a response to their lack of props. Props such as couches, dreams, interpretation, or withholding, are not options for the person-centred practitioner. However, this does not necessarily imply that the simplicity of their rituals, and they do have them, is superficial. On this subject Mearns and Thorne are intent on setting the record straight. They state:

. . . clearly and unequivocally our belief in the power, profundity, and subtle elegance of the approach[42].

Their response to practitioners such as Rollo May, who has accused person-centred practitioners of being naïve, and of being "wilfully blind to the "shadow" side of human nature"[43]:

We are increasingly weary of being told that all good therapist, whatever their tradition, offer their clients the core conditions before embarking on the business of the therapeutic enterprise . . .[44] . . . such statements clearly indicate a failure to understand the conditions as the attitudinal expression of a belief system about human nature and development , and about the healing qualities of the relationship ... They also fail to recognise that the relationship *is* the therapy and not preparation for it.[45]

Their pride and commitment and their need to state this is nothing short of a mission statement. Rollo May is but one practitioner who has made such accusations, there are others more vehement. Such a will to be heard is a significant development for the person-centred approach and the quotations above are examples of their raised voices. In the past they have been much less vocal in their challenges to critics and others claiming authority. Now they clearly articulate their criticisms of other traditions as well as in defending their own. This is not to say that they have not been critical at all in the past, only that now their criticism has been stepped up a notch and is clearly coming from a base of confidence, which has taken time to cultivate.

It is as if after Rogers' death there needed to be a time for consolidation, and perhaps of regrouping, followed by a time in which the new front runners would make their presence felt. It may be that Brazier, Mearns and Thorne are the new self elected advocates of person-centred counselling, in the UK, and until others within the tradition challenge them their views will appear to be representative of the approach. They have given the tradition, in the short term, a new foundation and a new confidence with their willingness to fight back against those who would be regarded as at the top of the hierarchy.

The quotation above also demonstrates a vehemence which is rarely heard in this tradition because of their policy on unconditional positive regard. For the person-centred practitioner to speak of their utter disenchantment with other approaches is a rejection of one of their core conditions, unconditional positive regard. Each tradition seems to imply that they have something to offer which is exclusive to them and at the same time that each therapy is just a different route to the same goal, a point made routinely about World religions. However, with the increasing commodification of therapy[46] their product must become more exclusive to them. The practitioners in person-centred tradition have through Rogers engaged in an extreme form of othering, trying to establish what they do as quite distinct.

Rogers and Mearns and Thorne have gone as far as to claim superiority over psychodynamic psychotherapy. So gone is the "different routes to the same God" attitude that they have pretended has existed. Blurring of boundaries between traditions, as we have seen although prevalent in practice, is not acceptable in theory. Each tradition is intent on maintaining its identity, thus a them and us attitude is maintained as a way of averting an identity crisis which is believed to arise if synthesising traditions. As noted above, purism is still desirable and as we shall see below there is concern for those practitioners who claim to be integrative or, even worse, eclectic.[47] Rogers himself cannot be described as a purist given his own admission to soaking up the Freudian views which were present at Columbia.

Mearns and Thorne are most affronted that Freud is regarded by some as the source of a person-centred concept and state:

> Ellingham has suggested that congruence is a concept fashioned essentially from a Freudian perspective and therefore out of harmony with a process—oriented view of therapy. (Ellingham, 1999)[48]

Ellingham is a practitioner who, it seems, has no right to trespass on the hallowed ground of the person-centred tradition. Although above we saw how Mearns and Thorne drew from the work of Irvin Yalom, and how they frequently use practitioners, who are not necessarily person-centred, to support their arguments of misunderstanding, when others engage in the same process of cross pollination it is threatening to them, certainly when it challenges the notion that congruence is peculiar to the person-centred tradition. As noted, Phillips also talks about psychoanalysis as a process, so it would seem that trespassing is inevitable.

This kind of defence through attack is an interesting one. John Shlien a person-centred practitioner has attacked the time honoured notion of transference, a concept which has been resisted by many person-centred counsellors, but which is one of the pillars of their greatest rivals, the psychodynamic tradition. Shlien claims:

> Transference is a fiction invented and maintained by therapists, in order to protect themselves from the consequences of their behaviour.[49]

This is an attack on the very foundations of psychoanalysis and much psychotherapy. Not only does it question the existence of transference, claiming that it is nothing more than fiction, but he uses it to attack the credibility of practitioners by stating that they need it to cover their own ineptitude, an ineptitude, which may have malevolent consequences, as Masson would also claim. Implied in this is the superiority of the person-centred approach for which he believes such tools are unnecessary and in fact a hindrance and that person-centred practitioners do not require the crutches which others have come to rely on. Such arguments are more than reminiscent of those between church denominations who when vying for supremacy, disregard their own tenets.

This process of arguing and counter arguing is necessary for the development of each tradition "without contraries there is no progress"[50]. With each attack there is a closer analysis of the subject which hopefully allows each to get to know their subject more. However, one of the issues arising in this work is the inability of each approach to have the tolerance which is, arguably, fundamental to their approach. As is the case between many churches and indeed faiths, the attention to qualities such as compassion and tolerance seem all too superficial. So for the person-centred to trust in the process of the psychodynamic tradition to go at their own pace and to use what ever their own potentialities happen to be, in this case the techniques of transference and counter-transference, is as yet, not possible. Rogers has set goals which are outwith the capabilities of person-centred practitioners. His core conditions are difficult to apply in any context even where people are trained with the expectation that such qualities are necessary. The psychodynamic tradition appear to have set themselves less challenging goals and as such look more successful.

Each approach is continually developing ways of arguing for the supremacy of their tradition and whilst this is in some way admirable, it begs many questions about purism and fundamentalism, when it could be argued that they all come from the same creator, and as such have more common denominators than each is willing to acknowledge.

No one person can be representative of an approach any more than one religious believer is representative of the whole tradition. However, those who publish are more influential by virtue of reaching a wider audience. Where Shlien, above, is a severe critic of transference there are some within the person-centred tradition who are less critical. Germain Lietaer for example, acknowledges the existence of transference whilst showing that it is of little relevance to the person-centred practitioner:

> Working through of transference is not thought of as a nuclear process, as the "pure gold", in client centred therapy.[51]

Lietaer would not be considered pro transference but demonstrates that Shlien's stance is extreme and it is therefore unsafe to take one person's word as representative. Lietaer is less defensive or more able to practice unconditional positive regard.

Mearns and Thorne claim:

> The person-centred approach is an entirely different therapeutic system from the psychodynamic and gestalt models which operate at a more superficial relational level.[52]

This is a fascinating criticism as the person-centred tradition is the one most often accused of superficiality. It does not belong to the Depth Psychology group, a group who have revelled in the status which the metaphor of "depth" has afforded them. Accusations such as this are due in part to person-centred claims of only working with what is here and now. In addition its unwillingness to work with unconscious processes renders it, according to others, lacking in depth. Another possible aspect is that person-centred counselling is often shorter term than psychodynamic and as time is equated, albeit mistakenly with depth, the accusation of superficiality has been applied. In the light of this the comments from Mearns and Thorne are more dramatic than they look. These person-centred practitioners are willing to standing up and fight back against other established schools and going as far as implying that they are deluded in their beliefs. Such an overt demonstration of disregard for their core condition of unconditional positive regard is new.

Mearns claims:

> The "responsibility dynamic" (Mearns,1997a) within the person-centred approach delineates the appropriateness of the

person-centred therapist/trainer being responsible *to* her client or trainee and the inappropriteness of the therapist/ trainer being responsible *for* her client/trainee[53].

As mentioned above, the same rules apply in the therapeutic encounter where any notion of inequality is discouraged and where parenting is clearly frowned upon. Parenting, and mothering in particular, are frowned upon in person-centred counselling, again demonstrating parallels with the Catholic church which is perceived to be parental(the priest is addressed as Father) and to keep control at all times. Other traditions in psychotherapy are less dogmatic about this and are chastised by person-centred practitioners for this. For example, in Mearns and Thorne there is an audible note of condescension when they state:

However in other therapeutic traditions, a more parental role is accepted and even expected.[54]

This criticism of the parental role is aimed directly at psychoanalysis as Rogers believed it was notorious for creating dependency. This note of condescension is nothing compared to the contempt towards the psychodynamic stance on boundaries:

The psychodynamic world is, rightly, more scared about boundaries than person-centred practitioners.

This is criticism indeed and one could easily hear such a sentiment coming from the Protestant church of Catholic priests. That the psychodynamic practitioner has more reason to be fearful about boundaries than the person-centred practitioner turns commonly held assumptions on their head, as person-centred practitioners have historically been the most likely to be challenged about their use of boundaries. As with the superficiality myth Mearns and Thorne have risen to the challenge over boundaries and dedicate a good deal of their new work to codes of ethics, which they believe to be biased in favour of psychodynamic practitioners. In that, existing legislation does not allow crossing the physical boundary. Touching is not an option, and one may be struck off for it. This is an accepted, but not always adhered to, rule for the psychodynamic practitioner whose tradition advocates both a rule of abstinence, which is the no physical contact rule, and has a recommendation of actively withholding personal information from the client. Each rule is set in the name of therapeutic success but as Mearns and Thorne have shown, does not necessarily guarantee the safety of the client if, as they also argue, withholding may be just as problematic.

The person-centred approach has no such rules internally and in practice has a different attitude to touch, as illustrated by the example of Thorne. There are so many paradoxes in the therapy world as to make it a daunting process to try to keep abreast and it seems that with each challenge there unfolds a myriad of further challenges. In the person-centred tradition they make claims about the minimal intervention of the practitioner, then counters this by arguing for the appropriateness of touch which must be regarded as an intervention.

In therapy, paradox is the norm. Mearns and Thorne imply that the reason for having such rules is more for the protection of the practitioner than the client. That person-centred practitioners share the same governing bodies, for example, the British Association of Counselling and Psychotherapy (BACP), and their Scottish equivalent COSCA, as psychodynamic practitioners is problematic. Each of these agencies includes a rule of abstinence in their code of ethics, codes which have been adopted from a psychodynamic model and as such renders them inappropriate for the person-centred practitioner. In the way that ethical codes in other faith communities have rules which are specific, so do these traditions of psychotherapy.

There is therefore a dilemma for the person-centred practitioner in carrying out their task, when they believe that at times to be fully human to the client may rely on making physical contact with them or disclosing personal material. Rogers was against the professionalisation of counselling. He, like Freud, believed that there are as many charlatans with qualifications as there are without. What he appears to have meant was that you can never legislate for the morality of practitioners: there will always be people who overstep the mark whatever the mark is. Underpinning this tension is the hierarchy which still thrives in therapy and the fact that Freud still drives governing bodies is a source of protest for those who have little affinity or are anti-Freud.

Mearns and Thorne, as mentioned above, argue that it can be just as detrimental to withhold from a client as it can be to touch a client.

However, there is no legislation which says you may be struck off for withholding. This is a burning contemporary issue between these two approaches. So much so, that Mearns and Thorne state:

> There is a greater gulf of understanding between person-centred and psychodynamic orientations on this matter than any other.[55]

In fact:

> This issue is so divisive between the approaches that it is almost impossible to sustain a dialogue upon it.[56]

This is an interfaith impasse.

Each of these approaches has a view of the other which is somewhat distorted. Their information is often based on their understandings of what outdated texts say that they do, rather than what practitioners actually do. For example, person-centred practitioners still hold that:

> [F]rom a classical psychodynamic perspective it is critical that the humanity of the therapist is hidden from the client and in the person-centred orientation it is crucial that her humanity be seen.[57]

It is questionable that such a thing as a classical anything exists other than in an epistolary way. The notion that practitioners of any approach really adhere to their book is unlikely. None the less person-centred practitioners find some solace in maintaining this myth in the same way that psychodynamic practitioners do with the superficiality myth mentioned above.

Whilst there may have been some foundation to Rollo May's accusation (above) of person-centred naivety it is possible to view it in another way. For example, that the person-centred tradition are optimistic and hopeful in ways which are not echoed by the psychodynamic tradition. The person-centred tradition still hold to Rogers' original supposition of the inherent goodness of the human being and this is what inspires and motivates their practice. If this is viewed in the light of their respective social and political environments one can understand that experience of and attitude to evil would be different. The dominance of Jews in the early Freudian camp perhaps makes this understandable[58]. Rogers in the USA was quite a distance from the rise of National Socialism with its culmination in the horrors of Nazi Germany and as such was perhaps protected to such a degree as to allow him to be more forgiving of human failure.

A spiritual dimension, as mentioned above, was to develop in the later part of Rogers' career and contemporary person-centred practitioners have recently taken up where they believe he left off. Rogers' work in this was very much in its infancy when he died, but Brian Thorne hopes to develop it in a way which he believes Rogers would have anyway. Mearns and Thorne discuss the fact that each individual comes to counselling with their own beliefs. For some this may be existential, as in the case of Mearns, and for others they may have a clear commitment to a religious tradition as does Thorne: Mearns notes:

Carl had plenty of disciples—but he also had people around him who enjoyed the tussle of ideas—pity I can't meet him now[59].

Rogers claimed:

I hate to have "disciples", students who have moulded themselves meticulously into the pattern that they feel I wish[60].

Rogers like Freud liked to influence the way he was received by people but did not have the power to prevent a discipleship developing. Such a statement makes Rogers sound as if he was not intent on having power. However, by making the statement at all he demonstrates his attempt to control his followers.

Thorne, who has been a devout Rogerian, believes himself to be one of the wayward, maverick, counsellors of this tradition. He claims to have had a revelatory experience when he was six years old and his religious conviction has stayed strong since then. He claims that this experience has set him apart from others and his allegiance to the church has been an ongoing challenge for him. His last publications have been attempts to reconcile his faith and his counselling. As noted above, Thorne has since (1991) had a number of publications in which he addresses the issue of faith in counselling and uses himself as the case study[61]. He is devoted to Julian of Norwich and has weekly visits to her shrine. His views about God in counselling have changed since his earlier experiences of personal turbulence, when he was unable to acknowledge his faith in the counselling encounter. From this we can deduce that Thorne has always looked beyond himself for a source of inspiration, going against Rogers' prescriptions about disciples and religion which, as noted, were taboo for Rogers.

Mearns makes the distinction between tusslers and disciples implying that disciples are not people of ideas. This is indicative of a fear of being associated with religious fervor. However, it is somehow acceptable if the fervor is named as secular. Mearns' attitude belongs to wider issues of maintaining divisions whilst appearing to be open and tolerant of others whose views are different. Such bipolarizing is a process of othering which relies on the use of extremes. Bipolarising tusslers and disciples follows in the tradition of either/or which ultimately seeks to keep an exclusive zone. There has been little advantage in promoting similarity which serves to dilute the exclusivity. There appears no way round this. Psychotherapists do have to rely on language which implies religiosity, spirituality and mysticism. However, they do not really accept this for fear that if they do they would have to relinquish their ties, tenuous though they are, to science. This process also follows in that tradition of binaries which declares, if not science then religion, with no middle ground. When something is familiar, and in some ways regarded as not in need of repair, it can be comforting and problematic at the same time. For example, one's discomfort zone can become one's comfort zone by virtue of familiarity, thus making it more uncomfortable to change than to stick with the familiar.

Mearns describes himself as an atheist, and Thorne as a Christian.

> Brian expresses himself in terms of his Christian faith while Dave's language is entirely secular.[62]

I think that such divisions are ultimately unhelpful. Language is man made and as such is both secular and religious at the same time. In fact, it is not language which is religious or secular but the way in which language is used: "let the use determines the meaning". The need to divide is a recurring theme in both the person-centred tradition and the psychodynamic tradition. Each needs to polarize in an either/or way which is so contrary to what they advocate for their clients for whom they would claim there is always a middle way.[63]

With the work of Thorne, and to a lesser extent, Brazier the idea of the spiritual or mystical aspect within the therapeutic encounter is gradually sneaking back. Rogers' declarations about his missing the importance of the mystical, although taking some time to be revisited, is now being addressed by a few mavericks who recognize its importance. Even Mearns, who is intent on secularising therapy notes:

> I use the term "meeting at relational depth" (Mearns 1996,1997a) as secular language to describe a powerful phenomenon. It is identical to Buber's notion of the "I-Thou" relationship (1937) even though Buber himself could not imagine that possibility within a therapeutic relationship.[64]

Here the atheist cannot use the words of the religious man but neither can the religious man conceive that they are talking of the same phenomenon. Buber, a Jewish mystical philosopher with whom Rogers had a dialogue[65] about this very phenomenon, had in the end to agree to disagree with Rogers. Neither Rogers nor Buber was able to move beyond their own paradigm and see, as Mearns claims, that "it" was identical. Thorne with his Christian theological background as well as a person-centred training, has no such difficulties. He believes that what happens in these times which Mearns calls relational depth is that God is present:

> God, it would seem, is a relationship and cannot exist except as an interrelated unity.[66]

The most important aspect of all therapy is the relationship and Thorne seems to be saying that for him when therapy is at its best God is present. Thorne is open to the mystical dimension where as Mearns names it as an existential experience which has no dimension beyond the here and now.

O'Hara, a person-centred practitioner, describes her own encounters:

It isn't the technique, it isn't the therapist, it isn't the training. It isn't the new wonder drug, it isn't the diagnosis. It is the clients' own inborn capacity for self-healing, and it is the meeting of two or more sovereign or sacred "I's" meeting as "we" to engage with the significant questions of existence (O'Hara, 1995,30)[67].

Such claims are very close to those of Bollas' descriptions of what he calls the noumenal encounter in psychoanalysis. O'Hara it seems is very clear about what "it" is not. She draws on Rogers' original concept that the client has inherent healing power and, against all odds, is able to move forward in development, but she also uses the same notion as Buber's "I–Thou" quoted by Mearns above. The healing power of the client is of course dependent on the right conditions for growth and these conditions require another human being in the same space who is capable of creating an environment in which the client feels safe enough to explore and develop themselves without judgment. These are more easily defined by what they are not. There is still much fear and confusion in this area. As is seen in O'Hara the spiritual and the so called secular collide. (And yet, as is apparent in the recent works of person-centred practitioners, there is still a good deal of work to be covered in this area).

Although the person-centred tradition has begun to acknowledge the possibility of the presence of spirituality within the therapeutic encounter, not all see it as a necessary development. However, they could learn from other disciplines, such as religious studies, where in the past to study a tradition and exclude its theology was common, where it is now recognized as unacceptable to leave anything out. As we have seen above, the psychodynamic tradition has also been reluctant to engage in this exploration.

The influence of their respective founders has had a significant effect on the attitudes of contemporary practitioners to spirituality. In the case of Rogers he was beginning to make space for the mystical, but this was not always the case. In fact he spent much time in his early years rejecting religion, a legacy which his disciples have found difficult to shake off. Freud on the other hand was always anti religion; a pathological state from which to be cured.

Above, we have explored some of the criticism about the person-centred tradition and some person-centred criticisms of other outside practice. There is however, also criticism of insiders who are not meeting the criteria for good practice and who are criticized almost as vehemently as outsiders. Mearns and Thorne have fierce words indeed for those practitioners who have failed to grasp the complexity of the core conditions:

> Sadly, those who falsely conceptualise the core conditions as techniques to be deployed are perhaps the most culpable deceivers, for their shallowness leads to prostitution of a life enhancing gift.[68]

These judgments recall the condemnation of deviants in the Old Testament and in addition when Mearns and Thorne talk about the "uncontaminated" it sounds even more fundamentalist[69]. The idea of contamination has parallels in the debate about eclecticism and that which is regarded as impure or unclean: terms with a long religious history. The source of the prescriptions for segregation in religion and the idea that if not segregated things become unclean, is a mystery and the debate about eclecticism versus purism appears equally obscure to psychotherapists.

Mearns and Thorne have noted the flaws of their colleagues, both inside and outside their tradition and are aware of the ways in which their theories have been misconceived and underestimated:

> ... even those who call themselves "person-centred" had an incredibly superficial view of the approach, seeing it as comprising only of the three therapeutic conditions of empathy, unconditional positive regard , and congruence.[70]

The underestimation to which they refer is reductionism and relies on selection, so one may see why it may pave the way to fundamentalism, in that those people who do not stray from what they believe to be original at least believe that they keep the original expressions of the tradition in evidence. However, others may believe that this is itself a way of distorting the process or system. The core conditions were the doctrine of Rogers and as such not open for development/distortion.

The above examples of contemporary work in the person-centred tradition indicate a kind of coming of age, a maturity and confidence which allows the work of the founder to be challenged as well as developed. Although this challenge is still often tentative it is present none the less. Person-centred practitioners are no longer willing to accept criticism without a fight and now have thought through responses for such criticisms.

As Mearns and Thorne and Yalom demonstrate above, the interplay between traditions is more common than each would like to think and the gap between them is ever closing. What once may have been regarded as their fundamental differences, are no longer as clear. That is, the practice of each of these traditions is often at variance to what their theory claims. Their adoption of the values of other traditions seems to take place by some process of osmosis making them less at odds than each believes. This demonstrates the discrepancy between theory and practice.

Those practitioners who have contributed to the texts mentioned above may be regarded as revisionists. They are all revisiting the original theories of Rogers and making suggestions for improvement. Or, as Mearns and Thorne they have tried to recontextualise the core conditions in order to counter the over simplistic and reductionist way in which they are regurgitated in most texts used in person-centred training. Now, Mearns and Thorne would no doubt argue that this is a necessary part of making an approach accessible, i.e. reducing the theory to a set of criteria. However, this can prove counterproductive if the theory becomes so far removed from that which it was intended as to render it false.

In the above we have discussed what contemporary practitioners of person-centred counselling are doing with the work of Rogers. Like Freud, Rogers' followers have had difficulty in coming of age where religion is concerned because it was such a taboo subject for their founder. Some have begun to take the risk and declare that they can see a place for the spiritual in psychotherapy but as yet these voices are still very much in the minority. Rogers' followers respond to him, as Freud's followers responded to Freud, not with reasoned evaluation but a passionate concern for protecting Rogers and his work and maintaining the façade of being what he prescribed they should be, scientists. The acknowledgment of the importance of the religiousness of both clients and counsellors is a major step forward. However, we have yet to hear them declare the necessity of taking account of religiousness, spirituality and the sacred, both for their practice and for their existence in a post-secular world. What they do is entirely underpinned by the religious.

Notes

1 Thorne (1992) *Carl Rogers*. London: Sage, p. 95.
2 Ibid.
3 Bond, T. (1993) *Standards and Ethics For Counselling In Action*. London: Sage. See also Peter Rutter (1989) *Sex in the Forbidden Zone*. London: Aquarian.
4 It is worth noting that there is both intra and inter squabbling as well as USA/European divisions. Even in my own training, which was described as a dialogue between the psychodynamic and the person-centred approaches, there was a definite east west division in so far as Glasgow has a hiher proportion of person-centred counsellors and Edinburgh more psychodynamic.
5 Ellenberger (1970) p. 863.
6 Brazier (1993).
7 Mearns & Thorne (2000) *Person-centred Therapy: New Frontiers in Theory and Practice*. London: Sage.
8 Mearns & Thorne (2000) p. 61.
9 Thorne (1992).
10 To be incongruent is expected in our culture. If people ask how you are they expect that you will say fine regardless of how you actually feel. If your reply is other than they expect they are often unsure of what to do with it. Market forces rely on the inauthentic, for example, not every one can buy a real Rolex watch but many can buy the fake. Fakes of anything may be found and since most want to be seen to own the label they buy the fake. The need for the real is desperate. People in practices up and down the country have come to seek out the authentic, "real self", fundamental self.
11 Brazier (1993) p. 34.
12 In psychodynamic practice there has been what is known as the rule of abstinence which is an "act" of withholding feelings and information from the client. This will be explored later in the chapter.
13 As if the notion of authenticity originated with Rogers and the person-centred tradition.
14 Brazier (1993) p. 274.
15 Yalom, I. (1989) *Love's Executioner and Other Tales of Psychotherapy*. London: Penguin. In this he gives examples of the role of transference and countertransference which are personal and explicit.
16 Mearns & Thorne (2000) *Person-centred Therapy: New Frontiers in Theory and Practice*. London: Sage.

17 Mearns & Thorne (2000) p. 4.
18 Ibid., p. 75.
19 Brazier (1993) p. 56.
20 Vanaerschot is a practitioner working at the University of Leuven in Belgium and one of the contributors to Brazier (1993).
21 We must not forget that it is conducted, however many claims there may be to non directiveness. The raising of an eyebrow can direct. So it is naive to assume that because there are not words directing that there is no direction being given.
22 Professor Liz Bondi, of the University of Edinburgh and a team of researchers (9/11/01 University of Abertay. Cosca research conference) revealed the results of their work and have so far concluded that counselling cannot be defined by what it is but is made clearer by saying what it is not.
23 Brazier (1993) p. 75.
24 *New Penguin English Dictionary.*
25 Mearns & Thorne (2000).
26 Jeffrey Masson has been one of psychotherapy's biggest critics. He claims that there is a malevolent aspect to benevolence which is particularly the case in person-centred counselling which keeps its power covert. Masson is himself somewhat despotic in his attitude to psychotherapy. Fundamentalism relies on blind spots and Masson has them just like the rest of us.
27 In a documentary entitled "Our Deepest Desires" (BBC ONE 30 October 2002) a study was carried out at New Castle University by Professor Robert Winston in which young men were asked to, blindly, smell their girlfriends' t-shirts which had been put into jars. Every single time the man identified the smell of his own girlfriend. This was a demonstration of the power of smell and our lack of consciousness to the influence it is having on us.
28 On an NLP training course the facilitator, Michael Spence, was using the work of American Life Coach Tony Robbins.
29 Brazier (1993) p. 97.
30 I hear this almost daily in the agency where I work.
31 Rachaels, J. (1993) *Elements of Moral Philosophy.* McGraw-Hill, Inc.
32 Ibid., p. 75.
33 Op. cit.
34 Ibid., p. 80.
35 Brazier (1993) p. 97.

36 This is a mine field of contention. Even the psychodynamic tradition have argued that they can with hold in a way which embodies the core conditions. Any thing can be argued.
37 Brazier (1993) p. 229.
38 Ibid., p. 12.
39 Mearns & Thorne (2000) p. ix.
40 Mearns & Thorne (2000) p. ix.
41 Ibid., p. 25.
42 Ibid., p. x.
43 Ibid., p. 62.
44 Ibid., p. 85.
45 Loc. cit.
46 Howard (1996). In this work he believes that counselling and psychotherapy are rapidly becoming commodities.
47 In Brazier (1993) there is a chapter by Hutterer on this very subject.
48 Ibid., p. 86.
49 Brazier (1993) p. 35.
50 Blake, W. *The Marriage*.
51 Ibid., p. 35. Lietaer also refers to this approach as Client centred which was the original name which Rogers gave to his approach before revising it to person-centred. Client centred is objectifying and person is not.
52 Mearns & Thorne (2000) p. 46.
53 Ibid., p. 46.
54 Ibid., p. 46.
55 Ibid., p. 46.
56 Ibid., p. 46.
57 Ibid., pp. 47–8.
58 Freud was intent that psychoanalysis should not become a Jewish Ghetto and it was for this reason that he wanted Carl Jung to be his next in line.
59 Mearns & Thorne (2000) p. 172.
60 Rogers, C.R. (1980) *Being Carl Rogers* Boston/New York: Houghton Mifflin, p. 19.
61 Thorne, B.(1999) *Julian of Norwich: Counsellor for Our Age*. Guild Lecture No. 265. This has been published as Chapter 17 of *Person-centred Counselling and Christian Spirituality* By Thorne, B. (1998) Whurr, pp. 105–116. Also Thorne, B. (2002) *The Mystical Power of Person-Centred Therapy: Hope Beyond Despair*. London/Philidelphia: Whurr. Thorne, B. (2003) *Infinitely Beloved: The Challenge of Divine Intimacy*. The Sarum Theological Lectures. London: Dartman, Longman and Todd.
62 Mearns & Thorne (2000) p. 55.

63 Phillips (1994) draws on the work of a feminist psychoanalysis Coltart, whose work is very influenced by Buddhism and this middle way is more prevalent.
64 Mearns & Thorne (2000) p. 56.
65 Kirschenbaum, H. & Land Henderson, V. (eds) (1990) *Carl Rogers Dialogues*. London: Constable.
66 Mearns & Thorne (2000) p. 61.
67 Ibid., p. 75.
68 Ibid., p. 88.
69 Ibid., p. 90.
70 Ibid., p. 26.

CHAPTER SIX (I)

Post-Secular Psychotherapy

Religious studies may seem like the least likely area where the much needed rescue package for psychotherapy may be found. However, if religious studies is brave and includes in its repertoire post-secular philosophy there could be a way forward. First, a somewhat reductionist word on the post-secular. Post-secular philosophy cannot be described in a nutshell any more than other philosophies can but it posits the idea of a return to God without church. Given that the problem which psychotherapists have had with religion has been, in the main, institutionalised religion it is possible that without the institutional trappings religion may be more accessible to them. For example, Phillip Blond, an advocate of post-secular philosophy claims:

> ... these secular minds are only now beginning to perceive that all is not as it should be, that what was promised to them—self liberation through the limitation of the world to human faculties—might after all be a form of self-mutilation.[1]

Blond sees the world through the eyes of a forward thinking theologian, who has observed the challenges of the secular, and is willing to risk the criticism of institutional religions by offering a further possibility for the already unchurched. He states:

> Always and everyday those trapped in such worlds practice the violence of denial. They deny that only one world or order might

precede them; through turning away from the transcendent they violate that which is present alongside and before them, and with intoxicating compulsion of ressentiment they complete it all with the refusal of a future, taking being-towards–death (sein zum tove) as the definitive mark of the only subjectivity to come.[2]

Blond above is referring to secularists, and psychotherapists may be included in this as they have been actively unchurched by virtue of their founders' vehemence towards religion. In psychoanalysis, psychodynamic psychotherapy and person-centred counselling to reject religion has become such an integral part of their functioning, their tacit knowledge that unless they step outside their skin they cannot see that what they do is religious.

Blond is a leader in the contemporary movement of post-secularists to reclaim God, albeit a very Christian God. However, in order to reclaim God one must first have lost God. Losing God is one thing, as is misplacing God. However, denying God involves intent, which is different, in so far as it is active not passive. Freud belongs to the latter category of those who were determined to denounce God by actively denying God. Freud's theory that belief in God was a sickness created a major problem for psychotherapeutic communities to come, although in post modernity it seems a disembodied God is, as we shall see, all the rage. On the one hand Freud's belief in such a wide spread sickness, whilst giving work to psychoanalysis and psychotherapy, also made religion a taboo for practitioners. This also applies to the followers of Rogers who have also remained faithful to him by, until very recently, not courting religion.

The post-secularist intention is to "recover a world before and beyond the secular"[3]. Although secular is ascribed such meanings as before and beyond church, and historically refers to an autonomous world free from the dominance of religious institutions, in common parlance the word secular has become allied to atheism. However, in order to have a concept of atheism, theism had to exist and as such is always part of the genealogy of any argument which is about pre, or post religion. As Foucault concluded, everything should be viewed in the context of the power created by its individual genealogy[4] and if the genealogy is as important as the thing itself it is surely essential to pay attention to each in equal measure. There is no pre-history, only histories which make histories. Freud believed that the answers to life's difficulties lay in our past and in finding the origin of our motivations we would have a greater understanding of our present. However, with this model, he would also have been interested in the origin of our origin. Although Freud would not have anything to do with the divine Regina Schwartz claims:

> Because of his faith in the explanatory power of science, this secular Freud is paradoxically compatible with the ontotheological tradition, with its search for origins, for meaning and purpose, for truth.[5]

Phillip Rieff claims:

> Regardless of how far he ranged outside the recognised boundaries of experimental science Freud was anxious to preserve the image of himself as a solid scientist rather than a freelance explorer poking around on the savage hinterlands of the civilized mind.[6]

For Freud to be religious was to be uncivilised, unsophisticated, however, as is often the case with Freud such beliefs did not prevent him from forging intimate friendships with men of faith. This said, to be Freudian or indeed Rogerian, and believe in God has been problematic as this in their founders' terms was an indication of, at the very least weakness, but in the main an illness and therefore, not a position from which to conduct science. The legacy of Freud's ideas on religion is that anyone with allegiance to him must collude with his denial of God. Resistance to accept any notion of God is commonplace in psychotherapy across the board. In this Freud is certainly alive and kicking[7]. His act of denial or, as Blond would have it, "self-mutilation", has created untold resistance. Ironic really when his ideology relies on the notion that the exploration of signs of resistance is what will lead to ones improved health. One could argue that for the followers of Rogers at least he left the possibility of the mystical. However, this came so late in Rogers own career that the damage had already been done and many Rogerians were already committed to atheism.

As we have seen above, there are some therapists from both traditions now willing to "improve their health" by beginning to court things religious. As noted above, Coltart explores religious parallels between Buddhism and psychoanalysis and declares the essential role of "faith" in the psychoanalytic process:

> How ever much we gain confidence, refine our techniques, decide more creatively when and how and what to interpret, each hour with each patient is also in its own way an act of faith, faith in ourselves, in the process, and faith in the secret, unknown, unthinkable things in our patients which, in the space which is the analysis, are slouching towards the time when their hour comes round at last.[8]

Is this a sign that the unchurched are embracing faith and the unknown in a way which is meaningful or is it yet more lip service to join the contemporary rush on things spiritual? To state that "slouching toward the time when their hour comes round at last", implies a slow, linear view of healing, one where there is a beginning, middle, and an end, and if one is lucky somewhere on the line, a view of "Eden". Eden, as Adam Phillips notes, again albeit ironically, is a moral imperative of psychoanalysis[9] and subsequent psychotherapies. That is, that each practitioner has their own agenda, motivated by a cultural norm which holds the image of a possibility of an "Eden" type of future, fuelled by a fantasy of "golden ages" of the past. That the past is always in the present and influencing the future is normative in psychodynamic psychotherapy. Coltart is saying more than just that faith is necessary, she is embracing the "secret unknown ..." and begins to relinquish a need to objectify this. Blond would argue that the objectification of the unknown is desirable and that truth, beauty and goodness are shared universal objects.[10] Rogers whilst having no notion that his person-centred therapy has a destination none the less claims that the individual has, what he calls, the actualising tendency which is development in a forward motion, not far removed from the Eden of the psychodynamic tradition.

Coltart has a way of bringing together different paradigms which is quite revolutionary. For example, she claims:

> The whole of our subject, psychoanalysis, can be, and often is, attacked on the grounds that it is unscientific and cannot be

supported by any scientific evidence. The most that can be claimed for it that it is *probable*, and what we use is not rigorous scientific investigation, but the act of faith, supported by rational and imaginative conjectures, themselves inevitably conditioned by our learning and our experience.[11]

In this Coltart transcends Freud by over-shooting the notion of science, and its associations with secularism, which others, such as Phillips appear to cling to, and she declares her belief that a combination of paradigms which have until recently been held in opposition can be synthesised successfully. Could this be seen as a return to God in a way that can be compared to the post-secularists? We shall see.

Coltart has developed her own ideas with her own genealogy which, as noted, include the works of earlier psychoanalyst Wilfred Bion who although keen to keep psychoanalysis in the scientific camp, was aware of their work on the soul:

> ... Psychoanalysis helps the spirit, or soul ... to continue ... we help the soul or psyche to be born, and even help it to continue to develop *after* it is born.[12]

Here a psychoanalyst claims responsibility for the conversion, rebirth, or reinvention of the soul and the possibility of a new life through psychoanalysis. To usurp religion in this way practitioners have had to adopt some of their, so called, enemy's tactics. Not exactly earth shattering news. However, the ease with which Bion uses the language of religion is testimony to his lack of fear. This fear which many of his time had and some still have of being regarded as too mystical and therefore too connected with the enemy, religion. Bion demonstrates that to describe the analytic process requires the concepts and the language of religion. In this he is not alone: as noted above Freud frequently borrowed the language of religion and relied on heroic religious figures to illustrate his own views. For example, he compared himself to Moses, Jung and Joshua.

For psychotherapists to remain scientific is a huge hoax, an exercise in delusion or acute disciplinary amnesia as Carrette would have it. Adam Phillips, in a recent debate, commented that it was Freud's bias that kept psychoanalysis in the scientific arena when actually it is an art[13]. Phillips blames Freud, but Freud could not have achieved this alone: he relied on others to support, and perpetuate his ideas and they continue to do this effectively and Phillips himself is but one example. Those closest to Freud had more of an excuse because the climate in which they worked was less open to ambiguity. Although Freud himself did not have a problem with ambiguity subjectivity was and still can be a significant taboo on the basis that one cannot be a real scientist and be subjective. Today, this lie, although exposed, is still difficult to relinquish, and the idea of what science is continually reassessed.

Coltart gives an example of what she and other contemporary psychoanalysts call "not knowing". She, like Bollas, acknowledges a dimension to which we do not have access, and that we must learn to accept this. The fact that we cannot see it, measure it, and repeat the observation does not mean that it does not exist or is not of value. And although this may mean that we cannot call it science, this does not render it redundant:

> Perhaps I may end here by saying that patients with such symptoms, and silent patients, teach us most vividly and memorably that there is always in our work a dimension that is beyond words.[14]

This dimension, silent, beyond words, can communicate that which words cannot. Such experiences, are cultivated by the mystic who would not be regarded as ill. That there are no words does not mean that nothing is being communicated, that it is possible to experience silence as deafening is testimony to this. There is a good deal implied in silence which is useful and indeed, as psychoanalysts argue, more important. Blond claims:

> In truth, however, the invisible is not separable from the visible; in fact (and here I get a head of myself), the visible is but a dimension of invisibility and the very clarity of the visible world rests upon the adumbrations of this higher discernible.[15]

Blond could just as easily and effectively replace "invisible" with silence and visible with dialogue. For each is an aspect of the other and the qualities of each make space for something beyond.

Coltart goes on to state that mystery resides in all of us and analysts are in the business of living with mystery. Mystery is clearly finding a place in psychoanalysis and psychotherapy but lest we become lulled into a false sense of security we must question the way in which it is being used. It may be that becoming open to mystery is a good thing and a sign that the resistance of psychotherapists is diminishing but it does not however imply an openness to everything mysterious. Bollas' *The Mystery of Things* is testimony to his selectiveness of mysteries.

Coltart's work differs from that of fellow analyst Bollas, whose *The Mystery of Things* lulls us into a false sense of security by implying an openness, which, incidentally, the book fails to live up to. Bollas, like Phillips clings to secular mysteries and he still resists the otherworldly. Neither has yet made a place for God in their work: their indices are testimony to this. However, the absence of God or religion may actually increase their presence as well as illustrating their continued protestations.

Whilst Coltart is willing to look at the parallels between religion and psychotherapy she also points out the differences and states categorically that psychoanalysis and psychodynamic psychotherapy are "non religious"[16]. This because they are based on centuries of rational thought dating back to Descartes, an idea, contested by Joel Kovel, an American psychoanalyst who claims that one of the main differences between psychology and psychoanalysis, and therefore psychodynamic psychotherapy is:

> Whilst psychoanalysis wandered into the realm of the excluded, psychology remained firmly within the bounds of Cartesianism, with its claims to positive, measurable knowledge . . . meanwhile psychoanalysis staked its claim on the dark immeasurable side of things: the realm of dreams, systematically false reasonings, obscure passions and neurotic compulsions[17].

Kovel at least acknowledges their less than scientific genealogy. However, he still believes in some form of psychoanalytic truth and that psychoanalysis is engaged in a battle with no less than civilisation itself:

> Beyond any particular truth, therefore, disclosed by psychoanalysis—the clinical theory, the insights into dreaming and child

mental life, and so forth—there is a truth of psychoanalysis as a whole: the uncovering of what had been repressed by "civilisation" itself.[18]

Religions claim that they have the truth, and in fact that Kovel makes a claim for a psychoanalytic truth presupposes homogeneity, a unified group that may be known as a psychoanalytic community by virtue of their conformity to such a truth. Although there are few who make this claim overtly, it is often implied. Kovel joins the minority in taking this step in what surely must be the right direction, the direction of deconstructing the layers of his community's defence and resistance to accusations of religiousness. Above, in taking on civilisation itself, Kovel is following in the founder's footsteps as Freud, in *Civilisation and its Discontents*, made a similar attempt to generalise about civilisation. At least Freud, being a product of modernity, was expected to make broad generalisations in the tradition of universalising. Kovel has no such excuse, and yet he is undeterred.

Phillips argues that psychoanalysis is a phenomenology,[19] and an "ideology of childhood"[20]. Whilst Phillips is moving away from the scientific illusion he is, as yet, unable to talk about psychotherapy as religious in any positive sense. A sign that Freud's legacy is more difficult to shake off than we imagine, even for the most evolved of analysts is the fact that the complete rejection of the founder's beliefs is not possible—yet.

Writers and practitioners have talked of psychotherapy as religion but have fallen short of embracing their parallels. For example, Mark Epstein who also writes on the similarities between Buddhism and psychotherapy claims that psychotherapy falls short of the expectations of Buddhism[21]. Such willingness to look at these similarities is new, as for years anyone on the inside who talked of such things found themselves criticised for being too mystical. We should, therefore not take this lightly. That Epstein has taken the risk of making such comparisons is useful for anyone concerned about the covert goings on in psychotherapies. In a recent publication from the Freud museum there is evidence of this continuing resistance by David Black, himself a practitioner who addresses the issue of the accusations of religiousness but who ultimately believes it to be a convenient analogy, and without real substance[22].

In today's climate of political correctness it is difficult to criticise anything without appearing to undermine it. As Blond states:

> The lowest has become the highest, and equality names itself as the only value which cannot be devalued[23]

In psychotherapy equality is problematic because whilst everything is, on the surface, regarded as being of value there is tension between the conscious and the unconscious material of the client. In psychoanalysis and psychodynamic psychotherapy there is more emphasis on the value of things which remain in the dark, things which are not yet conscious but are none the less believed to have powerful motivation. This is the paradox that the mysterious unknown is of such high value and yet has been denied, particularly when it is an aspect of the movement and not the client, because of its immeasurability. However, if the movement was the client things would be different. The exclusion of the mysterious from psychotherapeutic theory and practice, that they have actively shut it out, was, as noted, something which Rogers came to regret ignoring. His attitude, although late in its development, has left a door to the spiritual ajar for his followers.

Blond believes that turning away from the mysterious, and transcendent, as psychotherapy does is an act of violence. However, Blond assures us that all is not lost:

> This however, is not to say that that which remains unaddressed does not address us.[24]

Given that the major objective of psychodynamic psychotherapy is in addressing that which is other-wise believed to be unaddressable, or rather, unearthing denial and resistance, it is therefore all the more interesting that practitioners continue to engage in perpetuating a movement which has, since its founder, denied or resisted addressing its own religiousness. Psychoanalysis is not what it claims!

Coltart, although a forward thinking psychoanalyst, where the religious question is concerned, still has reservations which have their roots in her own attachment to Freud and the cumulative tradition of psychoanalysis, a sort of devotionalism. Coltart's views on spirituality belong to a modernist version of psychoanalysis and not to the post modern activity which some claim that it is. She seems not to view spirituality as an individual's response to their cumulative traditions, but rather, in the context of an orthodox, institutionalised tradition. That someone has a cumulative tradition does not mean that it is located either geographically or institutionally and yet this is what she seems to imply. For example, Coltart is critical of any notion that psychotherapy can provide an avenue for transcendence but does not define what she means by this:

> ... psychotherapy does not aim at "self transcendence", and there may be a sad confusion of concepts when, say, detachment leads to a kind of neurotic spiritual inflation, or a certain depth of awareness leads to a mistaken and crudely omnipotent notion that one is nearing enlightenment, or even has "it".[25]

Coltart gives the psychoanalytic game away. She is right. Very little attention has been paid to paying attention, because as she claims it verges on the religious. Her rejection of the notion that psychotherapy could have a transcendent element signals a lack of understanding of the vast possibilities which post modernity andpost-secularism have created for transcendence. In the same way that she views spirituality as being part of an institutionalised tradition: she holds a modernist view of transcendence. In the statement below she declares:

> In all our vast literature, very little attention has been paid to attention. In clinical discussion, public or private debate, one finds the same neglect. I think this may be to do with its being so taken for granted—*it* must be there as the essential invisible ingredient—this seems to be a sort of given. Or perhaps we have not yet developed any kind of language to speak about it. Or perhaps it verges on the religious.[26]

That there is an unidentifiable *"it"*, "the essential invisible ingredient" needs further exposition. That *"it* verges on the religious" is enough to make them deny it. This is indicative that even things which are not overtly religious, but may "verge" on it, are resisted as if a threat. Coltart herself is unable to see that their lack of a suitable language to speak of their own "it" indicates an affinity with religion which is more than illusory. It is worth quoting Blond again who states:

> In truth, however, the invisible is not separable from the visible; in fact (and here I get a head of myself), the visible is but a dimension of invisibility and the very clarity of the visible world rests upon the adumbrations of this higher discernible.[27]

Although Blond makes use of a binary system to make his point there is something at work in the invisible in psychotherapy. For example, silence and the unseen have a power, which any practitioner would testify, underpins them.

Coltart, in another act of lulling us into a false sense of her acceptance of religion, states:

> I believe being a good therapist is a vocation; it did not surprise me to discover that some communities, who offer holistic care for extremely disturbed patients have been nicknamed "psychiatric monks".[28]

Whilst the nickname "psychiatric monks" does not come as a surprise to her there is a sense of irony in her response. Although Coltart uses numerous analogies, she does not see that this is itself a form of resistance, denial, that if religious analogies are not only possible but necessary this may in fact be more than symbolic. The frequency with which analogies are used is alarming, and says more than she, among others, is willing, or is able to comprehend. We all have our limits and we visit these more easily when, as insiders, our own interests are being served.

Coltart commenting on the subject of attentiveness is complimentary about people who work in religious fields and claims:

> Certainly some of those who attend to it and write about it with clarity are found in the religious fields. And there is little more calculated to stir up anxiety and defensiveness in your average analyst than any hint of religion[29].

She admires the religious scholar and yet her awareness of the hostility of psychotherapists towards religion does not make her dig for reasons behind such defensiveness. Thus, whilst being aware of the very defensive responses which religion brings up in therapists her own insider position prevents her from seeing beyond this. She cannot see that it may also cause her to have limitations. When a client comes to an analyst with such obvious resistance the most likely inference would be that they have something to uncover, something to explore. It is no coincidence that Freud believed psychoanalysis to be the archaeology of the mind. He also believed that the stronger the protest the more worthy the exposition, but omitted seeing this about his own attitude to religion.

Coltart whilst beginning to get beneath psychotherapy and its motivations, as an insider, is unable to get beneath the givens. Each field has areas, which are tacit, normative, seemingly unavoidably accepted and it may be the task of the outsider[30] to attempt to get beneath. There is a great diversity of people who train to be psychoanalysts and psychotherapists, yet it is a profession dominated by so called atheists, or secularists who none the less appear to be called by this profession by virtue of its claims to being overtly secular. Psychotherapy as a profession has all the trappings of a religion, although not acknowledged, and as Phillips notes, without the obvious downside of a God. However, in post modernity, and indeed inpost-secular philosophy, the presence of God in any traditional sense is not a prerequisite for religion. No one, it seems, is asking whether the resistance and denial itself may be God or that God is in the testing, or rather, as Blond and the Radical orthodoxy group would have it, God is the testing.

Coltart talks of the discomfort which analysts have with religion and claims that the reason behind this is that it is a "competing system".[31]

> Many analysts come from secular backgrounds and are still inclined to hold Freud's own view—that all religion is neurosis— which betrays their discomfort and anxiety in the face of what they may regard as a competing system which threatens them[32]

Whilst Coltart is able to see the way which other practitioners have responded to religion and why, she is unable to see her own prejudices. That Coltart is on her own path, of Buddhism, is one thing, which whilst giving her insight into the parallels of these traditions at the same time distorts her understanding. That psychoanalysis is more than just like a religion remains out with her comprehension. Her Buddhism whilst allowing her the privilege of tolerance is limiting as are her other traditions: psychoanalysis with its genealogy belongs to a wider context of Judeo–Christian traditions. As psychoanalysis would have it, her past is in her present and as such her views are coloured. Of course religion is "a competing system". They do not talk of, or resist, the sciences in the way that they do religion.

Adam Phillips, in *Equals*, has a different attitude towards religion than in his earlier work, a sign that his views are dynamic. Like Thorne in the person-centred tradition he is in a process of working through how to locate, and be comfortable with, what he does. He talks liberally about psychoanalysis as an ideology because this is safe, secular territory. Phillips appears to suffer from similar insider blindness to that of Coltart and as noted above each uses religious analogies. However, each remains committed to the superficial ground of psychotherapy as "it is like a" religion but is not a religion. In a similar vein to Coltart, Phillips is critical of and is willing to expose the workings of psychoanalysis, but is equally selective:

And it has, perhaps, been an exemplary profession in the way that it keeps the whole question of superiority—of the nature of prestige and dictatorship—on the agenda.[33]

This is very honourable indeed, but my sense is that in paying attention to such things he is ignoring others, which are perhaps more fundamental. This delusion, which although inevitable when one has a question which directs the project, is bound to exclude things which on the surface seem of no significance. (The givens, the tacit assumptions of the insider). Freud was acutely aware of the importance of what we perceive as the ordinary. In all traditions there is so much taken for granted by those on the inside that it is only when questioned by an outsider that the extent of their tacit knowledge is exposed. The belief that talking about things is equal to acting on them is a common mistake and one which Phillips and Coltart both make, albeit in different ways. Simply by owning up to the hierarchy does not give psychoanalysis moral high ground. When psychoanalysis itself turns literacy into praxis things will have made a significant shift.

Phillips states:

> It is as though people are deemed to be something—to have something inside them—that is of equal value; and of a value greater than any worldly assessment can encompass.[34]

This "as though" statement is an "it is like a" statement, indicative of his resistance, unwillingness, in some areas, to move beneath the surface of what appears. The otherworldly thing, which he implies but cannot bring himself to say, would justify religiousness. The "noumenal" as Bollas calls it[35] is left largely unspoken.

Phillips is happy to condemn psychoanalysis for not acknowledging its participation in social and political spheres but does not mention religion in what he calls their illusion:

> Psychoanalysis of course was not conceived as, is not supposed to be, a political training camp; but that it has pretended not to be one, that it has at its worst created the illusion that it is possible to exempt oneself from group life, from politics, has, I think, been more damaging and misleading than need be.[36]

Psychoanalysis is a political training camp if only with a small p. Phillips although critical and forward looking cannot really make up his mind about where psychoanalysis belongs. So far he has had it in languages, in the arts, as "the only religion in which you are not allowed to believe in God", and as phenomenology and more recently has Freud as a literary giant[37]. However, he could just as easily locate it in religion if as he has said himself "psychoanalysis is the only religion in which you are not allowed to believe in God". Religion and its impact on psychoanalysis, as well as psychoanalysis as a religious movement, could be explored in ways which are more useful than the superficial treatment that they receive at the moment by insiders.

Phillips, even when describing the process of psychoanalysis, has to draw on words which he has to justify using. For example:

> ... if it is the unacceptable, paradoxically, that might make us more acceptable to ourselves and others, then a remarkable piece of magic, indeed secular alchemy, has been performed.[38]

His use of the word alchemy is immediately qualified by declaring it secular. Yet he is almost evangelical about his secularism and appears not to see it as a distancing ploy. He borrows such words but does not care to ask why this may be– to ask why his own discipline lacks words to describe their own work. If it is such a secular activity then why do they qualify it? Secularists do not describe themselves as such unless they are called to question. Psychoanalysis and psychotherapy are constantly being called to question, this in itself a sign that others require that it justify itself. In the same way as when people make the claim that they are atheists they, albeit inadvertently, give credibility to the idea of theism. Without theism there would be no requirement for atheism.

And yet later in this same work Phillips draws upon the work of T.S. Eliot whose criticisms expose the limits of psychoanalysis, with which Phillips is in agreement. Eliot states that with psychoanalysis:

> ... the material is so clearly defined ... there is no possibility of tapping the atmosphere of unknown terror and mystery in which our life is passed.[39]

Phillips states:

> and I think Eliot is right about this—psychoanalysis is too rational an account of irrationality. It displaces that atmosphere of unknown terror and mystery that is so precious to Eliot.[40]

It seems paradoxical to me that Phillips, whilst seeming to embrace this idea from Eliot, is elsewhere still intent on dismissing the dimension to which this belongs.

Phillips makes the mistake of generalising about both writers who are psychoanalytically informed, and writers who happen to be Christian. He seems to think that each will hold fast to a rigid framework, a very narrow view indeed. If we are to believe in Phillips' other work on contingency, led by their particular paradigmatic beliefs, and the language which accompanies this for example, he claims:

> My paraphrase of Eliot's remarks is: people who are psychoanalytically informed—people who have been convinced (if not

converted) by Freudian explanations—are likely to phrase their accounts in particular language . . . Where as the only conviction a Christian writer will bring to his work will be a conviction of mystery. As Augustine says in one of his sermons, "Since it is God we are speaking of, you do not understand it. If you could understand it it would not be God"[41].

In his last sentence Phillips gives more credibility to the idea of psychoanalysis as a religious movement in so far as psychoanalysts claim that psychoanalysis is itself beyond understanding. If God is beyond understanding and psychoanalysis is also beyond understanding then they have more in common than has been possible to entertain. Phillips, by referring to psychoanalysts as potential converts, and in using the quotation from St Augustine, highlights, and indicates the post-secular terrain which, arguably, psychoanalysis is entering. Demonstrated in the works of those contemporary, and past psychoanalysts, who advocate not knowing as an essential aspect of their work—in the way that Augustine speaks of God—if one can understand psychoanalysis it would not actually be psychoanalysis. It is the essence of the project not to understand but to keep open to its endless possibilities.

Phillips' oscillation between views, which may be described as both modern and post –modern, has echoes of Freud himself whose views were often contradictory and had similar extremes. The absence of a serious attitude to what psychotherapists do as religious has left a presence in Phillips work which has become glaring. Phillips, like his colleagues, simply protests too much. He does this by constantly making it clear to his reader just how secular he is, although he does not state exactly what he means by this. What can we infer from this? Is he anti religious and not merely without church as thepost-secularists would have it?

Phillips denies that what people want from Freudian psychoanalysis is to be saved:

What Freudian man and woman want is not to be saved, but to satisfy their forbidden desire . . .[42]

Yet a recent survey carried out by The University of Abertay[43] found that in therapy people are seeking "permission", "engagement", and "transparency". Psychotherapy and counselling seem to provide the approval which perhaps the church once did more widely.[44] Seeking permission is a prerequisite for being saved. Seeking "permission" can be about relinquishing power, looking for someone to whom we may abdicate responsibility. This is a return to a parental template, stored in our memory, whose appropriateness in adult life is open to question. However, it may also empower someone to do things from which they had hitherto been inhibited.

Phillips in making such a claim does not acknowledge that this process, paradoxically, can be the very saving of someone or that the satisfaction of desires may well "save" someone. Phillips also argues that the Christian God of salvation has a destination, whereas, in his view psychoanalysis does not. In this he echoes Rogers who believed in the direction of psychotherapy but that it is without destination. He does concede that psychoanalysis has a direction, but can only bring himself to describe this as a secular process. This secular process is "something akin to a conversion experience"[45] and Phillips asks how best this process may be described if not as a conversion. He has referred to this conversion experience as an experience of being "convinced"[46]. However, his description is less than convincing.

Phillips claims:

It is the valuing of the individual despite his social status, and not because of it, that both Christianity and democracy promote.[47]

Such values are among the core of psychoanalysis and psychotherapy. In his view the ideals of Christianity and democracy may be that of valuing the individual, in theory, but not without ties or judgment. He appears not to have noticed the views of the religious right in the USA and their promotion of such doctrines as the "gospel of health and wealth". Phillips takes risks in making generalizations, such as the above, and gets away with this largely because of the originality of his work. However, he does not, yet, go far enough with his observation. Phillips talks of us each having our own criteria by which we judge. In other words our individual ideologies lead how we regard things in the world and his own ideology excludes the religious. He sees the world through his secular tinted spectacles.

Because this is the case he appears not to have noticed that he is himself forging a reputation in psychoanalysis as a maverick thinker. Scaring the orthodox out of their wits, continually sought out by the media when ever they require an expert on psychoanalysis, he is, it would seem, on the path of messianism himself.

Phillips' religious blind spot is problematic, as he, like most, is selective about what he sees in any ideology. Those things, which are omitted from his views of Christianity, and democracy, are similarly omitted from psychoanalysis. His selectivity differs from one to the other but it need not. In this he is not alone as each person's anthropological lens inevitably influences what we are willing to see. Phillips' unwillingness to see psychoanalysis as a religion, prevents him from making comparisons which he could. His views are so tacitly imbued as anti religious as to make it impossible to see them. Every ideology is vastly different in practice to that which is advocated in theory. For example, Christianity, democracy, and psychoanalysis all suffer from a disparity between theory and practice and it is in their disparity that their common ground lies.

We have seen how Coltart and Phillips approach religion, let us now turn to Christopher Bollas whose *The Mystery Of Things*, seduces us into a false sense that he may have been able to relinquish his own resistance to the notion of religion. To choose the word mystery is to venture into a world which, as he points out is, "unknowable". This is the world over which religions have had a monopoly for some time, and have been content to live with the unknowable factor. Alas, Bollas is as resistant as the others to things religious. There is no mention of religion or comparison of psychoanalysis or psychotherapy with it. In fact there is only minor reference to anything connected, an absence which in itself should be a warning:

> This drive is an essential part of one's encounter with the mysteries of life, from the ordinary recurring mystery show of dreams, to the secret of the internal world, to the enigmas of the universe and of the physical world that inspires scientific curiosity and work . . .[48]

Further:

> Theological explanations of this world of ours and our place in it is an essential endeavour to think about the complexities of

life, but its premature vision, sustained now by anaemic faith, testifies to the strain of trying to know more than one does.[49]

Bollas leaves us in no doubt about where his allegiance lies. His views on theology indicate that he has not read too much contemporary theology where not knowing is lived, embraced. His promotion of science over theology, a theme which is common among psychoanalysts (who have not yet let go of Freud), echoes that of Freud whose raison d'être was to be a famous man of science. Like Phillips and Coltart, Bollas has to draw upon the language of religion in order to best describe experiences, which arise in psychoanalysis and for which there are no scientific words or explanations. For example, he talks about the "noumenal transference"[50], an experience, which he believes, is where one unconscious is connected to another:

a noumenal to noumenal encounter, a meeting of two immaterial logics engaging one another.[51]

Bollas describes psychoanalysis:

It is a site of mystery that will not vanish through the appropriate aims of categorical nomination.[52]

In this he echoes Phillips in so far as he implies that understanding psychoanalysis is beyond rationality and fixed categorization. Rudolph Otto reached a similar conclusion long before either of these men. Bollas' only overt mention of a connection to religiousness is in talking about the "spirit". And as noted above, he implies that even to mention such things, he is taking a risk. Both he and Coltart are aware of the resistance of their community to religion but do not question their own, as if they are not part of the community and as such immune to judgment. The community's resistance to religion remains for them something which is out there. And yet, it is the unmentionable which is the very fodder of psychoanalysis—as long as it has nothing to do with religion. Perhaps, like Coltart, Bollas is testing the temperature of the community before taking any further risk. However, Bollas, like Phillips, also attempts to rationalize that which we cannot in claiming:

In another essay I suggest that under special circumstances the term "spirit" should be introduced in to psychoanalysis , even though there would be many objections to a term laden with pre-psychoanalytic meanings ... If however, we understand spirit as the expressive movement of an individual's idiom through the course of his or her life, we may say that each of us is a spirit, and that we have spiritual effects upon others—who will indeed carry us as such within themselves, and we in turn will be inhabited by the spirits of others.[53]

It was worth quoting this again because for Bollas to say such a thing is progress indeed, although, it is still somewhat worrying to think that psychoanalysis is fearful of things which are pre-psychoanalytic. (They do not appear to have a problem with the railways). That to only use the term "spirit" in "special circumstances" implies caution, trepidation or fear of it. Phillips, Coltart and Bollas each realize that there is resistance within their community to religion but do not go beyond a tentative exposition and certainly do not go as far as to agree that it is one. (without qualification). As noted, Symington is the only psychoanalyst who has actually said that psychoanalysis is a religion, but qualifies this by saying that it is natural and not revealed, when it is entirely revealed. He uses the term as if it is inappropriate, that he is trespassing. There is more going on here than is being stated. As implied above, the denial of anything in psychoanalysis is regarded as a source of work. To unpack denial, or resistance, is what psychoanalysis and psychotherapy do. And yet their own is not tackled in any meaningful way in current theory. Bollas knows that any notion of the spiritual is a challenge not only to their scientific validity but to Freud himself.

Bollas comments on Freud's belief in "universal truths"[54] as if this is a thing of the past and not something which is still around in a different guise. As noted above Kovel still talks of the truth of psychoanalysis and is not the only therapist to invest in such an idea.

Notes

1 Blond, P. (ed.) (1998) *Post-Secular Philosophy: Between Philosophy and Theology*. London: Routledge, p. 1.
2 Ibid., p. 3.
3 Ibid., p. xiii.
4 Phoca, S. & Wright, R. (1999) *Introducing Postfeminism*. London: Icon Books, p. 94.
5 Schwartz, R. in Ward (1998) p. 281.
6 Footnote 4 on p. 302 of chapter 11 – Schwartz in Ward (1998). Schwarts is quoting from Rieff, P. (1959) *Freud: The mind of the Moralist*. Chicago: Chicago University Press, p. 23.
7 The aforementioned *Time* magazine survey was off the mark.
8 Coltart (1993) p. 3.
9 Phillips (1994).
10 Blond, P. (2003) In a paper given to the Art Society of University of Edinburgh 29/04/03 he argued that continued subjectivisation needs to be countered or redressed. He explored the work of the Impressionists and concluded that they began this process which modern art is trapped in. That art is anything that we want it to be. Blond disagrees.
11 Coltart (1993) pp. 96–7.
12 Coltart (1993) pp. 96–7.
13 *Start the Week* Broadcast on BBC Radio 4. 25/11/02 9am Adam Phillips, Anne Oakley, Andrew Marr . . .
14 Coltart (1993) pp. 96–7.
15 Blond (1998) p. 25.
16 Coltart (1993) p. 165.
17 Kovel, J. In: Elliott, A. & Frosh, S. (1995) p. 206.
18 Ibid., p. 206.
19 Phillips (1994).
20 Phillips, A. (2002) *Equals*. London: Faber & Faber, p. 150.
21 Epstein, M. (1998) *Going To Pieces Without Falling Apart: A Buddhist Perspective On Wholeness*. London: Thorsons.
22 Black, D. in Ward, I. (ed.) (2000?) *Is Psychoanalysis Another Religion?: Contemporary Essays On Spirit, Faith and Morality in Psychoanalysis*. London: Freud Museums Publications, p. 8.
23 Blond, P. (ed.) (1998) *Post-Secular Philosophy: Between Philosophy and Theology*. London: Routledge, p. 2.
24 Ibid., p. 3.
25 Coltart (1993) p. 168.

26 Ibid., p. 180.
27 Blond, P. (ed.) (1998) p. 25.
28 Coltart, p. 179.
29 Ibid., p. 180.
30 There are people who are both insiders and outsiders at the same time. People like myself who bridge the gap.
31 Coltart (1993) p. 184.
32 Ibid., p. 184.
33 Phillips (2002) p. 19.
34 Ibid., p. 21.
35 Bollas (1999) p. 10 The "Noumenal" was first coined by Emmanuel Kant but was explored in some depth by Rudolph Otto in *The Idea Of The Holy*.
36 Phillips (2002) p. 28.
37 Edinburgh International Book Festival, 17/08/05.
38 Ibid., p. 46.
39 Ibid., p. 105.
40 Ibid., p. 106.
41 Loc. cit.
42 Phillips (2002) p. 108.
43 This study was given at the Cosca research conference, which was held in The University of Abertay, 19/09/02, in a paper by Brian Rogers.
44 I expect that not only does psychotherapy provide approval—i.e the good bits of what the church did but also some of the constraints and disapproval.
45 Ibid., p. 131.
46 Ibid., p. 106.
47 Ibid., p. 21.
48 Ibid., p. 9.
49 Loc. cit.
50 Ibid., p. 9.
51 Ibid., p. 10.
52 Ibid., p. 14.
53 Ibid., p. 157.
54 Bollas (1999) p. 35.

CHAPTER SIX (II)

Post-Feminist Responses

It is important to say something of what feminists and post-feminists have brought to the study of religion, as well as to the study of psychotherapy. Their works have shown different means of exploring the unknowable unknown. This is exemplified in Ward's observations of Cixious:

> Cixious is less a theorist and more a practitioner, in her writing, of a religious way of viewing the world. Cixious's work performs a spirituality. She has written: "When I have finished writing, when I am a hundred and ten, all I will have ever done will have been to attempt a portrait of God. Of The God. Of what escapes us and makes us wonder . . . I mean our divinity awkward, twisted, throbbing, our own mystery"[1].

Cixious distances herself from the feminist model by claiming that she does not want to be part of the existing structures to which feminists aspire. Cixious is therefore allied with post feminism, although it is difficult to be such without acknowledging the role of feminism. Her work could prove crucial to the God work in psychoanalysis and psychotherapy. In so far as God is not something which is other, but is the "I", "our own mystery". So when Bollas discusses the mystery of things he could embrace Cixious's notion of "our own mystery" as God. This is a difficult concept to accept if your tradition has never made a place for God in any form other than as a neurosis.

Hélène Cixious and Luce Irigary are both versed in psychoanalysis and see beyond the church of Freud:

Contrary to much secular feminist thought, Irigaray is clear that religion cannot be ignored or written off; it has to be transformed[2].

Such transformation, she suggests, is already in the making if it has been recognized as necessary. However, talking of such things and acting on them are, as we have seen, different genres and require different motivations. Jantzen claims that Irigary would like to see religion being transformed rather than being ignored, but whilst this is a move in the right direction it belongs to an attitude which sees religion as the problem and not psychotherapy.

Post feminists are willing to transform their views about religion but at the same time rely on a template which could equally be applied to men and indeed religion. All categories have been devised as a means of constructing a social group with an agenda[3]. If God is dead and religion is a social construct, its role, and function today is determined largely by what people who continue to support it need. Jantzen's *Becoming Divine* has a good deal to say about psychotherapy and one wonders how much she has been unconsciously influence by it. For example, the title of her book sounds like a play on Rogers's famous *On Becoming a Person*[4] which has been hugely influential for psychologists in the USA. It might have been more useful for Rogers to have said that we are already persons in a process of becoming then Jantzen could have followed with "divine and still becoming". Jantzen is not the only one to demonstrate how we have each become part of a discourse whose boundaries are blurred. Such a blurring of boundaries allows the theologian to venture into discussions about philosophy and psychotherapy in ways which would not have been attempted in the pre feminist, pre post-secular arena.

For example:

Contrary to the sociocultural norms of his time, Christ approaches both men and women with the same freedom founded on wisdom rather than logical reasoning. Read or re-read the Gospels and try to find the logic of Jesus' words; he continually contradicts everything he says. Is this indicative of the importance of an age in transition, or is it these contradictions that allow his message to rise above understanding?[5]

Comparisons, such as she makes, are a sign of the fluidity of disciplines but also that the God without church is the religion of freedom. Reason is an example of perpetuating those binary, patriarchal needs of the modernist, which she so often condemns. However, her observations on contradiction, as a way of allowing knowledge to rise above understanding, may have parallels in the work of Freud who often contradicts his earlier work without comment. Freud is often accused of being dogmatic, and at times this is the case, but it does not do justice to his complete works which are riddled with contradictions which show he could be as open to contradiction as he could be dogmatic.

Irigaray claims that the:

... irrational in Jesus leads to the liberation of the spirit, not to love, not to nothingness or to the spiritual and mystical torture that probably originates in the stifling, paralysis of becoming, particularly along sexual lines[6].

Freud argued this in secular terms in that the unknown unconscious which he believed was the repository of the irrational, when uncovered, could allow the patient to feel a new kind of liberation.

Finally Pamela Sue Anderson on the work of Kristeva:

The psychoanalytic discourse of love takes the place occupied by religious discourse.[7]

This is problematic as it presupposes that there is such a thing as a psychoanalytic discourse of love and not that there are many discourses which may or may not include different types of loving. In this essay Anderson portrays Kristeva as having a "golden age" mentality, as she wonders whether this "therapeutic age" will be able to recover the "positive values once found in religion"[8]. This as if there is homogeneity in each age and that religion has at some point been without problems.

Anderson continues:

Today religious belief can be, if necessary, replaced by a fundamental trust in a loving analyst and eventual separation. Is this the agency of agape, the post modern God?[9]

This also a return to a religious golden age as if such a thing existed. This need in the writer to find something in the past which was superior and to which we should aspire is unusual in feminist discourse—and yet those post-secular scholars, drawn together in Ward's anthology, seem to. Their going "before and beyond church" seems dominated by their need to have an era which was Eden like.

Notes

1 Ward, G. (ed.) (1997) *The Post Modern God: A Theological Reader*. Oxford, UK: Blackwell, p. xxxix.
2 Jantzen in Ward (1997) p. 194.
3 Ortner, S. Sherry Ortner wrote about the way in which *Women are to Men as Nature is to Culture*. A paper which dispels biological determinism as the main source of our roles. Judith Butler's *Gender Trouble* is an analysis of trouble caused by gender stereotyping and has itself become a veritable sacred text.
4 Rogers, C.R. (1961) *On Becoming a Person*. Boston: Houghton Mifflin.
5 Jantzen in Ward p. 203. In this chapter Jantzen is discussing the work which Irigaray has done on Schüssler Fiorenza.
6 Ibid., p. 203.
7 Anderson in Ward (1997) p. 216.
8 Ibid., p. 219.
9 Ibid., p. 219.

Conclusion

It is ironic that, given their interest in the dynamics of the human mind, psychotherapists have until very recently failed to notice that their own relationship with religion has remained rather static. Psychotherapists have been influenced in a peculiar way by their founders a way which has prevented them from embracing religion and its associated spirituality. Yes, they have entertained the comparisons which others have made of psychotherapy with religion, and even gone so far as to agree but never with conviction, only with, as Jones noted, the certainty that the grain of truth in such a comparison was not really a threat. As so often is the case, with grains of truth, more becomes of them than is supposed and this has been the case with psychotherapy.

Whilst those psychotherapies discussed above have yet to relinquish themselves to a religious paradigm, they have moved some way from Freud's original criticism of all religion as neurosis. Those who have become forerunners in contemporary psychotherapy realise that making changes to the canon of their founder has involved risks, not least of which is expulsion from the community. That they have managed to do this and remain forerunners is perhaps indicative of the maturation of their tradition. Psychotherapists who have deemed such changes necessary have recognised the rise in demand for things spiritual but, more importantly, the absence of this phenomenon in their own work. To respond positively to this demand for the spiritual, without overtly rejecting the doctrine of their founder, has been problematic and has taken some time.

Contemporary psychotherapy has a problem with religion, in so far as it has censored out any positive significance religion may have, instead choosing to relate to it as something to be treated or ignored. However, as the prologue above testifies, psychotherapy has since its beginnings been compared to religion, although never as a form of flattery. The resemblance between psychotherapy and religion is more significant than those merely superficial analogies which have been made since its conception. Jones noted the grain of truth in such analogies but denied, as many others have, that the grain belies something more substantial. There are different levels of religiousness at work in psychotherapy; one level is the structure of these movements, or approaches, which is parallel to those of religious traditions; the second is their function as religious movements; the third is that what they do is religious: they cure souls, and the way in which this it executed is also religious. In addition, those meaning of life questions which they address have long been in the realm of religious traditions.

Freud's relationship to and beliefs about religion were the initial source of these difficulties. Freud and Rogers were each inspirational figures whose own negative relationship with religion prevented them from seeing a bigger picture. Although both were in the business of alleviating the bad faith of others, they were unable to see it in the discipline itself. Their intensity of feeling about religion has clouded their vision so much as to have left a damaged legacy. This legacy denies their indebtedness to religious traditions, especially to that of the cure of souls: confession. In addition, psychotherapy denies its parallel function to religion and demonstrates very little response to the spiritual needs of clients or practitioners. Freud and Rogers each claimed to be men of science. However, they each ventured into the domain of the unknowable which proved to be a particular kind of problem. As scientists it was impossible for them not to respond to the unknown as a challenge to be solved. Consequently each denied that the "it" or X factor was beyond knowing. Neither of them was motivated to experience more of the unknowable, as this would have forced them to relinquish their conviction that "it" was solvable, and in so doing rejecting the scientific paradigm to which they were committed. Each had his own reasons for his conviction to science and each left a legacy which required that their followers continue their scientific quest. Their quests have taken a long time to come to fruition. However, as with the great religions of the world, there are a few mavericks who have believed it to be worth the risk to relinquish their own convictions to psychotherapy as science and tentatively venture into the domain of mystery in a way which does not presuppose that they solve it.

Freud's followers had to overcome their adopted belief that all religion is indicative of illness, and Rogers' followers knew, until his final years, that religion was a taboo subject. The behaviour of these followers goes beyond that of people of science. The quality of a psychotherapist's commitment is not fully illustrated by simply exposing those superficial intra and inter tensions between purist and eclectic and integrative denominations. Even when practitioners display their inter-faith tolerance their underlying motivation relies on the perceived truth of their tradition. The commitment and conformity of practitioners to a specific founder and theory is a significant indication of their being part of a faith community and not to a scientific one. The absence of particular actions, for fear of being accused of blasphemy, is still present today. However, as we have seen, now there are those who have taken the risk to transcend the authority of their tradition and, as such, follow the mystics who, in order to become so called, had also to reject authority.

With the work of Neville Symington we have seen the beginnings of a dialogue in psychoanalysis which includes religion in a meaningful way. His claim of psychoanalysis as a natural religion is a good sign. However, it also remains superficial by denying the importance of those rich sources of the Judaeo Christian traditions which were the foundations upon which Freud, and others in his time, relied. Psychoanalysis is a revealed tradition which borrowed a good deal from these traditions: not least of which was the cure of souls.

Carl Rogers' movement was born of his disenchantment with Christianity and the patriarchal standards of psychoanalysis. His movement, although held in opposition to psychodynamic psychotherapy, has none the less followed a similar route to Freud and the Freudians. Rogers, like Freud, left a legacy of anti- religious sentiment beyond indifference: a complete dismissal which led his followers to realise that religion was an area which was not open for discussion. Rogers' eventual claim that omitting the mystical had been a mistake, has given tacit permission for practitioners to venture beyond theory.

Brian Thorne has been the most committed to this, and behaves as if he is the high priest of person-centred therapy. Although his ascendance could not be described as a trouble free journey, he appears to have survived his early turbulence and arrived at a position of self assurance which allows him to adopt a manner of address which is messianic. His lectures are delivered as sermons, and to have an audience with him is akin to being in the presence of a guru. Thorne's posture is reverential and his movements are deliberate and measured. His devotion to Julian of Norwich allows him to emulate a model of mysticism.

Until Thorne, the followers of Rogers have had a similar attitude to religion as to that of their psychodynamic counterparts. Each founder had set his scene by rejecting his own religion and disregarding its significance. The suppression of the importance of religion has been a serious mistake, and in today's world where spirituality is all around, it is difficult for psychotherapists, of whatever persuasion, to continue to ignore this area or to reinvent themselves as being pro religion. Post modernity has created a space in which psychotherapists can question the dogmatism of their own atheism and has exposed it as an unjustifiable way to survive. The exponential rise in things spiritual cannot be ignored by even the most committed psychotherapist. A walk down any high street is enough to demonstrate a market flooded with "spiritual" products which claim to rescue the ailing soul from impending doom, and the talking cure has become only one of many products on which disposable income may be spent.

In the so called post-secular era when almost anything, it seems, may be regarded as spiritual, and if God is without church, and no one has a monopoly on the spiritual, can psychotherapists continue to deny that which has become so pervasive? The answer is of course, "no", and as demonstrated above, psychotherapists themselves are beginning to address what they have termed the "unknowable", and they are talking about "moments of meeting". Freud himself even noted that no amount of skill or technique could in itself make his psychoanalysis work. It was the relationship between patient and practitioner that he believed tipped the balance of success. However, he could not identify what it was that would make it so. This "unknowable", these "moments of meeting", the "it", "relational depth", or the X factor are what people in therapy have repeatedly referred to as "revelatory", "spiritual", or "epiphanies". These changing attitudes are essential developments for the mental health of psychotherapy itself. In their continued denial of religion, active denial which suggests that there is something at stake emotionally, psychotherapists are denying social reality just as obviously as do their clients. Psychotherapists pride themselves on being the custodians of realities which their clients have yet to access: that they have the real and the client suffers delusions. In respect of religion this seems reversed. So their new uncovering of the spiritual, whatever they choose to call it, can only be of benefit to them. Psychotherapy has been suffering from this lying condition since Freud, and for it to survive must take this omission seriously. Such change can only be made from the inside. Symington and Thorne are beginning to make this happen.

As we have seen, even the most radical insiders have been unable to identify their own delusions by virtue of the mental attitude which had been prescribed for their approach, an attitude which has been beautifully preserved both by Freud's followers and by those who claim to have no allegiance to him. Psychotherapists have been blinded by their commitment to their founder, an attitude which goes well beyond the bounds of the scientific relationship.

Psychotherapists' resistance to religion is all the more bizarre in the light of what many of them do, which is to hear any manner of testimonies including those of criminals and will tolerate hearing of mental torture and, it seems, hear lies and assume that all are suffering. They appear not to be unduly disturbed by such testimonies. However, they are disturbed by religion: to be religious is still a self imposed taboo. To use Freud's own work *"Totem and Taboo"* as a template for how psychotherapy may improve its own health seems ironic. If psychotherapists could, if only metaphorically, devour their founder, they would be able to let go of their scientific pretensions and be what they are. They have made Freud their totem and have subverted the nature of their movement and practice, and as with most things which are subverted (driven underground) they eventually surface with more power than if they had been allowed space all along.

Bibliography

Professional Literature

Adams, W.E. Jr. (1984) "Rediscovering Trust: Towards an Alternative Psychotherapy". In: *Pastoral Psychology* 33: 5–14, Fall 1984.

Appleyard, B. (1992) *Understanding The Present: Science and the Soul of Modern Man.* Picador.

Balen (ed.) *Client-Centered and Experiential Psychotherapy in the Nineties.* Leuven University Press. Leuven, pp. 59–64.

Barnard, D. (1982) "The Gift of Trust: Psychodynamic and Religious Meanings in the Physicians Office". In: *Soundings* 65: 213–232, Summer.

Bergin, A.E. (1980) "Psychotherapy and Religious Values". In: *Journal of Consulting and Clinical Psychology* 48.

Bergin, A.E. & Jensen, J.P. (1990) "Religiosity and Psychotherapists: A National Survey". In: *Psychotherapy* 27: 3–7.

Bernheimer, C. & Kahane, C. (1985) (eds) *Freud, Hysteria, Feminism.* London: Virago.

Bettelheim, B. (1982) *Freud and Man's Soul.* London: Penguin.

Bion, W. (1970) *Attention and Interpretation.* London: Tavistock.

Blanton, B. (1996) *Radical Honesty.* New York: Delta.

Bollas, C. (1999) *The Mystery of Things.* London: Routledge.

Bollas, C. (2000) *Hysteria.* London: Routledge.

Bollas, C. (2002) *Free Association.* London: Icon Books.

Bond, T. (1993) *Standards and Ethics for Counselling in Action.* London: Sage.

Bowlby, J. (1988) *A Secure Base.* London: Routledge.

Bozarth, J. (1990) "The Essence of Client-Centered Therapy". In: G. Lieter, J. Rombauts & R. Van.

BIBLIOGRAPHY 201

Brazier, D. (ed.) (1993) *Beyond Carl Rogers: Toward a Psychotherapy for the Twenty First Century*. London: Constable.
Clarke, K.M. (1994) "Lessons from Feminist Therapy for Ministerial Ethics". In: *The Journal of Pastoral Care* 48(3), Fall.
Clarkson, P. (1996) *The Bystander*. London: Whurr.
Casement, P. (1985) *On Learning from the Patient*. Routledge (Reprint 1990).
Coltart, N.E.C. (1986) "'Slouching Towards Bethlehem' . . . Or Thinking the Unthinkable in Psychoanalysis". In: Kohon, G. (ed.) *The British School Of Psychoanalysis: The Independent Tradition*. London: Free Association.
Dryden, W. (1985) *Therapists' Dilemmas*. London: Harper Row.
Dryden, W. and Thorne, B. (1991) *Training and Supervision for Counselling in Action*. London: Sage.
Egan, G. (1985) *The Skilled Helper*. Brook/Cole.
Elliott, A. & Frosh, S. (eds) (1995) *Psychoanalysis in Context*. London: Routledge.
Elliott, A. (ed.) (1999) *Freud 2000*. London: Polity.
Ellis, A. (1980) "Psychotherapy and Atheistic Values: A Response to A.E. Bergin's 'Psychotherapy and Religious Values'". In: *Journal of Consulting and Clinical Psychology* 48: 635–9.
Epstein, M. (1998) *Going to Pieces Without falling Apart: A Buddhist Perspective on Wholeness*. London: Thorsons.
Epstein, M. (1996) *Thoughts Without a Thinker: Psychotherapy from a Buddhist Perspective*. London: Duckworth.
Feltham, C. (1997) *Time-Limited Counselling*. London: Sage Publications.
Feltham, C. (1998) *Witness and Vision Of Therapists*. London: Sage.
Feltham, C. (1999) *Controversies in Psychotherapy and Counselling*. London: Sage.
Fortune, M.M. (1994) "Therapy and Intimacy: Confused About Boundaries". In: *Christian Century* 111: 524–526, May 18–25.
Freud, E. & Meng, H. (eds) (1963) *Psycho-Analysis and Faith: The Letters Of Sigmund Freud to Oskar Pfister*. London: The Hogarth Press.
Freud, S. *Introductory Lectures*. Translated by James Strachey. London: Hogarth Press and The Institute of Psychoanalysis, Vols 1–16.
Friedman, M. (1982) "Psychotherapyin the Human Image". In: W. Sharkey (ed.), *Philosophy-Religion and Psychotherapy: Essays on the Philosophical Foundations of Psychotherapy*. Washington: University Press of America.
Fromm, E. (1951) *Psychoanalysis and Religion*. London: Victor Gallancz.
Fromm, E. (1942) *Fear of Freedom*. London: Routledge (Reprint 1997).
Fromm, E. (1957) *The Art of Loving*. London: Thorson (Reprint 1995).
Gendlin, E.T. (1978) *Focusing*. New York: Everest House.

Gendlin, E.T. (1990) "The Small Steps of the Therapy Process: How they Come and How to Help them Come". In: Lietaer, J., Rombauts, & R. Van Balen (eds), *Client-Centered and Experiential Psychotherapy in the Nineties*. Leuven: Leuven University Press, pp. 205–24.
Guntrip, H.J.S. (1977) *Psychoanalytic Theory, Therapy, and the Self*. London: Maresfield Library.
Guntrip, H.J.S. (1956) *Mental Pain and Cure of Souls*. London: Independent Press.
Hardy, J. (1987) *Psychology With a Soul: Psychosynthesis in Evolutionary Context*. London: Routledge and Kegan Paul.
Heisig, J.W. (1997) "The Quest of the True Self: Jung's Rediscovery of a Modern Invention". In: *Journal of Religion* 77: 252–267, April.
Heyward, C. (1993) *When Boundaries Betray Us: Beyond the Illusion of What is Ethical in Therapy and Life*. San Fransisco: Harper.
Heyward, C. (1995) "Fighting Boundary Fundamentalism". In: *Witness* 78: 25–26, May.
Horney, K. (1937) *The Neurotic Personality of Our Time*. New York/London: W.W. Norton & Co. Inc.
Irigary, L. (1993) *Sexes and Genealogies*. Translated by Gillian C. Gill. New York: Columbia University Press.
Jacobs, M. (1986) *The Presenting Past*. Buckingham: Open University Press (Reprint 1995).
Jacobs, M. (ed.) (1987) *Faith Or Fear: A Reader in Pastoral Care and Counselling*. London: Darton, Longman, and Todd.
Jacobs, M. (1988) *Freud*. London: Sage.
Jacobs, M. (1988) *Psychodynamic Counselling in Action*. London: Sage (Reprint 1996).
Jacobs, M. (1993) *Living Illusions: A Psychology of Belief*. Spck.
Jeske, J.O. (1984) "Varieties of Approaches to Psychotherapy; Options for the Christian Counseling Psychotherapist". In: *Journal of Psychology and Theology* 12: 260–9.
Jones, E. (1955) *Sigmund Freud:Life and Work*. London: Hogarth, Vols 1–3.
Jung, C.J. (1983) *Memories, Dreams and Reflections*. London: Flamingo.
Jung, C.G. (1991) *The Collected Works:11 Psychology And Religion West and East*. London: Routledge.
Jung, C.G. (1936) *Modern Man in Search of a Soul*. Kegan Paul.
King-Spooner, S. & Newnes, C. (eds) (2001) *Spirituality and Psychotherapy*. Ross-on-Wye: PCCS Books.
Kirschenbaum, H. (ed.) (1990) *Carl Rogers Dialogues*. London: Constable.
Kirschenbaum, H. & Henderson, V. (1990) *The Carl Rogers Reader*. London: Constable.

Kohut, H. (1971) *The Analysis of The Self*. London: Hogarth.
Kohut, H. (1977) *The Restoration of The Self*. Madison, C.T.: International Universities Press.
Koltko, M.E. (1990) "How Religious Beliefs Affect Psychotherapy: The Example of Mormanism". In: *Psychotherapy* 27: 132–141.
Lietaer, G. Rombauts, J., & Van Balen, R. (eds) *Client-Centered and Experiential Psychotherapy in the Ninties*. Leuven: Leuven University Press.
Lyall, D. (1995) *Couselling in the Pastoral and Spiritual Context*. Buckingham: Open University Press.
May, G.G. (1992) *Care of Mind Care of Spirit*. San Fransisco: Harper Collins.
McGuire, W. (ed.) (1991) *The Freud Jung Letters*. London: Penguin.
Mcleod, J. (1993) *An Introduction to Counselling*. Open University Press.
Mearns, D. & Thorne, B. (1988) *Person-Centred Counselling in Action*. London: Sage (Reprint 1994).
Mearns, D. & Thorne, B. (2000) *Person Centred Therapy: New Frontiers in Theory and Practice*. London: Sage.
Mearns, D. (1998) "Working At Relational Depth: Person-Centred Intrapsychic Family Therapy". Paper Presented To The Joint Conference Of The British Association For Counselling And The European Association For Counselling. Southampton, England, September 18.
Meissner, W.W. (1931) *Psychoanalysis and Religion*. Yale University Press (Reprint 1984).
Mihaly, C. (1992) *Flow: The Psychology of Happiness*. London: Harper Row.
Miller, W. R. & Martin, J.E. (1988) *Behaviour Therapy and Religion; Integrating Spiritual and Behavioural Approaches to Change*. London/California: Sage Publications, Inc.
Nelson-Jones, R. (1995) *The Theory and Practice of Counselling*. London: Cassells, 2nd edition.
Nelson, S.H. & Torrey, E.F. (1973) "The Religious Functions of Psychiatry". In: *The American Journal of Orthopsychiatry* 43: 362–7.
Orbach, S. (1999) *The Impossibility of Sex*. London: Penguin.
Orbach, S. (1999) *Towards Emotional Literacy*. London: Virago Press.
Phillips, A. (1993) *On Kissing Tickling and Being Bored*. London: Faber & Faber.
Phillips, A. (1994) *On Flirtation*. London: Faber & Faber.
Phillips, A. (1995) *Terrors and Experts*. London: Faber & Faber.
Phillips, A. (1996) *Monogamy*. London: Faber & Faber.
Phillips, A. (1998) *The Beast in The Nursery*. London: Faber & Faber.
Phillips, A. (1999) *Darwins Worms*. London: Faber & Faber.
Phillips, A. (2000) *Promises, Promises*. London: Faber & Faber.
Phillips, A. (2002) *Equals*. London: Faber & Faber.

Phillips, A. (2005) *Going Sane*. London: Hamish Hamilton.
Phillips, J.B. (1984) *The Wounded Healer*. London: Triangle Spck.
Pilgrim, D. (ed.) (1983) *Psychology And Psychotherapy*. London: Rkp.
Robinson, P.A. (1969) *The Sexual Radicals: Reich, Roheim, Marcuse*. London: Paladin.
Rogers, C.R. (1980) *A Way of Being*. Boston/New York: Houghton Mifflin Company.
Rogers, C.R. (1942) *Counselling and Psychotherapy*. Boston/New York/Chicago/Dallas/Atlanta/San Francisco: Houghton Mifflin Company.
Rogers, C.R. (1961) *On Becoming a Person*. Boston: Houghton Mifflin Company.
Rogers, C.R. (1951) *Client-Centered Therapy: Its Current Practice, Implications, and Theory*. Boston: Houghton Mifflin Company (First Published In Paper Covers In 1965).
Rogers, C.R. & Steven, B. (1967) *Person to Person: The Problem of Being Human a New Trend in Psychology*. London: Souvenir Press (British Edition 1973).
Sachs, H. (1945) *Freud Master and Friend*. London: Imago.
Sedgwick, D. (1994) *The Wounded Healer*. London: Routledge .
Symington, N. (1986) *The Analytic Experience: Lectures from the Tavistock*. London: Free Association Books.
Symington, N. (2004) *The Blind Man Sees: Freud's Awakening and Other Essays*. London: Karnac Books.
Szasz, T.S. (1979) *The Myth of Psychotherapy*. Oxford: Oxford University Press.
Szasz, T.S. (1972) *The Myth Of Mental Illness*. Paladin.
Temaner-Brodley, B. (1990) "Client-Centered And Experiential: Two Different Therapies". In: Lietaer, G., Rombouts, J., & Van Halen, R. (eds), *Client-Centered and Experiential Psychotherapy in the Ninties*. Leuven: Leuven University Press, pp. 87–107.
The Process Of Change Study Group (1998) "Non-Interpretive Mechanisms in Psychoanalytic Therapy: The 'Something More' Than Interpretation". In: *International Journal of Psychoanalysis* 79: 903.
Thorne, B. (1990) "Carl Rogers and The Doctrine of Original Sin". In: *Person Centered Review* 5(4): 394–405.
Thorne, B. (1991) *Behold The Man*. London: Darton, Longman and Todd.
Thorne, B. (1991) *Person-Centred Counselling Therapeutic and Spiritual Dimensions*. London: Whurr (1994 edition).
Thorne, B. (1992) *Carl Rogers*. London: Sage.
Thorne, B. (1994) *The Counsellor as Prophet*. Frank Lake Memorial Lecture, 1994, Lingdale Paper 21. Oxford: Clinical Theology Association.
Thorne, B. (1999) "Julian of Norwich: Counsellor of Our Age". Guild Lecture No. 265, The Guild of Pastoral Psychology.

BIBLIOGRAPHY 205

Thorne, B. (2002) *The Mystical Power of Person Centred Therapy: Hope Beyond Despair*. London: Whurr.
Thorne, B. (2004) *Infinitely Beloved: The Challenge of Divine Intimacy*. Sarum Theological Lectures. London: Darton Longman and Todd.
Yalom, I. (1989) *Love's Executioner and Other Tales of Psychotherapy*. London: Peguin.
Ward, I. (ed.) (1993) *Is Psychoanalysis Another Religion? Contemporary Essays on spirit, faith and morality in psychoanalysis*. London: Freud Museum Publications.
Wolff, W. (1955) Chairman of a Collection of Papers on *Psychiatry and Religion*. New York: Md. Publications, Inc.

Critical Literature

Bakan, D. (1958) *Sigmund Freud and the Jewish Mystical Tradition*. London: D. Van Nostrand. Co. Inc.
Bateman, A. & Holmes, J. (1995) *Introduction to Psychoanalysis: Contemporary Theory and Practice*. London/New York: Routledge.
Bettelheim, B. (1982) *Freud and Man's Soul*. London: Penguin Books.
Bhugra, D. (1996) *Psychiatry and Religion*. London: Routledge.
Bianchi, E.C. (1989) "Psychotherapy as Religion, Pros and Cons". In: *Pastoral Psychology* 38: 67–81, Winter.
Clare, A. (1976) *Psychiatry in Dissent: Controversial Issues in Thought and Practice*. Tavistock publications (2nd edition 1980).
Clark, R. (1980) *Freud: The Man and the Cause*. Jonathan Cape Granada Publishing.
Cohen, D. (1997) *Carl Rogers: A Critical Biography*. London: Constable.
Cooper-White, P. & others (1994) "Desperately Seeking Sophia's Shadow". In: *Journal of Pastoral Care* 48: 287–292, Fall.
Cousins, E. (1987) In: *Religion in Today's World* F. Whaling (ed.). Edinburgh: T&T Clark.
Danto, E.A. (2005) *Freud's Free Clinics: psychoanalysis and Social Justice (1918–1938)*. Columbia, USA.
Davis, P.G. (1996) "The Swiss Maharishi: Discovering The Real Carl Jung And His Legacy Today". In: *Touchstone: a Journal of Ecumenical Orthodoxy*. (Us) 9: 10–14, Spring.
DiCenso, J.J. (1999) *The Other Freud: Religion, Culture and Psychoanalysis*. New York/London: Routledge.
Ellenberger, H.F. (1970) *The Discovery of the Unconscious: The History and Evolution of Dynamic Psychiatry*. London: Fontana (Reprint 1994).

Frank, J.D. & Frank, B. (1993) *Persuasion and Healing: A Comparative Study of Psychotherapy.* Baltimore: The John Hopkins University Press London, 3rd edition.
Fisher, S. & Greenberg, R.P. (1996) *Freud Scientifically Reappraised: Testing the Theories and Therapy.* New York: Wiley and Sons, Inc.
Freud, E. & Freud, L., et al. (1978) *Sigmund Freud: His Life in Pictures and Words.* London: Andre Deutsch.
Gay, P. (1987) *A Godless Jew: Freud, Atheism, and the Making of Psychoanalysis.* New Haven/London: Yale University Press.
Gay, P. (1988) *Freud: A Life for Our Time.* London: Dent.
Gay, P. (ed.) (1995) *Freud Reader.* London: Vintage.
Glock, C. & Bellah, R. (eds) (1976) *The New Religious Consciousness.* University of California Press.
Godin, A. (1985) *The Psychological Dynamics of Religious Experience.* Birmingham, Alabama: Religious Education Press.
Grosskurth, P. (1991) *The Secret Ring: Freud's Inner Circle and the Politics of Psychoanalysis.* London: Jonathan Cape.
Gummere, R.M. (1988) "The Counsellor As Prophet: Frank Parsons 1854–1908". In: *Journal of Counselling and Development* 66: 402–5, May.
Halmos, P. (1959) "I Thou Relationship". In: *Journal of Individual Psychology* xv: 174–179.
Halmos, P. (1965) *The Faith of Counsellors.* London: Constable.
Heelas, P. (1991) *Indigenous Psychologies the Anthropology of The Self.* London/ New York: Academic Press.
Heelas, P. (ed.) (1995) *Detraditionalization.* London: Blackwell.
Heelas, P. (1996) *The New Age Movement The Celebration of The Self and The Sacralization of Modernity.* Oxford: Blackwell.
Heller, A. (1969) "Belief Or Trust". In: *Concurrence* 1: 325–333, Fall.
Howard, A. (1996) *Challenges to Counselling and Psychotherapy.* Hampshire/ London: Macmillan Press Ltd.
Howard, A. (2000) *Philosophy for Counselling and Psychotherapy: Pythagoras to Postmodernism.* London: Macmillan Press.
Janik, A. & Toulmin, S. (1973) *Wittgenstein's Vienna.* Chicago: Elephant Paperbacks (Reprint 1996).
Jones, J.W. (1991) *Contemporary Psychoanalysis and Religion.* Yale University Press.
Kahn, M. (2002) *Basic Freud: Psychoanalysis for the 21st Century.* London: Basic Books.
Krebs, R.L. (1980) "Why Pastors Should Not Be Counsellors". In: *Journal of Pastoral Care* xxxxlv, 4 December.

Lee, R.S. (1967) *Freud and Christianity*. London: Pelican.
Masson, J.M. (1988) *Assault on Truth*. London: Belknap Press.
Masson, J.M. (1989) *Against Therapy*. London: Harper Collins.
Masson, J.M. (1990) *Final Analysis. The Making and Unmaking of a Psychoanalysis*. Addison: Wesley Publications.
Masson, J.M. (1992) *The Tyranny of Psychotherapy*. In: Dryden, W. & Feltham, C. (eds), *Psychotherapy and it's Discontents*. Buckingham: Open University Press.
Masson, J.M. (1985) *The Complete Letters of Sigmund Freud to Wilhelm Fleiss. (1887–1904)*. Translated and editied by Masson, J.M. Harvard: Belknap.
Mitchell, J. (1974) *Psychoanalysis and Feminism*. London: Pelican.
Moyers, J.C. (1990) "Religious Issues In the Psychotherapy of Former Fundamentalists". In: *Psychotherapy* 27: 42–45.
Molnar, M. (1992) *The Diary of Sigmund Freud 1929–1939: The Final Decade*. New York: Scribner.
Murray, Cuddihy J. (1974) *The Ordeal of Civility: Freud, Marx, Levi-Strauss and the Jewish Struggle with Modernity*. New York: Basic Books.
Newton, P.M. (1995) *Freud: From Youthful Dream to Mid-Life Crisis*. NewYork/London: Guilford Press.
Neuger, C.C. (1995) "Review of When Boundaries Betray Us". In: *Princeton Seminary Bulletin* 16(3): 381–384.
Puner, H.W. (1947) *Sigmund Freud: his Life and Mind*. Transaction. New Brunswick, USA/London, UK (Reprint 1980). New York: Howell & Soskin.
Reisel, A. (1976) "To Trust or Not To Trust: Relaxing the Controls". In: *The Journal of Pastoral Counselling* 11: 70–75, Spring–Summer.
Remele, K. (1997) "Self Denial or Self Actualisation? Therapeutic Culture and Christian Ethics". In: *Theology* 100: 18–25, January–February.
Roazen, P. (1971) *Freud and His Followers*. Penguin Allen Lane (1974).
Roustang, F. (1976) *Dire Mastery: Discipleship from Freud to Lacan*. The John Hopkins University Press.
Rowell, E.K. (1996) "On Whom Can I Count Now?" In: *Leadership* 17: 82–88, Spring.
Rutter, P. (1989) *Sex in the Forbidden Zone*. London: Aquarian.
Sartre, J.P. (2003) *Being and Nothingness: An Essay on Phenomenological Ontology*. Routledge Classics (Reprint).
Schweiker, W. (1992) "The Good and Moral Identity: A Theological Response to Charles Taylor's Sources of The Self". In: *The Journal of Religion* 72: 560–572.

Segal, R. (2001) *Myth as Make Believe*. Paper given at University of Stirling, 07/05/01.
Shamdasani, S. (2003) *Jung and the Making of Modern Psychology; The Dream of a Science*. Cambridge, England: Cambridge University Press.
Shamdasani, S. (1998) *Cult Fictions: C.J.Jung and the Founding of Analytical Psychology*. London/New York: Routledge.
Shamdasani, S. & Munchow, M. (1994) *Speculations After Freud: Psychoanalysis Philosophy and Culture*. London/New York: Routledge.
Smail, D. (1987) *Taking Care: An Alternative to Therapy*. Dent.
Smail, D. (1996) *How to Survive Without Psychotherapy*. London: Constable.
Stafford-Clark, D. (1965) *What Freud Really Said*. Penguin (Reprint 1992).
Stephen Muse, J. et al. (1994) "Are Religiously Integrated Therapists More Empathic?" In: *The Journal of Pastoral Care, Spring* **48**(1).
Storr, A. (1996) *Feet of Clay: A Study of Gurus*. London: Harper Collins (Paperback edition 1997).
Sulloway, F. (1979) *Freud Biologist of the Mind: Beyond the Psychoanalytic Legend*. Fontana Paperbacks.
Taylor, C.(1989) *Sources of The Self: The Making of Modern Identity*. Cambridge University Press (Paperback edition 1992).
Taylor, C. (1991) *The Ethics of Authenticity*. Cambridge, Massachusetts: Harvard University Press.
Tipton, S.M. (1982) *Getting Saved From The Sixties*. California: University Of California Press.
Thornton, E. (1986) *The Freudian Fallacy: Freud and Cocaine*. UK: Paladin.
Vitz, P.C. (1977) *Psychology as Religion: The Cult of Self Worship*. William B. Eerdmans. Grand Rapids Mi.
Vitz, P.C. (1988) *Sigmund Freud's Christian Unconscious*. London/New York: Guilford.
Webster, R. (1995) *Why Freud Was Wrong. Sin, Science and Psychoanalysis*. Harper Collins.
White, J.E. (1995) "The High Road to Credibility: Gaining Trust Today is A long Hard Climb". In: *Leadership* **16**: 52–56, Fall.
Winnicott, D.W. (1986) *Home is Where We Start From*. Penguin (Reprint 1990).
Wittels, F. (1924) *Sigmund Freud: His Personality, His Teachings, His School*. London: George Allen Unwin.
Young-Bruehl, E. (ed.) (2002) *Freud on Women: A Reader*. London: Vintage.

General Literature

Allchin, A.M. (1988) *Participation in God*. London: Darton Longman and Todd.

Bailey Gillespie, V. (1991) *The Dynamics of Religious Conversion: Identity and Transformation*. Birmingham, Alabama: Religious Education Press.
Battin, M.P. (1990) *Ethics in the Sanctuary*. Yale University Press.
Bell, J. (1993) *Doing Your Research Project: A Guide for First Time Researchers in Education and Social Science*. Buckingham, Philadelphia: Open University Press (1997 edition).
Bellah, R.N. et al. (1986) *Habits of The Heart*. Perennial Library, 1st edition.
Berger, P.L. (1967) *Sacred canopy: Elements of a Sociological Theory of Religion*. Anchor Books USA (Reprint 1990).
Blond, P. (ed.) (1998) *Post Secular Philosophy: Between Philosophy and Theology*. London: Routledge.
Blond, P. (2003) Unpublished paper given to the Art Society Edinburgh University, 29/04/03.
Bocking, B. (2000) Unpublished paper "The New Queen of the Sciences" given to British Association for the Study of Religions. London: School of African and Oriental Studies.
Brunton, P. (1969) *The Wisdom of The Overself*. London: Rider & Co.
Buber, M. (1937) *I And Thou*. Translated by W. Kaufmann, 1970. New York: Charles Scribner's Sons.
Buchanan, J. (1995) "In Search of the Moral Identity: A Transversal Reading of Charles Taylor and The Communitarians". In: *Soundings* 78: 143–168, Spring.
Cantwell Smith, W. (1962) *The Meaning and End of Religion*. Mentor Books USA.
Carlyle, T. *On Heroes, Hero-Worship and the Heroic in History*. London: H.R. Allenson (India paper edition 1905).
Carrette, J.R. in Jonte-Pace, D. and Parsond, W.B. (eds) (2001) *Religion and Psychology: Mapping The Terrain: Contemporary Dialogues, Future Prospects*. London: Routledge.
Carrette, J.R. & King, R. (2005) *Selling Spirituality The Silent Take Over of Religion*. London: Routledge.
Colridge, S.T. *Biographia Literaria*, chapter XIV.
De Beuavoir, S. (1948) *The Ethics of Ambiguity*. Citadel Press 1972.
Derrida, J. (1972) *The Margins of Philosophy*. Chicago: University of Chicago Press (English edition 1982).
Derrida, J. (1967) *Writing and Difference*. London: Routledge (English edition 1978).
Dictionary of Pastoral Care and Counselling. Abingdon: Nashville.
Ellenberger, H. (1970) *The Discovery of The Unconscious: The History and Evolution of Dynamic Psychiatry*. New York: Basic Books.

Faber, H. (1976) *Psychology of Religion*. London: Scm Press Ltd.
Fitz, R. & Cada, L. (1975) "The Recovery of Religious Life". In: *Review for Religion* 34: 690–718.
Fitzgerald, T. (2000) *The Ideology of Religious Studies*. Oxford: Oxford University Press.
Fowler, J.W. (1981) *Stages of Faith*. San Francisco: Harper (Paperback edition 1995).
Haring, H. (1993) *Trust as Resistance Against Nothingness: The Question of God as Raised in Does God Exist?* In: Hans Kung (ed.) by Kuschel, K. and others, pp. 216–243.
Heyward, C. (1995) "Lamenting the Loss of Love". In: *Journal of Religious Ethics* 24: 23–28, Spring 1996.
Heelas, P. (1998) *Religion, Modernity, and Post Modernity*. Oxford: Blackwell.
Hooykaas, R. (1972) *Religion and the Rise of Modern Science*. Scottish Academic Press.
Jantzen, G.M. (1998) *Becoming Divine: Towards a Feminist Philosophy of Religion*. Manchester, England: Manchester University Press.
James, W. (1890) *Priciples of Psychology*. New York: Holt.
James, W. (1902) *The Varieties of Religious Experience: A Study in Human Nature*. London: Longmans, Green & Co. (Tenth Impression 1904).
Jenkins, D.E. (1976) *The Contradiction of Christianity*. London: Scm Press.
King, A.S. (1996) "Spirituality: Transformation and Metamorphosis". In: *Religion* 26: 343–351.
Kippenberg, H.G. (1990) *Concepts of Persons in Religion and Thought*. Berlin: Mouton De Gruyter.
Kopps, S. (1972) *If You Meet The Buddha On The Road, Kill Him*. Palo Alto, C.A.: Science and Behaviour Books.
Kuhn, T. (1962) *The Structure of Scientific Revolutions*. University Of Chicago Press (Reprint 1970).
Larzerlere, R.E. (1984) "Dydactic Trust and Generalised Trust of Secular Versus Christian College Students". In: *Journal of Psychology and Theology* 12: 119–124, Summer.
Macintyre, A. (1981) *After Virtue*. London: Duckworth Press.
Macintyre, A. & Ricoeur, P. (1969) *The Religious Significance of Atheism*. New York/London: Columbia University Press.
Malony, H.N. (ed.) (1983) *Wholeness and Holiness*. Baker: Grand Rapids.
Manuel, F. (1974) *The Religion of Isaac Newton*. Oxford: Clarendon Press.
Masson, J.M. (1993) *My Fathers Guru: A Journey Through Spirituality and Disillusion*. Addison: Wesley Publications.

McClellan, D. C. (1964) *The Roots of Consciousness*. Princeton: D. Van. Nostrand Co.
McKinnon, A. (1993) "Kierkegaard and 'The Leap Of Faith'". In: *Kierkegaardiana* 16: 107–125 (ed.) by Garff, J. and others.
McNeill, J.T. (1951) *A History of The Cure of Souls*. New York: Harper and Row.
Meghnagi, D. (ed.) (1993) *Freud and Judaism*. London: Karnac.
Midgely, M. (1992) *Science as Salvation: A Modern Myth and its Meaning*. Routledge & Kegan Paul.
Nussbaum, M.C. (1996) *Compassion: The Basic Social Emotion*. Off Print (Mg. Phil. Res). Edinburgh Unversity Library (Main).
Paskauskas, A.R. (ed.) (1993) *The Complete Correspondence of S. Freud and E. Jones (1908–1939)*. Harvard/Cambridge, Massechussetts/London, England: Belknapp.
Otto, R. (1917) *The Idea of The Holy*. Oxford, England: Oxford University Press (Reprint 1923).
Phoca, S. & Wright, R. (1999) *Introduction to Postfeminism*. London: Icon Books.
Penelhum, T. (1981) "Faith and Uncertainty". In: *The Scottish Journal of Religious Studies* 2(1): 28–37, Spring.
Rachaels, J. (1993) *Elements of Moral Philosophy*. McGraw-Hill Inc.
Rabinow, P. (ed.) (1991) *The Foucault Reader*. London: Penguin.
Sargant, W. (1957) *Battle for The Mind*. London/Melborne/Toronto/Cape Town/Auckland/The Hague: William Heinemann Ltd.
Scholem, G.G. (1949) *Zohar: The Book of Splendour, Basic Readings from the Kabbalah*. London: Rider & Co. (Reprint 1977).
Seligman, A.B. (1992) *The Idea of The Civil Society*. Princeton University Press.
Storr, A. (1996) *Feet of Clay: A Study of Guru's*. London: Harper Collins.
Taylor, C. (1989) *Sources of The Self: The Making of a Modern Identity*. Cambridge: Cambridge University Press.
Tremmel, W.C. (1992) *Human Kind and the Religious Dimension. In Empirical Theology* (ed.) Miller, R.
Vitz, P.C. (1977) *Psychology as Religion: The Cult of Self Worship*. England: Lion.
Ward, G. (ed.) (1997) *The Post Modern God: A Theological Reader*. Oxford, UK: Blackwell.
West, W.S. (2000) *Psychotherapy and Spirituality: Crossing the Line Between Therapy and Religion*. London: Sage.
Whaling, F. (ed.) (1984) *Contemporary Approaches to the Study of Religion* 1. New York/Amsterdam/Berlin: Mauton.

White, V. (1960) *God and The Unconscious*. Fontana.
Wyatt, N. (2001) *Space and Time in the Religious Life of the Ancient Near East*. Sheffield, England: Sheffield Academic Press.
Zeldin, T. (1988) *Conversation: How Talk Can Change Your Life*. London: Harvill Press.

Index

Adler, Alfred 42, 45, 71, 122
alienation 145–6
Allen, Frederick 117
analyst–patient relationship 29, 69, 76–7, 126, 132, 152, 155–6, 194, 198
  client as expert 127, 129, 130
  and Ferenzci 99–100
  hierarchical 76
  parenting 147, 156, 185
Anderson, Pamela Sue 193–4
authenticity 142–6, 149

Benedikt, Moritz 16, 27
Berger, P. 73
biological determinism 11
Bion, Wilfred 94, 105, 173
Black, David 176
Blond, Phillip 169–70, 174, 177, 179, 180
Bollas, Christopher 82, 85, 89, 92, 100, 104, 105, 162, 174–5, 182, 186–7, 191
  mystery 92–3, 175, 186, 191
Bond, Tim 139–40
Bown, Oliver 119

Brazier 141, 143, 146–9, 150, 152, 161
altruism 146–9
  and religion 148
Brentano, Franz 16, 27
Breuer, J. 16, 27
Brücke, Ernest Von 17, 27
Buber, M. 161–2
Buddhism 61, 86, 93, 105, 172, 176, 180–1

Carrette, Jeremy 73, 173
Charcot, Jean-Martin 11, 16, 27
Cixious, Hélène 191–2
Clark, Ronald 4
Claus, Carl 16
Cohen, D. 120
Coleridge, S.T. 105
Coltart, Nina 82, 93–4, 104, 105, 172–81, 186–8
confession 4, 16, 52–3, 57, 73, 196
  see also talking cure
congruence 69, 124–5, 127–30, 133, 142, 144–5, 153, 163
core conditions 120, 123–4, 127–8, 138, 142, 149, 152, 154, 164
Crews, Frederick 4

dogmatism 8, 37, 47–8, 60, 68–9, 83, 89, 95, 98, 100, 129, 142, 150, 156, 198

Ellenberger, Henri 27, 31, 32, 45, 61, 72
Ellingham, I. 153
empathy 58, 69, 123–4, 127, 145–6, 163
empiricism 12, 15, 30, 62, 73, 122–3, 141
Epstein, Mark 176
evolution 14, 18
eye contact 57, 73–4, 125, 135

faith 29, 62, 70, 94, 103
  bad faith 106, 124, 133, 140, 196
  and Bion 94
  and Bollas 187
  and Freud 14, 62, 71, 86
  religious 148, 154
  Rogers' 116–17
  and science 14, 62, 171, 197
  and Thorne 127–8, 133, 159–60
  in treatment 29, 72, 105, 126, 172–3
  and Vanaerschot 145–6
Ferenzci 45, 69, 99–100
Feuerbach, L. 16, 18, 27, 78
Fisher, S. and Greenberg, R.P. 83
Fleiss, Wilhelm 17, 28, 38, 43–4, 71
free association 72, 82, 85
Freud, Anna 22, 34, 64, 71, 75
Freud, Sigmund
  as an adventurer 28, 87–8
  and his biographers 4, 21, 22, 25, 26, 28, 33, 34, 42
  birth 21, 22
  and cancer 27
  childhood 21–3
  and distortion of facts 33–4
  and his father 21–2, 24

"Freudian pair" 82, 85, 100
and Judaism 11, 15, 17, 21, 24, 25, 49, 70, 87
and mythology 30–2, 34, 38
as a neurologist 11
and his personality xi, 23, 29, 46, 47, 49
and religion 11, 14, 25, 70, 85, 91, 103–4, 171
as a scientist 11, 16, 28, 59, 81, 196
Trinity 62, 64
Frosh, Stephen 96–7, 100
fundamentalism 25, 76, 85, 103, 154, 163

Gay, Peter xii, 13, 15
Gendlin, Eugene 138, 139
Graf, Max xii, 47
Grosskurth, Phyllis 42, 43, 51
Grunbaum, Adolf 4

Hardy, Alistair 122
Holdstock, Len 149–50
Howard, Alex 129
hypnotism 16, 27
hysteria 11, 16

inner conflict 63–4
Irigary, Luce 74, 75, 78, 192–3

Jacobs, Michael 60
James, William 122
Janik, A. and Toulmin, S. 56
Jantzen, Grace 192
Jones, Ernest xii, 4, 22, 28–9, 34, 42–3, 51, 195
Jung xi, 3, 26, 31, 43, 45, 46, 48–9, 64, 65, 68, 70, 71–2, 91–2
  analytical psychology 55, 72, 71
  and religiousness 71
  and the unconscious 71

Klein, M. 68
Kovel, Joel 175–6, 188
Kraus, Karl 19
Kristeva, Julia 193

language *see* religious, language
Levy, David 117
Liebault, A.A. 27
Lietaer, G. 155
Lowrey, Lawson 117

Masson, Jeffrey 4, 33, 46, 76, 77, 78, 133–4, 147, 150, 154
May, Rollo 151–2, 158
meaning of life 67, 90, 196
Mearns and Thorne 96, 102, 141, 144, 150–61, 163, 164 *see also* Thorne, Brian
 and authenticity 144
 relational depth 102
 and religion 159–61
modernity 98, 102, 121, 176
 post-modern 99, 180

National Socialism 18, 50, 159
Nietzsche, F. 17, 27
Noll, Richard 71–2

O'Hara, M. 161–2
Orbach, Susie 13, 81–2, 85, 89, 103
Otto, Rudolph 187

Perls, Fritz 68
person-centred counselling 118, 121–68
 as a religious movement 132, 160
 as a science 120, 123, 141, 146, 160
 and trust 126, 145, 148, 194
Pfister, Oskar 25, 43, 47
Phillips, Adam 4, 69, 80–4, 86–9, 101–6, 172–3, 175, 176, 180–8
political correctness 58, 177

post-feminism 191–4
post-secularism 169–70, 173, 180, 184
professionalising practitioners 66–7, 157
Proust, Marcel 104–5
psychoanalysis
 and anthropology 88
 and art 89, 103, 173–4, 182
 as a cult 47, 88
 as an ideology 2, 181
 and literature 88, 182
 and the medical profession 43, 56, 65, 89
 and meta-physiology 30, 80, 82, 88
 and phenomenology 89, 101, 176, 182
 and philosophy 89
 as a religious movement 1, 29, 43, 47, 47–8, 69, 86, 105, 180–1, 193, 195–6, 197
 as a science ix, 3, 10–19, 28, 81, 83–4, 92, 96, 102–3, 141

Rank, Otto 117
reason 36–7
religious
 analogies 36, 121, 132, 152, 176, 179, 181
 figures 1
 founders 13, 90
 language 1, 2–4, 43, 45, 91, 104, 140, 160, 173
Rieff, Phillip 171
Roazen, Paul 4, 29, 31, 32, 47
Rogers, Carl xii, xiii, 1, 2, 3, 4, 5, 6, 55, 66, 68, 115–168, 170, 177, 185
 as an adventurer 118
 birth 115
 "bracketing off" 122

childhood 115–16, 119
core conditions 120, 123–4, 127–8, 138, 142, 149, 152, 154, 164
encounter groups 116, 122
inherent goodness of humans 118, 127
and quick fix culture 131
and religion 115–17, 197
and science 120, 123, 150, 196
Rogers, Natalie 119, 149

Sachs, Hans 27
Salome, Lou Andreas 48
Sartre, Jean-Paul 124
Schlien, John 153, 155
Schwartz, Regina 171
science
　and atheism 14
　the God of all things 13–14
　and person-centred counselling 120, 123, 141, 146, 160
　and proof 12, 46, 62, 92, 96, 97
　and psychoanalysis 10–19, 28, 81, 83–4, 92, 96, 102–3, 141
　and religion 14
　and status 10–19
　and validity 10
secularity
　and Phillips 183
　of society 54
　of therapy 161
Segal, Robert 31
the Self 63, 68, 77, 78
self-concept 124
Sheerer, Elizabeth 117
Silberstein, Eduard 43–4
social and political context 18, 50, 56, 57, 65, 95, 182
the soul 50, 60, 62, 173
　cure of 49, 52, 78, 196, 197
　scientizing 48
　or unconscious 48

spirit 93, 173, 187–8
spiritualism 60, 161, 195, 198
Stekel, Wilhelm xi, 19, 42, 45, 51, 71
Storr, Anthony 26, 35, 44, 53
Sulloway, Frank 4, 19, 25, 27, 30, 31, 32, 47–8, 87
Symington, N. 90, 104, 188, 197, 199
Szasz, Thomas 25, 52

Taft, Jessie 117
talking cure 51–2, 54, 198
therapeutic
　environment 73, 75, 134–5, 139, 146
　props 151
　relationships 75
　rituals 74, 77, 134–5
　techniques 29, 59, 60, 72, 73, 76, 96, 125, 134, 154, 163, 172
Thorne, Brian 117, 127–9, 130, 132, 134, 138–9, 140, 159–61, 181, 198, 199 *see also* Mearns and Thorne
　and religion 128, 159–60
　and tenderness 138
Thornton, Elizabeth 33–4
transference 72–3, 75, 98, 102, 123, 144, 153–5, 187

unconditional positive regard 69, 119, 124, 127, 149, 152, 155, 163
the unconscious 31, 61–3, 72, 73, 101–2, 105, 177, 187
　dynamic 55, 58, 62, 68, 97
　and Freud 3, 11, 16, 62, 193
　and Jung 68, 71
　and Rogers 122
　or the soul 48

Vanaerschot, Greet 145, 146
Vienna 18, 33, 42, 56
 University of 16
Vitz, Paul 77, 78

Ward, G. 191
Watson, J.B. 118
Webster, Richard xi, 4, 32, 34–7, 44, 46–7, 49–50, 51, 91
Weininger, Otto 19

Weisz, George xii, 47
Winnicott, W.D. 31, 68
withholding 75, 98, 100, 128, 151, 157–8
Wittels, Fritz 4, 22, 48
Wittgenstein, Ludwig 3, 18, 86

Yalom, Irvin 143–4, 149, 153, 164

Zeldin, Theodore 106